How to Stop Fascism

PAUL MASON

How to Stop Fascism

History, Ideology, Resistance

ALLEN LANE
an imprint of
PENGUIN BOOKS

ALLEN LANE

UK | USA | Canada | Ireland | Australia
India | New Zealand | South Africa

Allen Lane is part of the Penguin Random House group of companies
whose addresses can be found at global.penguinrandomhouse.com

First published 2021
001

Copyright © Paul Mason, 2021

The moral right of the author has been asserted

Set in 9.75/13 pt Sabon LT Std
Typeset by Jouve (UK), Milton Keynes
Printed and bound in Great Britain by Clays Ltd, Elcograf S.p.A.

The authorized representative in the EEA is Penguin Random House Ireland,
Morrison Chambers, 32 Nassau Street, Dublin D02 YH68

A CIP catalogue record for this book is available from the British Library

ISBN: 978-0-141-99639-4

*To the anti-fascists – past,
present and future*

History teaches us the deathlessness of ideas.

Karl Loewenstein,
anti-fascist lawyer, 1937[1]

Contents

Introduction

Nazis: They're Back – But Why?

What if the Nazis invented a time machine? And in the last weeks of the Second World War, they decided to send a crack SS team into the future, to create a Fourth Reich? What year do you think they would aim for?

Seventy-five years is a round number; most witnesses to the Holocaust would be dead by then. So, let's do a thought experiment: suppose a group of Nazi time-travellers materializes in Europe in March 2020. They are shocked at the ultra-liberalism of Western society; they marvel at our digital technologies; they discover to their horror that black American music has conquered the world. But then . . .

. . . They watch Hindu mobs in Delhi beating left-wing students with iron bars. They see the far-right Vox party flood the Spanish media with violent rhetoric against migrants, feminists and the left, gaining 3 million votes in the process. They discover that 1 million Chinese Muslims are interned in something very like concentration camps, and that nobody cares.

Once they figure out the internet, and work out what a meme is, a cartoon frog saying 'Honk Honkler' makes them smile. Their smiles broaden as they read that a German army unit has been dissolved because it is irreparably infiltrated by neo-Nazis. Digging deeper, they realize that all the ideas in their own heads – racial purity, male supremacy, anti-Semitism and leader-worship – are circulating globally on Discord channels and WhatsApp groups between millions of angry people.

As they acclimatize, they realize something even bigger is brewing. There's a disease. It is killing people. As the Covid-19 virus rips through America, they watch far-right demonstrators take to the streets, some armed with automatic rifles, protesting for the right to catch it.

George Floyd is murdered. The alt-right bulletin boards seethe with anticipation: this is it, 'Boogaloo', the white supremacist code-word for a second American Civil War. As tens of thousands march to protest about Floyd's death, they are attacked by far-right militias, sometimes inter-operating with the police.[1]

Trump loses the election, but, being from the 1930s, our Nazis are not surprised at what happens next: he summons a racist mob to the US Capitol and incites them to storm the building. Nor are they surprised to see Republican lawmakers justifying the attack. Politicians fronting for violence is the standard operating procedure from their time.

As the far right begins a four-year insurgency against the Biden administration, what do our time-travelling Nazis do next? They relax, buy popcorn and watch the fun. Their mission was superfluous.

Fascism is back – but of its own accord. Something else got here first. But what, and what can we do about it? This book is my attempt to answer that question.

When my generation chanted 'Never Again!' at Nazi skinheads in the 1970s, we assumed this was a fact, not an aspiration. Fascism was history: the product of social hierarchies that could never return, triggered by a type of economic crisis that could never be repeated. We had good grounds for believing this. Ernst Nolte, the German historian who began the comparative study of international fascism in 1963, had declared the phenomenon 'dead'. We have seen all possible variants of fascism, said Nolte: it is a finished episode.[2]

As the digital age arrived, breaking the monopoly over information held by states and companies, it seemed that elites could never again manipulate public opinion in the way Hitler and Mussolini had done. As late as 2008, the historian Giuseppe Finaldi could write, in a university textbook on Mussolini: 'Fascism has little to say now and many of its obsessions seem not just absurd but incomprehensible.'[3] We assumed that, because we had recorded the truth about fascism, it could never re-emerge.

It is now clear that every one of these assumptions was wrong.

Over the past decade, three political movements have flourished to the right of mainstream conservatism: far-right extremism, right-wing populism and authoritarian conservatism. A whole sub-discipline in political science is dedicated to studying the differences between them, producing numerous typologies, definitions and labels.[4]

Far-right extremists typically advocate race war, commit violence and openly fight for the dissolution of democracy. Right-wing populists attack human rights, victimize minorities and stage mass mobilizations, but are usually non-violent and focused on winning elections, often through new political parties. Authoritarian conservatives, meanwhile, borrow the rhetoric of populism but operate within mainstream parties, elite networks and the traditional institutions of the state.

That's the theory. The problem is that, in reality, the three movements have begun to work in conscious synergy. Since the 1990s political scientists have assumed that right-wing populist parties would act as a firewall against real fascism. In fact, the opposite has happened. *The firewall is on fire.*

Since 2008, movements to the right of the mainstream have developed a shared language, a shared online space and a shared goal: to create *illiberal* democracies that can keep coalitions of populists and authoritarians permanently in power, erode the rule of law and torch the rules-based global order.

In the 2010s three of the most populous democracies on earth – the USA, India and Brazil – were rapidly and seriously undermined. More than half of the world's developed countries have seen the quality of their democracy decline over the past fourteen years. 'Functioning of government, freedom of expression and belief, and rule of law are the most common areas of decline,' says the monitoring group Freedom House.[5] This process, labelled 'democratic decay' has both weakened our defences against full-blown fascism and opened up a space for fascists to operate in.

The French neofascist Maurice Bardèche, who devoted his life to denying the Holocaust, predicted as early as 1961 that fascism would return in a different form:

> With another name, another face, and with nothing which betrays the projection from the past, with the form of a child we do not recognize and the head of a young Medusa, the Order of Sparta will be reborn.[6]

It was not the stormtroopers and the torture cells that formed the essence of the fascist project, Bardèche insisted, but its concept of 'man and freedom'. Today, whatever you are searching for on You-Tube, Facebook or Twitter, the fascist concept of man and freedom is only a few clicks away.

So my generation was wrong. Fascism, it turns out, was not rooted in the specific class dynamics of Europe in the 1930s. It does not take mass unemployment to produce it. It is not reliant on defeat in war or the existence of state-run radio stations. *It is a recurrent symptom of system-failure under capitalism.*

And the critical failure that fascism relies on is ideological, not economical. In normal times capitalism is sustained by a belief system that is both passive and pervasive. Simply in order to live our lives we need to believe that markets work naturally; that the government is fair and just; that hard work will be rewarded; that, as technological progress happens, life will get better for ourselves and our children. These beliefs, taken together, constitute an *ideology*. We replicate and reinforce them through our daily experience – at work, at home and in all the spaces in between.

Fascism takes hold when our faith in this everyday ideology evaporates, and no progressive alternative takes its place. But it is an ideology of a different kind: it can only be reinforced and replicated in people's heads by *extraordinary* experiences – of war, victimization and genocide.

Traditionally, historians have studied fascism from three vantage points: as an ideology, a movement and a regime. The premise of this book is that, though each of these viewpoints is valid, fascism can be fully understood only as the outcome of a process: specifically a process of socio-economic disintegration that leaves millions of people's lives in turmoil, their self-image in doubt, longing to believe a pack of lies, and indeed to take an active part in creating and spreading the lies.

The questions I will try to answer are: what's driving that process now? What drove it in the past? And how can we stop it?

The core of fascism's belief system today is clear: that majority ethnic groups have become the 'victims' of migration and multiculturalism; that the gains of feminism should be reversed; that democracy is dispensable; that science, universities and the media cannot be trusted; that nations have lost their way and need to become 'great' again; and that there will soon be a cataclysmic event which sets things right.

Every fascist believes all of this and more; every right-wing populist voter now believes some of it; every politician of the authoritarian right has used coded language to play to some part of this agenda. In fact, a good way to tell if you are dealing with an *anti*-fascist conservative is if they are prepared to repudiate all of it, in clear words and actions.

But what separates modern fascists from the populists and right-wing conservatives is their ultimate goal: a global race war that reshapes the world into ethnic monocultures and ends modern society.

Fascism's current strength cannot be measured through voting figures: in most Western countries, fascists usually vote for right-wing populist parties, content to exploit the connections and the political space provided. Nor can it be judged from the size of its street mobilizations: the real mobilization is happening online. For now, fascism's strength is best judged through the salience of its ideas, which have spread rapidly via social media.

The reason why they're spreading is clear. Over the past decade, as the free-market economic system failed, as globalization went into reverse, as climate change demanded radical alterations to our priorities, and finally as the Covid-19 pandemic hiked economic and geopolitical tensions, the ideology that made sense of the world for many people crumbled into dust. In its place, fascism offers a new Utopia based on racism, misogyny and violence.

At its most granular, this is a process taking place at the level of individuals. In the 1940s, some claimed Nazism was the product of 'the German character'. In fact, countered the philosopher Hannah Arendt, it was caused by the *disintegration* of the German character.[7] Today we are facing something similar: the disintegration of a global character – the typical 'self' that emerged during the period of free-market globalization, which is now lost in the dark as it all implodes.

In the search for an enemy, the new far right has declared war on 'cultural Marxism', echoing the rhetoric of Nazism in the 1920s. But since the number of actual Marxists is small, it is feminists, people of colour, climate scientists, refugees, lawyers and LGBTQ people who have to be stigmatized, harassed and 'doxxed' (i.e. forced out of public life by the release of their personal information). During the pandemic, public health officials were added to the target list: in far-right folklore even masks are 'Marxist'.

If we learn one lesson from the twentieth century it should be this: once the fascist way of thinking is adopted by millions of people, nothing satisfies them short of total destruction. In 1945, reporting from the site of the Treblinka death camp, the journalist Vasily Grossman pleaded with us, the future generations:

> Every man and woman today is duty bound to his or her conscience . . . to their motherland and to humanity as a whole, to devote all the powers of their heart and mind to answering these questions: what is it that has given birth to racism? What can be done to prevent Nazism ever rising again?

He did not ask us to consider how bad was fascism, how great its cost, how irrational its ideas, but *what caused it*? His answer goes to the heart of what is happening now:

> What led Hitler and his followers to construct Majdanek, Sobibor, Belzec, Auschwitz and Treblinka is the imperialist idea of exceptionalism – of racial, national and every other kind of exceptionalism.[8]

Another word for this exceptionalism would be *supremacy* – of white people over black people; of men over women; of the 'native' population over immigrants; of colonists over indigenous peoples of the global south. Grossman understood that inside every supremacist ideology there lurks a genocidal impulse, which – as we will see – conceals an even deeper desire for self-destruction.

Six million Jews died in the Holocaust.[9] Sixty million people died in the Second World War, three quarters of them civilians.[10] Though our brains struggle to comprehend these numbers, the price of a second fascist era could be higher.

In 2018 I visited Majdanek, a former concentration camp near Lublin, Poland, where at least 80,000 Jews, Poles, Russians and others were murdered. What struck me was the flimsiness of its construction:

some rough concrete posts a few inches thick, a double barbed-wire fence and some watchtowers made of pine.[11] Five hundred prisoners escaped from Majdanek. Nobody would escape a facility built for the same purpose today.

A twenty-first-century Majdanek would use facial recognition, biometric tags, electrified razor wire and tasers to keep its inmates under control. Its boundaries would be guarded by lethal autonomous weapons, not dogs and searchlights. It would be run as a business, with its own PR department, a certificate to offset its carbon emissions and – just like Guantanamo Bay – a gift shop for visitors and staff.

In fact, all it would need to turn a modern penitentiary or migrant detention centre into a death camp is what the Nazis brought to places like Majdanek: a pitiless logic of dehumanization.

Majdanek was liberated by the Red Army. But who would liberate a modern Majdanek? This time around the jeopardy is absolute. A second victory by fascism in a major country would be a survival-level event for humanity.

The only thing that's going to stop it are resilient institutions and the anti-fascism of ordinary people. But what should anti-fascism mean?

From the 1970s to the 1990s I was an anti-fascist activist – first in the Anti-Nazi League and then in Anti-Fascist Action. We disrupted fascist events in ways designed to discourage future attendance. We marched with tens of thousands of people to shut down the HQ of the British National Party (BNP) in Welling, London, getting our heads kicked in by riot police in the process.[12] We suffered surveillance, harassment and infiltration by undercover police. And to what end?

By forcing the fascists off the streets, we obliged them to make a detour into electoral politics, where the ideas associated with the BNP in the 1980s are now mainstream in the Conservative Party. Tory leaders openly celebrate Britain's history as a slave power and contemplate the mass deportation of refugees to island prison camps. More than half its members think Islam is 'a threat to Western civilization' and to 'the British way of life'.[13]

As a child in the coal-mining town of Leigh, Lancashire, I played in disused air-raid shelters whose walls were still scrawled with anti-Nazi graffiti from the war. In 2019, while campaigning there for Labour in the general election, I heard men of my age openly fantasize about the ethnic cleansing of Romanian migrants. 'Go round to their houses at midnight, lock them in a van with their children, and drive them to Dover,' was the demand. 'And then what?' I asked. Their response was an embarrassed smile.

All the bricks, bottles and abuse we hurled at skinheads in the 1970s didn't stop the garbage of white supremacy flooding into people's minds once the global financial crisis triggered an ideological meltdown.

To stop fascism, we need to answer the same questions that confronted progressives in the 1930s. How do we unite the left and the political centre to fight the threat? How do we defend the rule of law and the state's monopoly of force as far-right movements undermine them? Can police forces and intelligence services designed to protect the elite against the working class ever be used effectively to protect democracy from fascism? How do we persuade people radicalized by hopelessness and the romanticism of violent action to de-escalate? How do we revive democracies that are so corrupt and decayed that they seem, in the eyes of many disillusioned people, not worth saving?

None of the answers are easy, because every one of them involves *risking our own status*. If you are reading this book on a train, in a café, at the beach or in a classroom, its cover has already politicized the space you are in. Thanks to Donald Trump, declaring yourself anti-fascist now carries a stigma everywhere.

I can remember vividly the first moment when I understood that fascism existed. It was in the mid-1960s and I was around five years old. The TV was on and a programme about the liberation of Bergen-Belsen started. My mum, the daughter of a Polish Jew, leapt to her feet and switched it off. 'We're not watching *that*,' she shouted.

Born in 1935, she'd spent her childhood knowing that if the Nazis invaded Britain she would be killed. Later I realized that it wasn't my eyes she was trying to protect from the pictures but her own. But she failed. For a few short moments we saw a bulldozer pushing a pile of emaciated bodies into a pit.[14]

It is now widely understood that, for the first decades after the war, both the memory of fascism and the desire to study it were sup-pressed. From the movies we learned that the Nazis had put people in barbed-wire camps, and sometimes killed them; but the victims in the movies I watched as a child were for the most part British prisoners of war, not Jews.[15]

Then came the thaw: in the 1970s, TV series like *Holocaust* and movies like *Cabaret* turned the popular image of the Nazis inside out.[16] The people who'd perpetrated the horror were no longer depicted mainly as prison guards in jackboots; they were the ordinary people of Germany – the landlady, the cleaner, the bisexual cabaret host.

Finally came the long period – from the 1980s onward – in which fascism was commodified in popular culture. A generation that had nothing to fear, and harboured no post-traumatic stress, could hap-pily consume movies, novels, drama series, comedies and even porn themed around the Nazis.

Meanwhile, the Auschwitz memorial expanded, and major global museums and monuments were erected to the Holocaust, replete with new evidence gathered from the archives of the Soviet Union, which had collapsed.

As a result, today we know more about what fascism did while in power than any previous generation. But many people are woefully ignorant about how it came to power. Despite the countless movies and drama series, we are almost never shown how millions of people were swept up in the thrill of murdering Jews, gypsies, gay people and socialists; how they had *imagined* doing it, even as they cast their votes for what seemed at the time like protest parties.

That is why, in this book, I focus not on regimes but on the *process* that brings fascism to power, asking: how did far-right parties break out of their isolation? What were the psychological traits they preyed on? And why did the left fail to stop them? If we can answer all this we can design strategies to stop it happening again.

To understand fascism requires a theory; a collection of facts won't do. But with the re-emergence of today's far right, almost every theory of fascism produced during the past sixty years needs revision.

Until the 1980s, you could justifiably argue that fascism was what happened in the 1930s, and the surviving far-right groups are hangovers from that. In the 1990s you could say: a new right-wing populism has emerged but it is not fascist. Today we are witnessing a real and serious fascist resurgence. And though its organizational forms and language are different, its philosophical roots are exactly the same.

'Why did it happen once?' is a very different question from 'Why is it happening again?' The latter begs the question: will we have to go on defeating fascism over and over until the capitalist system itself departs? I fear the answer is yes.

The most fragile theories of fascism are those that emerged straight after the Second World War, rooted in pre-existing disciplines. Psychiatrists explained fascism as mass psychosis; political science evolved the Cold War theory of 'totalitarianism' in which fascism and communism are essentially the same thing; moral philosophers explained it as 'radical evil'; anthropologists categorized it as a 'political religion'. There was no coherence, just a tangle of competing claims.

As for Marxism, at least in its orthodox form, its theory of fascism was wrong in the 1920s, half-baked in the 1930s and has been rendered incoherent in the past decade. Classic Marxism saw fascism as the agent of the financial elite, whose mission was to smash the highly organized labour movements of the interwar period in order to head off a revolution. Today there is no revolutionary proletariat, no mass unemployment, and no serious faction within high finance wants or needs fascism. And yet it's back.

Since the 1970s, academic historians have created the discipline of 'comparative fascist studies', while social scientists have offered behavioural explanations. I will explore their insights critically in this book because, with the sudden resurgence of the threat, this is no longer an academic issue.

Our task is to piece together a new theory of fascism that builds on the work of academics but is 'owned' and maintained primarily by activists, based on experience as well as theory, and can respond to the threat in real time.

We need something more than a definition, because definitions are not explanations. A checklist of the features common to historic fascist parties won't explain why one ends up as an irrelevant sect and another is able to conquer mainland Europe. Nor can a definition easily encapsulate a process by which individuals, parties and movements that were not fascist become fascist.

Nevertheless, since the demand for definitive statements is strong, here's mine. *Fascism is the fear of freedom, triggered by a glimpse of freedom.*

It is the violent mobilization of people who do not want to be free, around the project of destroying freedom. It is, as the Italian anti-fascist Enzo Traverso wrote, 'a revolution against the revolution'.[17]

Throughout history people have believed in the possibility of human self-emancipation. It was the subtext of all humanistic religions, the explicit project of the Enlightenment and the declared objective of Marxism. Fascism is an attempt to stop it happening.

The Nazis' stated aim was to erase all progress since the French Revolution of 1789 and then to freeze historical time so completely that no new modernity, or Enlightenment or progress could ever emerge. That is what today's far right wants too.

In the search for what makes people want to reject and prevent freedom, I will argue that we need to look much deeper than the contingent factors of economic crisis, or class antagonisms, which have been the traditional focus of the left.

Though there is no fascist party with a viable route to power at time of writing, that could change. From climate change to deglobalization, the mid-twenty-first century will generate pressures bigger than those that destroyed the fragile democracies of the twentieth century. On the upside, if we address these challenges bravely and collectively, we could be nearer to freedom than we think.

This book is structured around three themes: the ideology and practice of modern fascism; the process through which the original fascists formed their movements and seized power, and its similarities to today; and the search for effective ways of resisting them.

It is not a work of critical theory, nor of political science, nor of academic history. It will be of no use at dinner parties hosted by post-modernists, unless you want to throw it at someone. Nor will it provide a comprehensive guide to the far-right organizational landscape: that morphs and mutates so rapidly you will need to consult the websites of activists and monitoring groups to keep up to date.

The simplest way to stop fascism is to put your body – not your internet avatar – between fascists and their objective. I have done this, and can attest to how powerful it can be.

But physical resistance, which has been the core activity of anti-fascists since the 1920s, works only if it's part of a wider political strategy. If they're carrying guns, incited by the president and backed by the biggest news network in the country, you're going to need something more powerful than your own courage – namely a theory, a strategy and a lot of like-minded people.

This book explains how we get from here to there.

PART ONE

Ideology

I

Symbolic Violence

What Do Twenty-first-century Fascists Want?

Let's call him Hans, because the researcher doesn't name him: the first Nazi convert in an Austrian village. Hans is an orphan, raised in a devout Catholic community in the alpine region of Vorarlberg. By the time he's a teenager, in the mid-1920s, thanks to his lowly birth he's the village outcast. He does menial jobs for the priest and is the butt of everyone's jokes. 'It's a lot of work with no joy and the constant feeling of being in people's debt,' he says. He has no future and no way out.

In 1929, he meets a German tourist – an enthusiast for mountaineering and Nazism in equal measure. 'All of a sudden, the scales fell from my eyes,' says Hans. 'I saw how they had abused me, and the uselessness of the morals they had taught me. I recognized my situation.'

Hans picks up National Socialism fast. He holds secret meetings with a few friends, then bigger ones in public. The priest disowns him, but now the villagers are keen to lend him money because they like what he is saying. He is, the researcher reports, 'a passionate speaker when inspired by hate'.

Wall Street crashes, the economy slumps and Nazi ideology strengthens: 'an atmosphere of expectation was created, of a thousand-year dream', writes the researcher. Soon, only three out of thirty-eight families in the village are still devoutly Catholic; for the rest, their active religion is Nazism. For Hans, his conversion to fascism gave the world a new meaning:

> He was no longer a pariah: he found his place within the community again ... The new convert belonged to the great German people; he was a master just by participating. He was superior to the majority, he

was chosen, initiated. Through political activism the face of the world was changed.[1]

We know about Hans because of Lucie Varga. In 1935, faced with the spread of Nazism in Austria, Varga – a Jewish historian from Vienna – went undercover to investigate. She adopted the techniques ethnographers use when studying unfamiliar cultures: take nothing at face value; listen for the nuances and unspoken meanings; decode the language, behaviour and imagery you encounter, but abandon your preconceptions.[2]

People in the alpine valleys, she wrote, operated with two broad concepts of time: 'Before' and 'Now'. Before the Depression, life was good. Now it was intolerable. Before, people believed in Catholicism, the priest blessed the fields at harvest time and there was an eternal order. Now there was penury and disorder and total hostility to the Church; the ideological framework of people's lives had collapsed. For people like Hans, Nazism had filled the void:

> The optimistic, progressive people of the village; their millennial polit-
> ics, their desperate bravery; all that is ready to change, from one
> moment to the next, into apathy, disgust at life, into fatalistic pessim-
> ism. The consequences? We observe; we are not prophets . . . [3]

Varga did not live to see the consequences. She died in France in 1941, on the run from the Gestapo, because – with no money and a fake ID – she could not procure insulin to treat her diabetes. The family that sheltered her were sent to Auschwitz.

We, however, know how the story ends. More than 900,000 Austrians served in Hitler's armies. One of them was Josef Vallaster, a farm labourer from the same valley Varga studied. He, like Hans, was recruited as a teenager and became a fanatical Nazi.

Files uncovered in 2007 revealed that Vallaster had been a 'stoker' at the Hartheim euthanasia facility, where he oversaw the gassing of 18,000 mentally and physically disabled people, before graduating to the same role at the Sobibor death camp, where he helped to murder 250,000 Jews. He was killed in an uprising by the prisoners in 1943 and had been listed as a 'victim' on the village war memorial (now removed).[4]

Some 108,000 Austrians – one in nine of those who served – were charged with war crimes by special courts installed by the occupying powers; 28,000 were brought to trial, of whom half were convicted. Because the tribunals were cancelled at the start of the Cold War in 1948, most of those charged were never tried. All those jailed were pardoned in the mid-1950s.[5] By then, few people wanted to remember what a sudden collapse into 'fatalistic pessimism' can set in train.

We, too, have learned to divide historical time into 'before' and 'now'. For the generation I grew up with in northern England, 'before' means before the coming of Margaret Thatcher in 1979: a time defined by prosperity, rising wages, decent jobs, a settled community and hope for the future. For Generation X and the Millennials, 'before' means before the financial crash of 2008, when it seemed that the upswing of digital technology, globalization and liberal attitudes would go on for ever. For today's teenagers, 'before' might mean before Trump, before the Australian bushfires, before Covid-19.

Yet we all share the same 'now'. As we enter the 2020s we're living through a multi-layered disruption of normality, in which every new crisis adds to the disorientation triggered by the last.

In the midst of this situation, a new kind of fascism has emerged. Its organizational forms morph so fast that any book on the topic runs the risk of quickly becoming dated. In this chapter I will try to answer three questions. What does the modern far right typically do? What is it trying to achieve? And why should we fear the consequences?

Like Varga, I am interested not just in what far-right extremists say, but what they mean: the subtext of the videos they post, the memes they spread and the brands they wear. We need to understand the symbolic character of their violence to discover what they are trying to achieve.

Just as in Varga's alpine valley, the most important function of extreme-right ideology today is as a replacement belief system, an *active* ideology built on the ruins of a passive one that has failed. In our case, it is the religion of the market that has failed – and with it some people's belief in democracy.

Though fascist organizations today are small, the fascist ideology is much more widely accepted than many of us realize. Taking them together, you can read the actions of right-wing extremists not as a series of futile, disconnected gestures, but as improvisations around a common script. They are designed to tell the same story over and over again, rather than – at this stage – to take power.

Fascism, of course, is not the only challenge to liberal democracy. The global period of instability that began after 2008 has thrust right-wing populists into government. In Hungary, Poland, India, Brazil and Turkey, such parties have cemented their position in power through the erosion of democratic rights and judicial independence. In Italy, Slovakia, Switzerland and Austria, they have governed in coalition with conservatives.[6] In other countries – Sweden, Finland, Germany, France and Spain, for example – right-wing populists enjoy double-digit support but are, at the time of writing, frozen out by mainstream party alliances. In Britain and the USA, right-wing populist movements (Vote Leave and the Trump movement) operate as 'shadow parties' within the Conservative and Republican parties, setting them on a collision course with the judiciary and constitutional law.

The extreme right believes that, as future instabilities emerge, it can move the populists further – from 'illiberal democracy' to full-blown ethno-nationalism. If we want to stop this happening, we need to look the practice of modern fascism squarely in the face. Let's start with some snapshots from around the world in the year 2020, and study the pattern of action and intention that emerges from these interactions between fascism, populism and the state.

A POGROM IN INDIA

On 12 December 2019 the Indian parliament passed a law granting citizenship to all undocumented migrants – except Muslims. It was the first time in the country's history that the law had formally discriminated against the 172 million-strong Muslim population. Many saw it as a signal that the ruling BJP, a Hindu nationalist party led by Prime Minister Narendra Modi, was about to turn the world's biggest democracy into an ethno-state.[7]

Protests erupted against the new law, with students demonstrating in at least fifty university campuses and local communities taking to the streets. Muslim women began peacefully occupying roads, blocking the traffic while reading out passages from India's secular constitution.

One chant dominated: *Hum kya chahte, Azadi!* – 'We want freedom!'. The *Azadi!* (*'Freedom!'*) slogan originated in Kashmir, a 97 per cent Muslim region whose borders are disputed with Pakistan, and which India placed under severe martial law in August 2019. During the protests against the migrant citizenship law, the slogan morphed into a universal expression of resistance: a cry for freedom from religious intolerance, freedom from the caste system and, for some left-wing students, freedom from capitalism.

And that was the trigger for the far-right backlash. Pro-government channels and websites whipped up an anti-*Azadi* movement.[8] BJP politicians called for the protesters to be shot and threatened to remove them in a 'surgical strike'. On 23 February 2020 – with Donald Trump set to arrive for a presidential visit – Kapil Mishra, a prominent local leader of the BJP in Delhi, made a speech telling police that unless they cleared the protesters, his supporters would do it themselves.[9] As videos of the speech spread via Facebook and WhatsApp, what followed was a pogrom.

Several large mobs, ranging from 100 to 1,000-strong, rampaged through north-east Delhi, killing at least fifty-three Muslims and hospitalizing more than 250. They torched twenty-two mosques and Muslim religious schools, hundreds of shops and homes, and numerous copies of the Quran. The targets were meticulously chosen: Hindu homes and shops were left unburned amid the wreckage. The rioting lasted three days. Numerous victims reported collusion and even participation by the police, in evidence submitted to human rights organizations.[10]

Calls to participate spread on WhatsApp groups run by members of the RSS, a century-old far-right Hindu nationalist movement with millions of members, originally founded by admirers of Mussolini.[11] Though the RSS did not appear officially in their khaki uniforms, their chant *Jai Sri Ram!* ('Glory to Lord Ram!') was heard continually from the mouths of the attackers. 'Brother, RSS people have come here in support,' said one message in a WhatsApp group used to organize the massacre.[12]

Teenagers took selfies, and posted videos of their part in the attacks, apparently in order to boost their status with the movement.[13] Many of the murders were not investigated individually, but in the case of just one – a Muslim man shot as he left his home – a total of sixteen activists from the RSS were arrested.[14]

In this single outbreak of mass violence, all the standard operating procedures of modern fascism were on display. The attackers used social media and messaging apps both to instigate the violence and to advertise what they'd done. The violence was politically symbolic, designed just as much to terrorize the wider Muslim population as to harm those present. It was incited by elected politicians of the populist right but executed by the foot soldiers of the extreme right. And it served a wider political purpose.

Trump, who arrived on the second day of the rioting, had only praise for Modi. 'They have really worked hard on religious freedom,' he said of Modi's government, making no reference to the mass killing in progress just eleven kilometres away from the press conference. 'We talked about it for a long time and I really believe that's what he wants.'[15] The BJP rewarded Trump's loyalty by mobilizing its networks to support him in the November 2020 election, just as they had done for Boris Johnson's Conservatives in Britain, in December 2019.[16] Though the Hindu community in the USA is just four million strong, and not all support the BJP, nearly half a million Hindus live in Texas, with six-figure populations in Georgia, North Carolina and Florida; elections in these states were decided by much smaller margins.[17]

All over the world the main driver of far-right extremism is the fear that people who are not supposed to be free might achieve freedom, and that in the process they might redefine what freedom means. Listen carefully to the attackers' words and you'll hear this fear expressed. As they beat the Muslim street-traders, the crowd shouted: 'Take *Azadi*, we are giving you *Azadi*.'[18] As they torched a mosque and blinded those inside with acid, they taunted their victims: 'This is *Azadi*.' At one point the police dropped their trousers and showed their genitals to a group of Muslim women, shouting: 'You want *Azadi*, we'll give you *Azadi*.'[19]

Psychologists studying fascism in the 1930s described its primary motivation as the 'fear of freedom'.* If so, the north-east Delhi attack

---

* See Chapter 7 below.

provides a literal case in point. The Muslim protesters used the word 'freedom' in an amorphous and expansive way. In return, their attackers told them: the only freedom you're going to get is to be raped, beaten or killed.

There is nothing new about intercommunal violence in India; it was encouraged for centuries by colonial divide-and-rule tactics, and is deeply rooted in the caste system.[20] These intercommunal tensions were restrained during the post-1947 period by a secular constitution, a firm judiciary and a democratic political culture, with the secularist Congress Party as the dominant political force. But from the 1980s onwards, a combination of corruption, urbanization and rising inequality fuelled rivalries between religious groups, allowing the BJP to become a powerful opposition party, eventually taking power in 2014, with Modi at its head.

The wider Hindu nationalist culture – labelled Hindutva – has existed for decades, with the RSS and other grassroots extremist groups operating symbiotically with the BJP, underpinned by a quasi-religious philosophy that is drilled into activists in daily lessons. It is, in a way, an arrangement that all other forms of far-right politics aspire to.

After Modi came to power, the question facing India was: can the judiciary, the electoral system and the constitution hold him in check, or will he redefine India as a Hindu state, with a permanent BJP government? If the 'text' of the February 2020 massacre was that Muslims should forget freedom, the subtext was that – at a time of Hindutva's choosing – the secular basis of India's post-independence society will be destroyed. That threat, on its own, casts a long shadow over the twenty-first century.

VIGILANTES AT THE GREEK BORDER

In March 2020, during a diplomatic standoff, the Turkish government encouraged thousands of refugees to storm the country's border with Greece, threatening a return to the refugee crisis of 2015, when more than 1.5 million migrants entered Europe.

As Greek security forces struggled to contain the refugees, people in the border city of Volos formed a Facebook group called 'The

Association of Illegal Migrant Hunters'. They posted snapshots of the firearms they intended to use to 'clear the city of migrants' and defend the border. Ioannis Lagos, a former leader of the fascist party Golden Dawn, now an independent member of the European Parliament, arrived with 'volunteers' clad in military camouflage to patrol the border.[21]

Soon, contingents from extreme-right groups across Europe began to arrive. Prominent among them was Martin Sellner, the former leader of Generation Identity, an Austrian group which shot to notoriety after receiving a donation from the man who murdered fifty-one people in two Christchurch mosques.[22] Sellner posed with a banner at the fence telling refugees to go home.[23] Also present was Jimmie Åkesson, leader of the Sweden Democrats, a right-wing populist party that achieved 17.5 per cent of the vote in the 2018 election. He handed leaflets to the refugees with the same message: go home.[24]

Away from the cameras, groups of right-wing European extremists joined armed Greek villagers in tractor convoys to hunt down migrants by night. Photos in the Italian media showed armed civilians 'guarding' a group of refugees whose shoes they had confiscated.[25]

This, in short, was a mobilization of the European far right. By October 2020 Lagos would be facing a long jail sentence, convicted of leading a criminal organization. His form of closet Nazism represents the far-right's past, but Sellner and Åkesson are its intended future: slick, presentable and oriented to electoral politics, they communicate through gestures like the one at the border.

If the text of their intervention was, literally, 'Europe is full, go home', the subtext was even more chilling. The ultimate far-right fantasy is of an ethno-religious civil war in Europe, with white Christians on one side, refugees and Muslims on the other, with the Greece–Turkey border one of its main battlefields. This border standoff was designed as a small-scale demonstration of what it might look like.

A FAR-RIGHT MILITIA IN BRAZIL

On 3 June 2020 the Brazilian far-right activist Sara Winter arrived outside the country's Supreme Court with fifty armed followers.

Proclaiming their support for Brazil's right-wing president, Jair Bolsonaro, and calling themselves the '300 Brazilians' – a reference to the small force of Spartans at the battle of Thermopylae – they pitched tents, attacked journalists, launched fireworks at the building and then stormed it, getting as far as the roof while the police stood helpless.[26]

In a YouTube video, Winter – a 27-year-old former sex worker turned anti-abortion activist – promised potential recruits they would become part of a far-right guerrilla movement and receive training in 'subversion'. The stunt was part of a wave of protests against the Supreme Court, over its attempts to investigate President Bolsonaro for interference in a police investigation concerning his business dealings.

Winter's avowed aim was to 'Ukrain-ize' Brazil – that is, to overthrow its Congress and Supreme Court in a revolution modelled on the Euromaidan protest of 2013.[27] She threatened one judge via Twitter:

> We are going to make your life hell. We will find the places you go to. We will find the cleaners who work for you. We will discover everything about your life.[28]

Winter herself does not conform to the typical image of a fascist. Nonetheless, her group fits the typology of the fascist militia perfectly. They were armed, in face masks, with burning torches; even Winter's name, a pseudonym, is borrowed from that of a wartime British Nazi. But Sara Winter was not the main problem for Brazil's beleaguered judiciary. For among the wider mass of demonstrators who assembled outside the Supreme Court to demand its dissolution early that June was President Bolsonaro himself.

Bolsonaro rose to power because of a double collapse: the collapse in commodity prices and wages after 2008, which ended a decade of growth and improvements for the poor; and the collapse in support for the ruling left-wing Workers' Party (PT) as its leading members were engulfed in a corruption scandal in the mid-2010s. This scandal culminated in 2016, with the impeachment and removal from office of Brazil's then president, Dilma Rousseff, as millions of right-wing demonstrators took to the streets, while prosecutors also jailed the PT's iconic leader, Luis Inácio Lula da Silva (known as Lula).

The anti-Rousseff movement mobilized all those who had lost out under the left's redistribution programme: landowners, big farmers, the financial elite and parts of the urban middle class. But it also mobilized poor people who felt betrayed after the global economic downturn made further social reforms impossible.[29] And now, alongside its traditional propaganda channels – the Evangelical churches, newspapers and clandestine publications advocating military rule – the right-wing elite had social media, above all YouTube, which helped to create a mass, popular, far-right ideology.

A 2019 investigation by the *New York Times* found that YouTube's algorithm, whose rules for video recommendations have never been disclosed, systematically promoted and expanded the far-right video universe in Brazil, facilitating its merger with a pre-existing subculture of anti-vaccination ('antivaxx') conspiracy theorists. In the process it normalized the practice of *linchamento*: online lynch mobs targeting doctors, teachers, journalists and left-wing politicians, sometimes inciting physical attacks. One of *linchamento*'s main exponents was Bolsonaro himself.[30]

Long before Covid-19, Brazil became a laboratory for what happens when social media algorithms reward, amplify and bring together ideologies promoting irrationalism and hate. Even the atmosphere in schools changed, with teachers suddenly finding basic scientific facts challenged in the classroom by pupils who'd been exposed to far-right propaganda on YouTube. The result was Bolsonaro's 2018 election victory, after which he set out to intimidate and degrade the judiciary and parliament, repeatedly inciting violence and calling for a military coup.

Is Bolsonaro a fascist? Not by most definitions offered in political science. But if he is a right-wing populist – sharing the same category as Nigel Farage or Italy's Matteo Salvini – he is at the extreme end of it.

The main problem, ultimately, is neither Sara Winter *nor* Jair Bolsonaro, it is the process of political disintegration and polarization they are exploiting. A quarter of Rio de Janeiro, the country's biggest city, is effectively controlled by 'community self-defence' militias, armed and trained by the police and prepared to kill left-wing politicians who get in their way.[31] In the Amazon, meanwhile, vigilantes protecting the interests of farmers, mining companies and loggers killed twenty-four environmental activists in 2019 alone.[32]

When Covid-19 hit Brazil in 2020, all Bolsonaro had to do was mobilize the pre-existing machinery: the parties, the Evangelical churches, the junior officer networks, the extreme right and the paramilitary groups. Defying science, Bolsonaro declared the virus was 'mild flu' and, despite catching the disease himself, began agitating against the public health lockdowns desperately mandated by regional governors. Bolsonaro led his supporters to protest outside army bases, calling for military interventions to lift the lockdowns, at one stage appearing on horseback. At the time of writing Brazil has suffered one of the worst death tolls from Covid-19, at 384,000 and rising.[33]

Sara Winter's attack on the Supreme Court was intended as a stunt. Police action eventually dispersed the 300 Brazilians and broke up their camp. She was then arrested and banned from Facebook. By October 2020 she was posting tearful videos on Instagram, claiming that Bolsonaro had abandoned her.[34] But Winter's protest had served its purpose: to send a message that if Lula, now released from prison, makes any kind of serious bid to form a democratically elected left government, all the forces of disorder are prepared to attack Brazil's democratic institutions for real.

A NAZI CELL IN THE *BUNDESWEHR*

In May 2020 German police dug up an arms cache containing two kilograms of plastic explosives, a detonator, an AK-47 rifle, knives, a crossbow, thousands of rounds of ammunition, an SS songbook and a pile of Nazi memorabilia. Its owner was a sergeant-major in the country's elite special forces unit, the KSK.[35]

An investigation by German security services found that the soldier's unit was so thoroughly infiltrated by the extreme right that it had become 'partially detached from the chain of command' – a polite way of saying 'out of control'. The unit was duly dissolved.

The security services announced, moreover, that they were watching 550 suspected neo-Nazis in the *Bundeswehr*, twenty of them in the KSK. For years, the German authorities had denied the existence of a far-right network in the army; now they had to admit it was real, and extensive. Four months later, twenty-nine police officers in the Ruhr city of Essen were suspended after they were found exchanging swastikas, Hitler photos and faked photos of refugees in gas chambers.[36]

The discoveries were part of a rising tide of terror threats emanating from the German far right. In September 2019, German security forces had uncovered a secret network of soldiers, police and veterans known as *Nordkreuz* (Northern Cross). Its members were using the Telegram messaging service to coordinate the compilation of hit lists, using data stolen from police computers, of 25,000 German citizens deemed to be too supportive of refugees.[37] One message said that, in the event of a crisis, those on the list should be 'collected and taken to a place where they are to be killed'. The group members continually fantasized about the collapse of the German state and made active preparations for 'Day X' – which they expected to be triggered by a climate catastrophe, a Muslim uprising or a new financial crash.[38] They are part of an international right-wing subculture known as 'preppers' – people preparing to survive a catastrophic event.

Separately, throughout 2020, more than a hundred left-wing politicians, lawyers and celebrities were bombarded with death and rape threats from a neo-Nazi network calling itself NSU 2.0 (National Socialist Underground 2.0), again using personal data traced to police or judicial computer systems. Meanwhile, over the same period, Germany saw three lone-shooter attacks, which killed, respectively, an anti-racist conservative politician in Hesse; two people at a synagogue in Halle; and nine Kurdish people in a café in Hanau. In each case the perpetrator had expressed far-right views online.[39]

This is the extreme end of the radicalization process: armed, secret networks operating inside the state, with lists of targets and the means to kill them. Though the numbers were small, the violence they imagined or executed was deadly.

Because Germany has an overtly anti-fascist constitution and a police force dedicated to the surveillance of extreme-right groups, the political space for those advocating violence is tightly constrained. But the political space below that is huge. The right-wing populist Alternativ für Deutschland party (AfD) is the third biggest party in Germany: at time of writing it has ninety-four members of parliament and 34,000 members.

Though a few of the *Nordkreuz* activists were members of the party, there is no proven link between the AfD and terrorism. Nonetheless, it contains thousands of people who think what fascists think. Around 7,000 members of the AfD were, until March 2020, part of a subgroup called *Flügel* (Wing), which was shut down after police formally designated it extremist.

A survey of AfD members in the central German region of Hesse showed that a large majority were fully subscribed to the mythology of the new far right: that migrants are responsible for crime; that they 'feel alien in our own country because of Muslims'; that 'gender madness has to be stopped'; and that 'global warming is exaggerated'.[40]

Like all right-wing populist parties, the AfD remains unclear in its direction (whether deliberately or unintentionally is itself opaque), subject to the pull of parliamentary respectability and waves of radicalization washing over its support base. The main obstacle to its advance has been mainstream German conservatives' refusal to collaborate. This position wobbled early in 2020, when conservatives in Thuringia tried to use the AfD's votes to form a regional coalition government, ousting the left.[41] But after concerted political pressure from Berlin, and some resignations, the policy of non-cooperation held. There is a lot riding on whether it holds in future.

DEFENDING WINSTON CHURCHILL

London, 13 June 2020. 'If you'd done your jobs we wouldn't be here,' the man next to me yelled at a group of riot police. About 5,000 people had gathered in Parliament Square: white, male and mainly over the age of fifty. The far right had mobilized to 'protect' the bronze statue of Winston Churchill, which, standing in the square's north-east corner, had been sprayed with graffiti by Black Lives Matter protesters a week before. I went undercover among them to report.

London is an obviously multicultural city. But a good half-mile away from the Churchill statue, I entered a zone of white monoculture. Suddenly there were no students, no people of colour, no tourists, no out gay people. I was back in the world I grew up in. White men, working class and from the suburbs, walking close to each other despite the pervasive presence of Covid, shouting profanities and swilling lager.

Self-appointed guardians of Churchill, they were executing their mission by urinating against the gates of Parliament, littering the road with discarded cans, surging into pointless scuffles with the police, posing for selfies with uniformed military veterans, and ranting.

'Call us racists? We're all fucking racists!' one shouted at the cops. The rest cheered raucously. Another, a postal worker in uniform, held a white feather in the face of a policeman: 'That's what you deserve. We should all be here. Cowards the lot of you! Why are you protecting *them*?' Another – shaved head, cheeks flushed, drunk – yelled into the face of a police officer: 'Arrest *them*!' – 'them' being the term for Black Lives Matter protesters, none of whom were in sight. He threw a punch and was arrested himself.

The violence is what made the headlines, but as a snapshot of the far right it was these monologues of self-pity that mattered. The longer I listened, the clearer their subtext became. This is the sound people make when they fear the wages of whiteness will not be paid.

The black American sociologist W. E. B. Du Bois wrote in the 1930s that racism persisted beyond slavery because white American workers, though paid the same low wages as black people, were 'compensated in part by a sort of public and psychological wage' consisting of the minor privileges that come from being white.[42] In addition, Du Bois noticed, their concept of whiteness was structured around 'ownership of the earth forever': the right to invade and own countries populated by non-white people.[43]

For a conservative minority of Britain's working class these twin sources of racism have gone unchallenged for decades. But events that summer made something snap. First, the sight of tens of thousands of young, articulate, black people marching through London and other cities in protest at the murder of George Floyd. Second, that, amid one such protest, in the former slave port of Bristol, demonstrators toppled the statue of slave-trader Edward Colston and dumped it into the harbour, as the dumbfounded police stood by.

Black people in Britain are nine times more likely to be stopped by the police than white people. At least 40 per cent of young people in prison are black or Asian. Twice as many black and Asian households live in persistent poverty compared to white households. White people receive consistently shorter jail sentences than black and Asian offenders. Black women are five times more likely to die in childbirth than white women. There is, in short, a structural racism in Britain that endures, despite formal legal equality.[44]

For the white men on the Churchill demo this structural difference – which is so abstract if you are salaried and educated, but so concrete if you are not – is all they have left from the world they grew up in. As in the Delhi riot, their rage was triggered by fear: fear that a group that is supposed to be subordinate to them might be on the verge of achieving freedom and equality.

There were far-right extremists on the Churchill demo: members of Britain First, whose fake news videos attacking Islam had been retweeted by Donald Trump, posed with their banner. Other significant right-wing figures – Tommy Robinson and the leaders of the newly formed Patriotic Alternative – stayed away, aware that the inevitable violence and drunkenness would be a reputational disaster. The majority of those on the protest, however, were mobilized by a group called the Democratic Football Lads Alliance.

Founded in 2017, the DFLA has organized thousands of older football fans to march against 'Muslim rape gangs' and 'returning Jihadis', while always claiming to be non-racist.[45] The more they marched, the more the posts in their 12,000-strong secret Facebook group expressed explicitly extremist ideas, notably that immigration threatens British identity and that a civil war is coming.[46] Now, in June 2020, in response to Black Lives Matter, they were for the first time rallying round overt anti-black racism.

The crowd was a microcosm of the way the far right works. The extremists were there because they subscribed to fascist theory: they were younger, calmer and had a purpose; they wore regalia coded with international fascist symbols, such as the flag of 'Kekistan', modelled on the Nazi war flag, or the full-face skull mask favoured by the banned terrorist group AtomWaffen Division. The 'football lads' were mostly driven by emotion, not theory: they were older, drunker and once they had occupied the space they struggled to know what to do, other than sing and fight. But though they may not yet subscribe to fascist theories, they were co-creating fascism's folklore.

These are snapshots of events that took place in big and once stable democracies in the space of a single year. The connections they demonstrate – between right-wing populism, the extreme right and authoritarian conservatism – form a pattern repeated in many other countries. And each of the incidents described has to be understood as a form of symbolic action: action designed to tell a story, using both text and subtext.

They show that the organizational norm for right-wing extremism in the 2020s is not a single hierarchical party. Rather, it consists of the interplay between online networks, symbolic violent actions, loose and mercurial organizations, and an inner core of theorists, leaders and influencers calling the shots.

The base layer of modern fascism is the online space, on platforms such as Telegram and Signal and on the '*chans' – anonymized bulletin boards – where discussions of ethno-nationalism, anti-Islam, conspiracy theories and fantasies of violence take place. Anonymity is the critical factor here. Most far-right activists are immersed in daily conversations where no identifiable person ever has to take responsibility for what they say or do.

The movement enters the physical world through demonstrations, short-notice mobilizations, symbolic actions, fake journalism operations and stunts like the one Winter pulled with the 300 Brazilians. And, as we've seen, such actions often find covert support within certain police and military units.

The sharp end of modern fascism consists of planned, intentional violence: anti-migrant provocations, lone-shooter attacks, death threats and 'prepper'-style training. Most actions are filmed, to be used as propaganda that cascades down to the base layer and boosts the status of the activists taking part.

Because the structure is composed of networks, not fixed and solid entities, communication is just as easy vertically as it is horizontally. Lone-shooter attacks are livestreamed to thousands of people; symbolic acts of violence are shared on video channels and end up on the smartphones of schoolkids.

And the power of the figureheads is, as with Islamist terror networks, 'stochastic': what they say is statistically likely to trigger somebody, somewhere, to commit violence – but it will leave no chain of responsibility. For example, when Trump tweets a video of himself 'body-slamming' a wrestler representing CNN, and a Trump supporter then mails a pipe bomb to CNN, claiming (unsuccessfully at his trial) that he has been inspired by Trump, that is a clear example of stochastic terror.[47]

The classic form of fascism – the 'militia-party' with uniforms, symbols, parades and a charismatic leader – still exists, but is not as important as the online space. Its vulnerabilities were illustrated by the conviction of Golden Dawn's leaders in 2020. The Greek neo-Nazi group, despite enjoying parliamentary immunity, and operating out of front businesses selling martial arts clothing, were still found to have run a criminal organization.[48] The downsides of hierarchy, with a traceable command structure between the incitement and the actual violence, should ensure that the perpetrators – once seen as the most successful far-right group in Europe – serve long jail sentences.

The attraction of online activism, via platforms such as Facebook, Telegram and YouTube, is not just that it allows the rapid spread of far-right ideas, but that it allows the activists, even new recruits, to co-create the ideology as they go, adding their own thoughts to the outpouring of amateur philosophy, DIY science and bogus journalism produced by the movement's influencers. In addition, fake social media identities and the widespread use of anonymous bulletin boards allow activists to plan, coordinate and execute violence and intimidation without prosecution.

What is common to these snapshots of fascist activism? First, that they centre on *symbolic, violent action*. Every action is designed to tell a story.

Second, that they are *prefigurative*. They are meant to show the peripheral activists and the vaguely interested that this is how things could be. The message is that India could become an ethno-state; that Greece will be the frontline of an ethnic civil war; and that Germany might, once again, see left-wing activists disappear into what Hitler called 'night and fog'.

Third, that the most persuasive communications use *subtext*. In Parliament Square, because I've spent years engaged with the far right, I could read the flags, masks, tattoos, obscure foreign football regalia as they did – a self-reinforcing system of meaning. To casually engaged journalists and bystanders it just looked like an odd collection of hieroglyphs.

Fourth, that it allows *co-creation of the narrative*. From the teenagers filming themselves stoning Muslims to death in Delhi to the drunken boneheads of Parliament Square, the taking and sharing of transgressive selfies while engaged in violence is the building block of the story. And that's because of the fifth and most important similarity.

What the fascists were doing, from Brasilia to New Delhi, is *myth-making*. We will explore in detail the inner logic of the modern fascist myth in the next chapter, and trace its historic roots later in the book. Here it is important to understand that, for fascists, a myth is not a fantasy or superstition, it is *a story you can make come true* by believing in it hard enough, and centring your life around it.

The short-term strategy common to every incident described above was to install or maintain right-wing populist politicians in power; to make the cost of voting them out high, because of the violence it will provoke; to degrade the rule of law and operate in the space that opens up; and to intimidate minorities, liberals, lawmakers, judges and the left.

But the long-term strategy is to trigger, fight and win *an ethnic civil war*. Each of the actions described above was, in its own way, an investment in that long-term project. By popularizing the myth of a coming civil war, today's fascists want people to start expecting it, hoping for it and preparing for it – and to make their opponents resigned to its outbreak.

So, as we resist fascism today, whether as counter-demonstrators, politicians or law enforcement, we are not just trying to prevent a series of violent actions. We are also trying to falsify the inner logic of the myth they are trying to create, and to disrupt their attempt to tell the story. For, as Lucie Varga found in the 1930s, once such myths take hold on a mass scale, with quasi-religious fervour, their consequences can be incalculable.

2

Dreams of the Ethno-state

The Thought-architecture of Modern Fascism

If right-wing populist leaders have one thing in common, it is that they despise theory. From Nigel Farage to Matteo Salvini and Donald Trump, we are dealing with anti-intellectuals, content to mobilize the prejudices of conservative-minded voters against Muslims, migrants, feminists and the 'woke'. They have no need for sophisticated theories.

The extreme right, by contrast, has become intensely theoretical. During the past forty years, when progressive values were dominant in the West, and the main challenge to the elite came from the anti-capitalist left, the far right was obliged to survive primarily on a diet of ideas, not action.

What twenty-first-century fascists *want* is clear: to destroy liberal democracy, human rights and the rule of law; to cancel the rights won by women since the 1960s; and to create monocultural ethno-states using cataclysmic violence.

The problem they face is how to persuade people to accept this. Given the radicalism of their objective, it's not going to happen simply through mobilizing people's prejudices. In the past, when fascism succeeded, it did so because millions of people adopted it as a worldview, and were swept into quasi-religious activism around it.

But the theories the far right inherited from the 1930s were shaped in a very different world of hierarchy, obedience, overt imperialism and controlled access to information. Plus, Hitler's *Mein Kampf* and Mussolini's *The Doctrine of Fascism* were indelibly structured around the logic of specific, national imperialist projects. That's why most attempts to build 'neofascist' movements in the 1970s and 80s failed: they looked like tribute bands for a kind of society that no longer existed.

As the far right revived in the 1990s, the search began for thinkers who had cleaned up their language, and for a form of fascism that made sense in a more globalized economy and a more networked society. The most obvious candidates came from within the so-called European New Right (ENR), a movement inspired by right-wing French writer Alain de Benoist.

De Benoist had been the rising star of French neofascism in the early 1960s, but in 1967 broke publicly with far-right political action, to start a think tank researching 'European civilization' and to begin a long battle of ideas in favour of ethno-nationalism. His views are summarized in the 1999 *Manifesto for a European Renaissance*.

De Benoist says, first and foremost, that modernity was a mistake. The eighteenth-century revolution in philosophy and science unleashed a process that, he says, allowed the individual too much freedom, elevated rationality over emotion, destroyed traditional religious narratives and legitimized universalism, which asserts that all human beings have equal rights.[1] The Nazi propagandist Joseph Goebbels had already put this idea more succinctly in proclaiming that with the victory of Nazism, the year of the French Revolution, 1789, 'has been expunged from the records of history'.[2]

But if reversing modernity was an aspiration for the Nazis, it has become a necessity for their twenty-first-century successors. Because, according to de Benoist, modernity is about to collapse. It has reached its final form in globalization, free markets, multiculturalism and feminism, and can go no further. It will be replaced not by a single fascist regime, but by thousands of 'sovereign spaces liberated from the domination of the modern'.[3]

This is the first pillar of extreme-right theory today: a complete reversal of the Enlightenment triggered by a coming global catastrophe. It will not happen, as in the projects of Hitler and Mussolini, in a single state, nor will it be enacted through conquest: it will take the form of a simultaneous global meltdown of states and institutions.

So-called 'Traditionalist' thinkers allied to de Benoist have expanded on this idea. They include the Russian far-right leader Alexander Dugin, Bolsonaro's mentor Olavo de Carvalho, and de Benoist's one-time collaborator Guillaume Faye, who died in 2019.

In *Why We Fight: Manifesto for a European Resistance*, published in 2001, Faye alleged that Europe is 'rapidly and massively being occupied and colonised by peoples from the South and by Islam' and is therefore 'at war'.[4] The aim of the war, for Faye, was to create and defend a white, pan-European identity.

Though de Benoist went to considerable lengths to avoid crude racism, Faye did not. For Faye, history *is* the struggle between races. Their strength lies in their genetic purity, so Europe has to be 'reconquered' by its white inhabitants in order to regain its strength. Faye called on the people of Europe and Russia to 'form a land army, made up of native Europeans and adequate to fighting a possible religious-ethnic civil war'.[5] Then, 'once the twenty-first century succumbs to the approaching crises, the slate will be wiped clean'.[6]

Echoing the philosopher Friedrich Nietzsche, Faye believed a new warrior class of Supermen would be needed to fight the coming civil war. He advocated 'positive eugenics' to breed them, and, in a startlingly frank passage, he outlined their purpose. In the coming crisis, the job of the Superman is to 'transgress':

> . . . for the dangers threatening his people demand solutions that are as
> unthinkable as they are indispensable. As such, he transgresses not for
> the sake of pleasing a dictator . . . but of serving his people's survival,
> that is, in defending its future lineage and ancestral heritage.[7]

These words take us to the dark heart of twenty-first-century ethno-nationalism: what happens if, during the process of creating what Faye described as a 'white, pan-European identity', migrants, Muslims and ethnic minorities refuse to leave? What is the 'unthinkable solution' other than genocide, and what are Faye's words if not an advance justification of it?

In Alexander Dugin's writings, we find the same argument for an ethno-state, but focused on the geopolitical interests of Russia. Dugin wants Russia, not a united Europe, to be at the centre of what replaces modernity. In the 1990s he helped form the National Bolshevik Party – a left nationalist group emerging from the Stalinist tradition. Though he quit the party, he still advocates an alliance of the anti-democratic left and right to crush liberalism, and the creation of a disciplined 'international' of extremists.

What Dugin adds to the anti-modernism of de Benoist and Faye is a call for the 'reversibility of time'. In the contemporary world, he argues, 'everything is bad. The idea of progress is bad; the idea of technological development is bad.' In fact, he says, the entire scientific tradition since Isaac Newton is bad, and all teaching based upon it.[8]

This is something more than nostalgia. Dugin believes that, if a country like Russia can reverse out of the predicted historical sequence, from communism back to capitalism, then it can reverse further, into feudalism or a slave society, or even a hunter-gatherer existence. In these earlier forms of society, Dugin notes, time was conceived as cyclical: if you could roll back 250 years of progress you could then freeze human history at a chosen stage of development – creating a permanent feudalism out of which a new Enlightenment could not emerge.

The ideas of these self-styled 'philosophers' of the far right are not simply grotesque, they would not last five minutes if subjected to the rigours of logic and analysis in an actual philosophy department. That's why they communicate in obscure, long-winded and often unintelligible prose. However, they are persuasive.

As the 'end of history' theory, which had become central to liberal thinking, collapsed, the writings of the Traditionalists became foundational texts for the international alt-right movement that blossomed after 2008. Their works initially crossed over into the American right via the activist Richard Spencer, where they found a ready audience among followers of 'paleoconservatism' – a nostalgic, nationalist and white supremacist movement left over from the Cold War, which was already obsessed with 'cultural Marxism' and anti-feminism.[9] Traditionalist writings were then popularized through internet message boards and through niche publishing houses, and in the late 2010s were publicly embraced by the former Trump adviser Steve Bannon.[10]

Though labelled 'Traditionalists', these thinkers have in fact made an important change to the traditions of both fascism and conservatism. Hitler and Mussolini were, above all, nationalists: they proposed to replace the class struggle with a struggle to the death between nation states. For de Benoist, Dugin, Faye, Carvalho and their followers, the primary focus is ethnicity. Spencer's alt-right movement emerged from a paleoconservative milieu that had been obsessed with preserving white *America*, and turned it into a global project to mobilize the 'white race', from Seattle to Vladivostok, for war against the rest of the world. And whereas twentieth-century fascism, as we will see, contained a strong dose of 'reactionary modernism' – extolling the virtues of machine power, fast automobiles and the cinema – the Traditionalist right is profoundly anti-modern.

Their intent, from the outset, was to create a far-right 'metapolitics' – a new common sense that would filter out of their alt-academy into culture and then into politics itself.[11] They have succeeded. Today, the Traditionalist view of history forms the first ideological pillar of extreme-right thought and can be seen and heard everywhere in cyberspace.

The second pillar is pseudoscience about race and gender. Though it presents itself as science, its conclusions are the same as those arrived at through speculation in the nineteenth century: that 'races' exist and can be defined genetically; that cultural differences between ethnic groups are the product of genetic difference; and that racism is the result of biological inequality, not social injustice. Women's oppressed and subordinate position throughout history is similarly conceived as 'natural', and feminism unnatural, since – it is argued – women have evolved to be subordinate to men through behavioural strategies that shaped the structure of their brains.

All of this, of course, is in conflict with the actual conclusions of science. Today, an overwhelming majority of geneticists and anthropologists accept that 'race is not a genetic concept'.[12] The international community, via UNESCO, declared that 'the human race is one' and that, while ethnic groups can be defined, and define themselves, 'for all practical social purposes "race" is not so much a biological phenomenon as a social myth'.[13]

Yet in the decades after the war, racist pseudoscience and its concomitant strategy, eugenics, survived within semi-private academic networks, often funded by white supremacists in the USA.[14] But it was the emergence of the academic subdisciplines of 'sociobiology' and 'evolutionary psychology' that created a new space for pseudoscientific claims about the social status of black people and women.

Given that our understanding of human behaviour remains incomplete, it is legitimate to ask whether advances in genetics should change our view of what determines behaviour. But if you create a new scientific discipline, fusing empirical research with speculative assumptions, you open a gateway for racists and misogynists that cannot be adequately policed using the traditional methods of academic peer review.

In the view of the new scientific racists, white Europeans are genetically superior because the stress of moving out of Africa 45,000 years ago, into the colder environment of Europe, meant that only the most intelligent survived.[15] Since white skin pigmentation evolved only around 8,000 years ago in response to the environments humans moved into, this racist argument runs that black and white people's brains may have evolved differently over the same timescale. As a result, the argument concludes, different average IQ scores between ethnic groups have a genetic basis, rather than being the result of social inequality or the racist framing of the IQ tests themselves.[16] Unsurprisingly, these bogus claims have been widely and repeatedly debunked.[17]

In the 1990s, the return of race science was closely allied to conservative social policy. In their controversial book *The Bell Curve*, political scientist Charles Murray and psychologist Richard Herrnstein argued that welfare programmes for the poor should be ended in the USA because, being heavily used by black people, they 'subsidised births among poor women who are disproportionately at the low end of the intelligence distribution'.[18]

But as scientists rubbished *The Bell Curve*, the far right noticed the utility of operating within highly fragmented, often speculative scientific disciplines. A new figure emerged, generally white and male, with genuine scientific credentials, who could make a genetic 'hypothesis' about behaviour that enjoyed the same status as other hypotheses until it was disproven. As a result, major, peer-reviewed journals were, as the science writer Angela Saini records, bombarded with substandard and tendentious racist research.[19]

When this research was routinely rejected, a new kind of academic journal emerged: one in which peer review is nonexistent or carried out by 'independent researchers' – i.e. amateurs. A group of journals named *OpenPsych*, for instance, specializes in articles claiming to trace criminal behaviour or low intelligence to genetic racial difference.

But while it's easy (though exhausting) to gatekeep a scientific discipline against a DIY journal, it's impossible to guard the floodgates of the public sphere. Which is why the standard practice of 'race science' is to publish an outrageous claim, cause a public political furore, and turn this furore into an issue of academic freedom.

This is precisely what happened when the Cambridge University researcher Noah Carl, who wrote for *OpenPsych* and had spoken at a secretive eugenics conference in London, was sacked from his post in 2019. The *Daily Mail* ran headlines claiming he was a victim of political correctness, while a crowdfunder organized by a white supremacist-aligned computer programmer in the USA raised $100,000 for his defence. (At the time of writing, Carl remains in dispute with the university over unfair dismissal.)[20]

With anti-feminist science, meanwhile, it is the emerging discipline of evolutionary psychology, dubbed 'EvoPsych', that does the heavy lifting for the far right. Its premise is that while 'races' are the product of relatively recent human evolution, gender relationships should remain as they were programmed in the Stone Age. The behaviours that have been coded as 'female' over 40,000+ years of women's oppression are, say some EvoPsych proponents, the result of brain structures inherited from women's prehistoric social 'tactics'.

In this view, the structure of the female brain explains why men are more likely to sleep around, have casual sex, pay for sex and regard women possessing the traditional attributes of 'beauty' as attractive. 'It's all completely hardwired, guys,' is the message to misogynists. Year after year, the EvoPsych bandwagon produces new hypotheses, always premised on the assertion that social norms, cultures and conditions have no bearing on the tendency of men to oppress, rape and physically assault women.

The usefulness of EvoPsych to the far right is obvious. If 'race science' shows that laws mandating racial equality are unnatural, then it is also against nature for women to have equal property rights, civil rights and control over their own bodies.

Not all those involved in pseudoscience are motivated by right-wing politics. But the far right has greedily amalgamated their work into its project. In the process they have created a 'counterscience' movement: dedicated teams of amateurs, armed with long lists of scientific 'references' torn out of context, churning out what one psychologist called 'little turds of tainted data'.[21] Their narrative is that science has been hijacked by political correctness, cultural Marxism and wokeness, and that the scientific method itself is a defence mechanism for the elite.

If Traditionalism functions as the far right's theory of history, pseudoscience functions as its theory of injustice: one in which the main victims are white men. All it needs to be a complete worldview is a theory of politics, and for this it has returned to the Nazi source material.

Until the second Iraq War, political theorists to the right of mainstream conservatism were heavily libertarian, demanding a minimal state and maximum individual freedom in pursuit of people's 'natural rights'. But from the mid-2000s – and especially after the financial crisis hit – libertarianism became a gateway drug to right-wing authoritarianism.

Observing what he called the 'libertarian to alt-right pipeline', journalist Matt Lewis advanced a sociological explanation: both ideologies attract young, white men critical of the status quo. But there is a simpler explanation: the logic of libertarianism just does not work in conditions of crisis.

Ultra-libertarian economics says that a market, left to itself, creates a spontaneous order. Where disorder exists, it's because states intervene to provide welfare for their citizens, or because pressure groups (such as black people, women, trade unions and the poor) distort the market's priorities. The libertarian prescription for all economic crises, then, is 'less state'.

But the collapse of the financial markets in 2008 made the whole of capitalism suddenly dependent on 'more state'. Economic libertarianism under these circumstances would produce more chaos, not order. And as the crisis triggered resistance, filling the public spaces of the world with tent camps and anti-capitalists, a large, militarized and repressive state looked like the best option for defending the 'natural rights' of billionaires.

Some libertarians were ahead of the game. In 2001, the right-wing thinker Hans-Herman Hoppe wrote a book arguing that even the smallest democratically run state is too restrictive for capitalism.[22] Though all states were bad, said Hoppe, if you have to have one, better to make it a monarchy.

Then in 2007 Curtis Yarvin, a software engineer in Silicon Valley, started a highly influential blog under the pseudonym Mencius Moldbug, pushing Hoppe's ideas to their logical extreme. Yarvin, like many in the tech industry, had started out as a libertarian. Now he wanted an autocratic state.

Libertarianism, he wrote, works only where there is order. Amid the disorder following the 2008 crash, democracy could benefit only the left: human rights laws, judges and democratic voting systems would always constrain the executive in its task of sweeping away barriers to the market. So, argued Yarvin – and not ironically – the right should become 'royalist':

> As a royalist, I favor absolute monarchy in the abstract sense: unconditional personal authority, subject to some responsibility mechanism. I am not an adherent of any particular dynasty, nor do I favor the hereditary principle as a method for royal selection . . . I feel the State should be operated as a profitable corporation governed proportionally by its beneficiaries.[23]

The task of the monarch would be to launch a savage crackdown on all sources of disorder. Riffing on lines from the movie *Taxi Driver* and the Dead Kennedys single '*Kalifornia Über Alles*', Yarvin wrote:

> Unleash the blue wave! As Travis Bickle put it, someday a real rain will wash all the scum off these streets. That rain is on the way. Its name is President Brown. 'You will croak, you little clown / When you mess with President Brown!' And after that rain, preventive-detention facilities will spring up like puffballs, as America's streets are scrubbed clean as diamonds and left as safe as the White House lawn.[24]

This lyrical paean to fascism proved influential, especially in Silicon Valley. In 2009 Yarvin's friend the Paypal entrepreneur Peter Thiel wrote that, because of the scale of state intervention required after the crash, 'I no longer believe that freedom and democracy are compatible.' The extension of voting rights to women and welfare to the poor, he wrote, meant that a libertarian party could never win elections in conditions of crisis.[25]

At this stage Thiel, despairing of a political solution, urged libertarians to create communities of survival, not resistance; this is the rationale for Silicon Valley's obsession with building undersea cities and space travel. Yarvin, too, advised his followers in the Neoreactionary (NRx) movement to remain passive and wait for liberalism's eventual collapse. But on election night in November 2016, they would together celebrate the victory of a man who made their political fantasies come true. 'President Brown' turned out to be real. Only his name was different: Trump.

From 2016 to 2020, Trump's 'blue wave' of police and immigration crackdowns was like a laboratory experiment for the form of governance advocated by Thiel and Yarvin. He did, indeed, try to rule like a monarch, nominating his own children to key posts, overriding the constitution, and acting as if he personally embodied the state. As Yarvin had envisaged, he ran the state like a private business. He also followed the NRx playbook by unleashing a 'hard rain' of Federal law enforcement against anti-racism protesters and migrants, separating thousands of innocent immigrant children from their parents as families attempted to cross the US border, and locking them in detention centres. Though Trump was voted out democratically, his administration created a template that will be used throughout this century, both in the USA and elsewhere, wherever right-wing populists gain executive power.

However, a blog and some intuitions do not constitute a full-blown political theory. And so, as electoral successes multiplied in the mid-2010s, far-right ideologists inevitably returned to the fountainhead of authoritarianism: the works of the Nazi legal scholar Carl Schmitt.

In the last years of the Weimar Republic, Schmitt provided successive right-wing governments with the legal justification for suspending parliamentary rule. Once Hitler took power Schmitt joined the Nazi Party, became its most influential legal scholar and issued a series of opinions backing its actions, ranging from the extrajudicial murder of Nazi dissidents in 1934 through to the 1941 Nazi invasion of Russia (on the grounds that 'great spaces' need a single government).[26]

Schmitt survived the war, avoiding trial despite his culpability, and installed himself in West German academia. There he continued to riff on his three main themes: that every state is defined by its enemy, that sovereignty is determined by the ability to suspend democracy, and that mixed societies don't work.

The authority of a state, wrote Schmitt, derives not from laws or constitutions but from its power to impose dictatorship. Rejecting the separation of powers between judges, ministers and parliaments, he taught that sovereignty resides only with the person who can pull the plug on democracy. And the authority for pulling the plug is ultimately derived from the existence of an enemy:

> The political enemy need not be morally evil or aesthetically ugly; he need not appear as an economic competitor, and it may be advantageous to engage with him in business transactions. But he is, nevertheless, the other, the stranger; and it is sufficient for his nature that he is, in a specially intense way, existentially something different and alien, so that in the extreme case conflicts with him are possible.[27]

It is hard not to read that passage, written on the eve of the Nuremberg Laws, which in 1935 withdrew German citizenship from the country's Jewish population, as justification for what followed.

Of course, ruling by decree while overriding the rule of law, through a state defined by continuous war against its internal enemies, is not the preserve of fascism alone. In the early twenty-first century, Schmitt's political philosophy has also become a manual for authoritarian conservative rule. Today he is as popular in the Kremlin and among the intellectuals of the Chinese Communist Party as he was in Trump's White House.

But it is Schmitt's third concept, logically underpinning the other two, which puts those who follow him today on a trajectory towards fascism. Schmitt believed democracies can work only if they are 'homogeneous'. There can be no radically conflicting values within a democracy, he wrote: it requires 'first homogeneity and second – if the need arises – elimination or eradication of heterogeneity'.[28]

There were two main sources of 'heterogeneity' in the Weimar Republic: Jews and Marxists. So it was entirely, if grotesquely, logical – and not some kind of excusable accident, as claimed by his supporters – that when the Nazis imposed his theory of 'homogeneity' Schmitt rushed to legitimize and support them, organizing a conference designed to purge Jewish ideas from German law and to get Jewish books listed in a separate library catalogue.[29] Unsurprisingly, both the American fascist Richard Spencer and the AfD in Germany claim Schmitt as an inspiration.

The resurgence of Carl Schmitt is a danger signal. His mission was to convince Hitler to present a legal justification for the crimes of the Third Reich. He failed because, as we will see, fascism in power was radicalized and amorphous. It had no use for a regularized legality – and this lack of a legal underpinning became the source of extreme instability within the Nazi regime once it went to war.

Yet Schmitt's work outlived the Nazi regime. Today, it provides right-wing populism, extremism and authoritarian conservatism with a common theory of what constitutes political legitimacy. Their attachment to Schmitt's ideas signals that this time around the fascists intend to 'do it right': to achieve through legal rigour the thousand-year structure that Hitler failed to cement.

If they ever gain power, twenty-first-century fascists intend to create a permanent and orderly dictatorship – not the chaotic and unstable muddle that was the Third Reich – and with the textbooks of Carl Schmitt as their handbook. All the actions of the ethno-state against its enemies will be justified using Schmitt's arguments. It is his theory of politics that forms the third pillar of the fascist thought-architecture.

THE MYTHOLOGY OF MODERN FASCISM

Over the past twenty years, then, far-right thinkers have assembled an internally coherent theory of history, justice and political power. It is systematically both anti-liberal and anti-Marxist, and – though deranged – attracts people precisely because liberal ideas are in disarray, the orthodox version of Marxism unpersuasive, and social democracy an ideological dead-zone.

However, few people have the time to read the works of elderly mystics like Dugin or the rambling invective of Guillaume Faye. To achieve mass effect the theory has been condensed into something more accurately described as a 'social myth': something that you *want* to happen, that you *believe* will happen and – by taking violent action – you can *make* happen.

Myth creation, as we will see, was an important tool for historical fascism. Today, though it differs from country to country, the fascist mythology can be condensed into five propositions, which are easily understood by recruits:

1. **The Great Replacement Theory**, a unifying idea popularized by the French writer Renaud Camus, wrapping together racism, anti-feminism and hostility to the left. It says that immigration constitutes a 'genocide' of the white race; that feminists are helping them by depressing the birth-rate; that 'Cultural Marxism' – the socially liberal left – is to blame for its promotion of feminism and migration; and (in the most paranoid versions of the theory) that Jews are secretly facilitating it all through their ownership of Hollywood, finance and the media.[30]

2. **Liberalism is the main enemy.** Liberal democracy has facilitated mass immigration; human rights protect the 'invader'; the judiciary and the legal profession are willing accomplices; and all political parties except the populist right are to blame for the country's decline. Any attempt to reform liberal capitalism in a more humane direction – such as the 'Great Reset' programme proposed by the World Economic Forum – is reinterpreted as a plot by the elite (dubbed the New World Order) against the people.[31] Democracy must be replaced: either by a strong ruler, overriding the rights of minorities through a state of emergency; or (for the pessimists who believe they have already lost that battle) by 'survivor' communities, operating at small scale, run by oligarchs and warlords.

3. **'Cultural Marxism' is destroying the West.** This aspect of the mythology claims social liberalism was introduced to the West by Marxists in the 1960s as a deliberate plot, after the failure of communism. Since they could not overthrow capitalism through class struggle, so the claim goes, the left would undermine it using ideas attributed to the Frankfurt

School of social theorists. In this view, social liberalism is pernicious because it justifies the 'pollution' of the gene pool through migration, destroys the 'natural' relationship between men and women, promotes homosexuality and transgender rights, and destroys 'free speech'.[32]

4. **The primacy of metapolitics.** There is no need yet for a Hitler-style project of street violence in support of a direct fascist bid for power. For now, the right-wing populist parties and figureheads can be used to exert pressure within the official system. The tactic of the ethno-nationalists is to do 'metapolitics' – to spread their ideology and win the arguments, primarily via the Internet – and wait for multiple catastrophes to trigger the decisive phase. The ideology can be spread in two ways: through exemplary action (as with the manifestos issued by lone shooters or the symbolic stunts described in Chapter 1); or by inhabiting 'online antagonistic communities' – networks of people angry about their own lives, who can be convinced to join the dots between one grievance and the next so that they become angry about everything.

5. **Day X.** The expected catastrophe – a mass outbreak of racial civil violence – differs according to which country the far right is operating in. In the USA, it will be 'Boogaloo' – code for a second American Civil War; in Brazil, it might be a military coup to head off a further election victory by the Workers' Party, which sees the left jailed *en masse*; in Europe, it could be triggered either by a 2015-style wave of refugees, or by a conflict between law enforcement and an increasingly alienated Muslim population. Whatever the catalyst, the outcome – the fascists hope – will be societies characterized by ethnic purity and traditional gender roles.

If you condense modern fascist mythology to these five points, you can understand why its theorists never do so. They express themselves at length, metaphorically, through irony and allusion precisely because fascist mythology needs to be sub-rational, and unchallengeable by logic, analysis or reality.

Because, in reality, there is no 'white race' to be subjected to 'genocide'. Nor did anyone 'design' inward migration as a modern phenomenon. It is what happens if you globalize the world economy, having first impoverished some countries through centuries of colonization and decades of Stalinism. Nor did the Frankfurt School plot the downfall of the West; they were resigned to its survival. Nor did they 'invent' social liberalism – black people, immigrants, women and gay people fought with their hands, with barricades, with lawsuits and mass campaigns for the rights they have today – from Selma, Alabama to Stonewall through to Black Lives Matter and #MeToo. Nor is 'liberalism' the primary source of people's disempowerment. It was in the main *conservatives* who demanded the globalization treaties that diluted national sovereignty and ripped the heart out of industrial communities. As for Day X, there is nothing in the dynamics of the present that makes it inevitable *other than the victory of fascism itself.*

Chillingly, however, every one of these themes can be heard resonating not only on the extreme right, but through mainstream conservative politics.

In Britain, for example, Conservative ministers depict refugees as a threat, Muslim men as prone to paedophilia, and Conservative MPs accuse 'Cultural Marxism' of undermining the British way of life.[33] In 2019, Boris Johnson attacked the Supreme Court and illegally shut down Parliament, and has repeatedly threatened to break international law.

The metapolitics of the far right resonates with the Tory membership – not least because many of them, before 2018, were themselves members of the right-wing populist party UKIP. During 2018, when the nationalist and globalist wings of the Tory Party were at war, pro-EU MPs reported new members surging into their local associations, after a call by a major UKIP donor for them to do so.[34]

The fully formed mythology is, of course, pushed overtly by an ever-changing group of small far-right parties: the British National Party, For Britain and most recently Patriotic Alternative, whose entire narrative is constructed around the threat of migration to 'indigenous' demographics. But the myth's permanent home is on social media, in the headlines of the racist tabloids, and in the 24/7 babble of prejudice facilitated by talk radio channels.

In numerous countries, the spread of the fascist myth has, during the 2010s, allowed activists in the right-wing populist movements to 'back-fill' their prejudices with a coherent ideology and long-term project. With the rise of the AfD in Germany, for example, forms of racism and anti-feminism that were formerly instinctive, or leftovers from the days of East Germany, gained a structure, a language and a means of expression – one which crossed over from the realm of the blog, via YouTube, to the bar, the football terrace and the street.

This process whereby old prejudices become imbued with a new logical structure went largely unobserved except by anti-fascist activists who recognized it in the changing vocabulary heard on right-wing street mobilizations and bulletin boards. Today it is vital that everybody understands the logical structure we are up against.

In this book I use the term 'thought-architecture' to describe the far-right ideological space. As a metaphor it suggests a building with many entrances, different façades and floors, but in which there is always a room marked 'fascism'. You can spend many years wandering through the building without entering that room, but you will always meet fascists in its corridors. And when a crisis happens, it turns out that fascism is the panic room. Everybody knows where it is and can – as Carl Schmitt did – rush towards its door.

Like a building, the thought-architecture of fascism has to be maintained. That's why modern fascists keep producing books that say the same thing over again, at great length. They are teaching people how to build the architecture in their heads, so that if it is demolished it can be rebuilt from memory. That is the function of the myth.

The strength of the fascist thought-architecture is that it is consistent – so long as it is never exposed to logic, science or complexity. That's why the essential task of anti-fascists is to dismantle the structure in people's heads, brick by brick, both through logic and experience, and to continually challenge the myth.

This, I will argue, cannot be done simply through appeals to people's common economic interest, or to post-1945 democratic traditions; the myth is stronger than both of them. Nor can it be done by deploying any kind of irrational counter-myth. Though emotion, narrative and collective solidarity will be vital to anti-fascist strategy, and to the revival of progressive politics, busting open far-right mythology requires persuading large numbers of people to return to the terrain of logic and evidence.

Nowhere is the challenge clearer than in the dramatic radicalization of Donald Trump's mass base towards fascism in the run-up to the Capitol Hill riot of 6 January 2021. I have left it until now because, as a potentially historic turning point, it has to be understood as a case study, and indeed proof, of the argument advanced above.

Capitol Hill was a textbook example of how conservatism, right-wing populism and fascism have begun consciously to interact. Though it took the political mainstream and law enforcement by surprise, it was perfectly predictable – and indeed predicted – by those who understand what fascists want, think and do.

TRUMP, QANON AND CAPITOL HILL

If things go badly in our century, the storming of the US Capitol by a far-right mob may be seen as a detonator event, equivalent to John Brown's attempt to start a slave uprising in America in 1859 by seizing a Federal armoury. In fact, the two events could come to be seen as symmetrical in history: the first as a tragic prelude to the Civil War, the defeat of slavery and America's century of advance to the status of a democratic superpower; the second as the trigger for the collapse of US democracy and civil order, and with it any kind of rules-based order in the world.

If we want to avoid that fate, we need to see the events of 6 January as a worked example of how a fascist social myth guides people towards symbolic violence, and how – through such violence – relatively small groups of people can destabilize systems that have been solid for decades.

After losing the election in November 2020 Trump created the fiction that it had been 'stolen' through the use of fraudulent postal votes and rigged electronic voting machines, and that the Biden presidency would be 'illegitimate'. His initial strategy rested on a blizzard of legal actions and defamatory claims, culminating in a lawsuit by the state of Texas which aimed to cancel the results in four Democrat-voting states. The Texas lawsuit was backed by attorney-generals in seventeen states, and 126 members of Congress, but was thrown out by the Supreme Court.[35]

On 18 December, after the electoral college cast their votes for Biden, Trump's inner circle held a fractious crisis meeting to discuss their options: martial law and the seizure of electronic voting machines were both considered and rejected. But it was straight after this meeting that Trump tweeted: 'Big protest in DC on January 6th. Be there, will be wild.'[36] From the available evidence (more will emerge), we can impute that this was the moment Trump decided to stake everything on stopping the ratification of the electoral college vote.

Trump called the 6 January rally outside the White House; his organization paid for the infrastructure to stage it, while far-right media networks mobilized their supporters to attend it. Its aim was to convince a joint session of the US Congress to vote down the election result, and to pressure Mike Pence, the vice president, into annulling it. It was Trump's last chance to retain power and, he had calculated, his best. Two days before the event, on the main bulletin board for the mobilization, more than 50 per cent of promoted messages featured 'unmoderated calls for violence'.[37] Indictments against the leaders of both the Proud Boys and the Oathkeepers militia show both groups mobilized for violence on the day in the belief Trump had called them to an insurrection.

In a speech beginning around noon, Trump told demonstrators to march on Congress and to fight like hell: 'If you don't fight like hell, you're not going to have a country any more.' Even before the speech ended, several hundred demonstrators detached from the rally and began to march, chanting 'Storm the Capitol!'

At around 1 p.m., members of the Proud Boys, a violent far-right movement, broke through the police lines and dismantled the barriers, allowing thousands of others to cross behind them. At around 2 p.m. a group of about thirty uniformed activists from the Oathkeepers militia, a far-right group mainly composed of army veterans, formed a military-style assault group and broke their way into the actual building.

Court indictments record one Oathkeeper (unidentified at time of writing) telling the others: 'You're executing citizens' arrest. Arrest this assembly, we have probable cause for acts of treason, election fraud.'[38]

However, once prevented from capturing key lawmakers (or, as they had fantasized about on the messaging boards, executing them), the mob occupied the Senate, fought the police, and milled around taking selfies and damaging property, content to have stopped the vote and awaiting direction from the man who called them there.

National Guard reinforcements were denied by the US Department of Defense, whose entire leadership had been replaced by Trump after the election. After a two-hour delay, the National Guard deployed and drove the protesters from the building. Pence refused to overturn the election result and, when Congress reconvened at 8 p.m., they ratified the electoral college vote.

Trump, in short, mobilized, funded and incited a mass event aimed at coercing Congress to defy the US Constitution; fascists at the sharp end used force in pursuit of the same objective; and a layer of Republican activists radicalized by the #StopTheSteal rhetoric swarmed behind them to occupy the buildings.

The event triggered a pointless debate about whether Trump, himself, is a fascist. Distinguished historians wheeled out definitions formulated thirty years ago, to show that Trump does not meet the criteria that made Hitler and Mussolini fascists. Fascism, wrote the historian Richard J. Evans, was 'the creation of the First World War, which militarised society' and was driven by 'the desire to refight the First World War'. In addition, fascism had deployed systematic street violence. Since Trump had started no wars, and his support for street violence was unsystematic, he could not be classed as fascist.[39]

Meanwhile, writers from the orthodox left pointed out that classic conditions for fascism identified by the Communist International in 1935 were not met, and concluded that the threat of American fascism was therefore illusory. Fascism, wrote Daniel Bessner and Ben Burgis, is not defined by its ideas at all, but by 'its ability to dominate many of the most important institutions in society'.[40] George W. Bush was 'worse' than Trump, they argued, and since the actual fascist groups were small, this was not a serious coup attempt, but something more like theatre: a chaotic shambles that would leave American democracy intact.

We will explore below what drives this wilful refusal to recognize the threat, both among liberal historians and the far left, but for now let's state what should be obvious: *Trump is not a fascist.*

The ideas in his head during his four-year term did not correspond to those of the fascist philosophers discussed above, nor did his actions conform to the demands of the actual fascist groups. That's why he limited himself to incitement, disinformation and funding the 6 January mobilization, and why he failed – at the crucial moment of 18 December – to launch a military coup or extra-constitutional actions. Nor was America under the Trump administration a fascist state.

But there is a plebeian mass base for American fascism and Trump has chosen to lead it, even though his own political project was not initially fascist, and even though there is scant support among the mainstream corporate elite for that project. Trump consciously facilitated and accelerated the collaboration between fascism, the MAGA movement and the authoritarian conservative wing of the Republican Party. It is also true that both Trump himself, and his movement, are a work in progress, and that numerous of his original aides – such as Steve Bannon and Mike Flynn – moved into the far-right ecosphere after being criminally indicted once out of office.

Once we move beyond sterile definitions, and understand fascism as a *process of social breakdown*, we can identify Trump as a product of the process and a driver of it. And we can see the nit-picking formalism among some historians and the left as an obstacle to comprehension.

Trump, in short, swung a wrecking ball through the finely constructed typologies of political science. His project, clear throughout his years in office, was to end globalization and reinvent neoliberalism as a nation-centric game, enriching himself and sections of the business elite in the process. He used the Treasury and the Federal Reserve to fuel a surge in asset prices, benefiting the super-rich and the upper middle class. He manipulated the weaknesses of the US Constitution to create formidable obstacles to his removal.

But in doing so, from the 'Unite the Right' demo in Charlottesville in 2017 onwards, he advanced the fascist process. Stunningly, he was able to transform the Republican Party – one of the oldest democratic political formations in the world – into the willing host for fascist activism.

From June 2020 onwards, Trump's support produced a step-change in far-right confidence. Militia groups appeared alongside neo-Nazis, the Proud Boys and the 'Boogaloo Bois' movement, to oppose and repress anti-racist protests, cheered on by the Trump-supporting media, and in some places with police collusion.

By the autumn of 2020 Trump had achieved what Charlottesville failed to do. He 'united the right' around an objective: to create so much symbolic violence across America's TV screens that conservative voters would turn out massively, spurred by fear. The fear would be the same fear I saw in Whitehall: that the 'wages of whiteness' would no longer be paid, and that the vestiges of white supremacy might disappear. That strategy mobilized 10.2 million more votes for Trump in the 2020 presidential election than in 2016.[41]

So, while neither Trump nor the Republican Party are 'fascist', the Trump movement – as it radicalized in office between 2016 and 2020 – co-opted many of the signature elements we will recognize when we explore historic fascism: the armed militia, the civilian 'squad' dedicated to attacking the left, the mesmeric rally with transgressive speeches, physical attacks on mainstream journalism, the stigmatization of judges and challenges to the legitimacy of the constitutional state.

And the most important factor driving this conservative-populist-fascist synergy was the adoption of a shared conspiracy theory.

'Before they seize power and establish a world according to their doctrines,' wrote the philosopher Hannah Arendt, 'totalitarian movements conjure up a lying world of consistency which is more adequate to the needs of the human mind than reality itself'. Arendt understood that the purpose of conspiracy theories is to make people knowingly complicit in irrationalism: to shut them off from facts, analysis and reason, and to create a closed world in which everything makes sense. In the 'lying world' created by Nazi propaganda, she wrote, 'through sheer imagination, uprooted masses can feel at home and are spared the never-ending shocks which real life and real experiences deal to human beings and their expectations'.[42]

Nowhere was that better illustrated than by the QAnon conspiracy theory, which during 2020 spread from the USA to become a worldwide signifier for the far right, drawing niche and peripheral movements deeper into its core.

QAnon was fuelled by cryptic 'Q-drops' posted on internet

bulletin boards by a supposed White House insider. The essential claims of QAnon are that a cabal of paedophile Satanists runs the world; that they kidnap children and harvest their blood for a chemical called adrenochrome which helps them live longer; that much of Hollywood and the Democratic Party are at the centre of it; that between 2016 and 2020 this elite was running a 'deep state' aimed at sabotaging the Trump administration; and that Trump would unleash 'The Storm' – a coup against them, jailing large numbers of liberal figures in Guantanamo and executing others.

Despite the outlandish nature of these claims, its followers were, by the time Trump left office, estimated in the tens of millions worldwide. Trump, though he claimed not to know about QAnon, described its supporters as 'people who love our country' and, according to a media monitoring group, tweeted QAnon-related propaganda 256 times.[43]

In 2020, as the Covid-19 pandemic hit and the Black Lives Matter protests spread around the world, QAnon-branded clothing and placards began to appear on anti-vaxx protests, anti-lockdown protests and far-right mobilizations against BLM. Far-right activists increasingly colonized the QAnon movement and exploited it.[44]

For example, a US militia movement that patrols the Mexican border to intercept migrants began running QAnon propaganda on its YouTube channels. In Germany, on 29 August 2020 a joint mobilization of neo-Nazis, anti-vaxxers and QAnon supporters tried to storm the Bundestag building. Meanwhile, using the slogan #SaveTheChildren, the conspiracy's supporters began to mobilize women, via Facebook groups and messaging applications, to attend demonstrations supposedly against child trafficking, in the process exposing them to the full panoply of far-right ideas.

If we examine the logical structure of QAnon, it is simply a version of the fascist social myth adapted to the Trump project. At its core is the 'blood libel' propagated against Jews by Christians since the Middle Ages, which claims that Jews steal and kill children in order to drink their blood. QAnon is also obsessed with the Rothschild family, the Hungarian Jewish financier George Soros and key Jewish figures in Hollywood, who are part of a supposed secret world government.

Once this core idea was established in the minds of millions of people, the rest of the fascist thought-architecture could be assembled around it, ranging from ludicrous add-ons – the idea that the elite are in fact lizard people from outer space – to the more mundane proposal that locking your opponents in prison camps or executing them is an acceptable solution.

The act of interpreting the Q-drops became a form of collaborative multiplayer game among the myth's adherents, allowing relatively uneducated people to take part in 'metapolitics' without having to read any book-length fascist texts. 'The Storm', meanwhile, was just a metaphor for the long-expected racial civil war.

Law enforcement and anti-terrorism experts quickly identified the specific danger of QAnon. First, by colonizing all other conspiracy theories and crank movements, from the lizard alien folks to the anti-vaxxers, it would turn them into a conveyor belt towards violent extremism. Second, by radically compressing the timescale to 'Day X' – which in fascist mythology is usually projected to happen in the medium term – it would trigger physical violence in the here and now.

Though QAnon gained audiences in the hundreds of thousands in many countries, it is significant that its two strongest showings outside the USA were in Germany and Japan – the defeated countries of the Second World War. In both, QAnon merged with conspiracy theories regarding the legitimacy of the states imposed by the Allies in 1945.

In Germany, the 20,000-strong *Reichsburger* movement, which believes the German government is a private corporation still run by the Allied countries of the Second World War, was the first to spread the theory, claiming that Trump would soon invade Germany and topple Chancellor Angela Merkel. In Japan, it was spread by supporters of an existing cult, which believes that the entire business elite are foreigners secretly occupying the country, and that 'smart cities' whose systems are run by artificial intelligence are a mechanism of foreign domination.[45]

If we read QAnon literally, what are its adherents actually promising each other? That just as the 'elite' secretly rules the world now, through ruthless subterfuge, so we – the ordinary, white, conservative Americans – can rule it in future, and in the same way. Internment camps, prisons, secret detention centres would be built – and, of course, they would be filled not with Hollywood stars, but with black, Muslim, Hispanic and Jewish Americans, together with the 'cultural Marxists' who are alleged to be conspiring to 'replace' the white race.

QAnon, in the end, was just a part of the mythology of modern fascism encoded and embedded into broader conspiracy theories. Its spread – in Germany, Japan, Brazil and above all the USA – was one of the surest barometers of where the fascist risk is strong.

But ludicrous though it is, QAnon is the key to understanding how rapidly Trump radicalized his followers from traditional populism towards violent, proto-fascist forms of action. Polled in October 2020, at the height of the election campaign, around half of all Trump voters agreed with QAnon's core assertions.[46] It had become their self-justification for supporting a deranged, dynastic crook.

In her research into the fascist radicalization process in the 1930s, the historian Lucie Varga recognized its similarities to religious conversion. The process begins with:

> a group of people in dynamic despair, for whom life in the old framework, according to the old scale of values, has lost all meaning. At the bottom of the despair and solitude lies the illusion of a golden age and the nostalgia of a paradise lost. [Then come] the first meetings, the key to a discovered world: the gift of yourself, giving oneself over to the new doctrines which prepare those persuaded to reject any other logic, symbol, myth or holy book.[47]

If she had witnessed QAnon's effects in 2020, Varga would have found every word of that passage vindicated.

A similar insight into the role of irrationalist theories was provided by Karl Mannheim, a sociologist writing in Germany in the 1920s, when he described the emergence of fascism as a form of 'Utopian thinking', which can exist only as an active, self-reinforcing doctrine divorced from facts. When a group of people want radical change, he wrote, they start to frame the whole of reality around that desire, ignoring all facts that contradict it. The Utopian mentality, he said, 'guided by wishful representation and the will to action, hides certain aspects of reality. It turns its back on everything which would shake its belief or paralyse its desire to change things.'[48]

Today's far right call this process of rejecting reality 'redpilling'. The metaphor is drawn from the movie *The Matrix*, in which the hero has to take a red pill in order to see as fake the reality in which he lives. Redpilling became a popular metaphor for conversion to right-wing extremism in 2012, via a bulletin board devoted to online misogyny.[49] At that point, to take the red pill meant to realize that men are oppressed by women, not the other way round. Today, it signifies a more general conversion to the wider spectrum of right-wing thinking.

In all cases, it requires the acceptance that everything you thought was true about the world is false. And since the ideology you're rejecting – democracy, market forces, globalism, science and the rule of law – formed a totalizing thought-system, the human brain requires a similarly complete alternative, not just a set of partial and disconnected theories.

It is likely, with Trump's defeat, that the QAnon theory will mutate, in order to explain the non-occurrence of 'The Storm'. In March 2021 the British anti-fascist research group Hope Not Hate outed a man they claimed was behind a replacement ideology, called the Sabmyk Network.[50] It is safe to say only that there will be other iterations, and that their function will be the same.

But in a short space of time QAnon provided modern fascism with a synthetic ideology, beyond the control of any one leader or influencer. Like a black hole in space, its gravitational pull attracted all other discontents and conspiracy theorists into a central vortex. Its internal logic may be busted, but the political energies that flowed into the Trump-QAnon narrative in late 2020 will not be easily dissipated.

QAnon, despite its continuities with twentieth-century fascist lies, illustrates how the threat has changed. It is a mercurial ideology, not a fixed one; the product of many minds connected via an online network, not a single Führer or a tsarist secret policeman churning out fake documents. Hitler, for certain, was able to absorb ecofascism and Norse mythology into Nazism, but ultimately he was its gatekeeper.

Today the ideology is co-created. And that makes it potentially more resilient to short-term political defeats.

During the 2010s – and above all during the four toxic years of Donald Trump – the extreme right's thought-architecture penetrated Western culture so strongly that one of its chief ideologists, the far-right Swedish publisher Daniel Friberg, could claim:

> Our liberal-leftist opponents have already lost. They have just not stopped breathing yet.[51]

How did we get to a situation where that claim should be taken seriously? Because the once dominant ideologies of neoliberalism, liberal democracy and globalization no longer explain the world for large numbers of people. No matter how ludicrous, internally contradictory and disproven far-right mythology is, it will go on replicating itself unless liberalism and Marxism – the twin offspring of the Enlightenment – can build resilient and persuasive thought-architectures of their own.

And that's a problem. Because, though fascist organizations are small today, the crises we face in the mid-twenty-first century are huge. We've seen how fascists fight; we've understood what they think they're fighting for. Now we have to carry out a brutal audit of the society that is to be their battlefield.

3

Five Kinds of Trouble

The Forces Driving the Far Right

Fascist ideas are spreading because we're facing five kinds of trouble at once. We have an economic model that no longer works; evaporating support for democracy; and a crisis of technological control, in which some states, businesses and non-state actors are using information networks to suppress truth and deter rational thinking. Looming above it all is the coming climate catastrophe. Add in the after-effects of the Covid-19 pandemic, which have accelerated the breakdown of globalization, and we have a multi-layered crisis unprecedented in the history of capitalism.

The problem with simultaneous crises is that they interact, in unpredictable ways. As a result, several countries at once are displaying symptoms of the kind of disintegration process that produced fascism in the 1920s and 30s. What follows is an audit of the forces driving modern fascism, and the future opportunities they will create for the far right.

NEOLIBERALISM IS BROKEN

The most fundamental problem is that the West's economic model has failed. Forty years ago the world's major governments adopted a strategy of privatization, globalization and the commercialization of everyday life. It worked for a while, for some people, but has now stopped working. The result, long before anyone had heard of Covid-19, is the projected long-term stagnation of advanced economies. Productivity growth has slowed, while interest rates on government debt – the most fundamental measure of capitalism's dynamism – have slid from 5 per cent to sub-zero in the space of twenty years.[1]

The model that has failed is called neoliberalism. But its achievements were real: between 1989 and 2008 it doubled the size of the world economy and quadrupled the value of global trade.[2] During this time GDP per person doubled in Brazil, rose fourfold in Indonesia, fivefold in China and sixfold in India.[3]

But the biggest winners were the super-rich. Over the past forty-five years, the richest 1 per cent of people on the planet have captured 27 per cent of all this growth, through rising incomes and the massively expanded value of their assets: property empires, investment portfolios, patents, yachts, fine art collections, gold deposits and cryptocurrencies.[4] Even a global pandemic, which took down airlines, shopping malls and steel mills, could not stop this process of wealth accumulation for the rich. By December 2020 the world's billionaires were together worth $12 trillion, around a third of that 'earned' during the pandemic simply by doing nothing.[5]

I have told the story of why the neoliberal model failed in detail elsewhere.[6] The short version is that prosperity for working people in the advanced economies became reliant on credit rather than on rising real wages and productivity; and the global financial system became a machine for miscalculating the risks involved in lending. This led to repeated financial crises, which central banks always countered by cutting interest rates, stimulating another surge in borrowing, and unwittingly paving the way for an even bigger financial crash.

When Lehman Brothers went bust in September 2008, it came close to taking down the global banking system; the entire edifice of mortgage, credit card, corporate and government debt could have collapsed, leading to mass bankruptcies. Without massive state intervention, millions of people would have lost their savings, homes and jobs.

To avoid a Depression, governments were forced – yet again – to cut interest rates and borrow money. But it was not enough. Now they had to print money via the policy of quantitative easing and in some cases to nationalize the banks. From this point onwards, the neoliberal way of doing things was on life support.

The result was an even bigger pile of debt. Between Lehman

Brothers' collapse in 2008 and the outbreak of the Covid-19 pandemic, we added $87 trillion to the debts of people, companies and governments, while central banks printed around $12 trillion to keep the economy afloat.[7] By February 2021, thanks to the pandemic, global debt had risen by a further $24 trillion (to $281 trillion), and central banks printed a further $10 trillion, mainly to lend to their governments.[8]

As capitalism switched to a model of growth based on creating money and borrowing, it fuelled rising inequality. Across twenty-five advanced countries surveyed by McKinsey in 2016, 70 per cent of households – some 580 million people – saw their real wages fall over the decade.[9] In the ex-industrial towns of eastern Germany, northern France, England and the American rust belt, not only did the quality of life deteriorate, there was no obvious way it could improve, especially for people with lower skills and qualifications.

The implicit deal that globalization had offered to working-class people in the West was this: the good industrial jobs are gone and will not come back, but a mixture of easy credit and welfare spending will make life bearable. The 2008 crisis tore up the deal. There was little money left for welfare or public services. For the first time since the 1930s, young people realized they would end up poorer than their parents.

Something had to give, and what cracked first was the commitment to globalization. From around 2015 a split took place within the elites themselves. One faction wanted to revive neoliberalism by globalizing faster: using trade deals to integrate their economies, relentlessly eroding regulations that protect wages and public services in the process. That was the programme of Barack Obama, Nicolas Sarkozy and then Emmanuel Macron in France, Justin Trudeau in Canada, Angela Merkel in Germany and the then British prime minister, David Cameron.

Another faction wanted to break with the rules-based global system: to switch from a policy of collaboration, free trade and open standards to a form of *neoliberal nationalism*. They would go on promoting inequality, wage stagnation and privatization, but now competitively, and under the rhetoric of 'national interest'. In each country, this nationalist faction of the elite would try to dump the social costs of the failing system onto other countries, through immigration controls, trade wars and technology bans. As a result, the second half of the 2010s was dominated by a struggle between the two visions, with the nationalists mobilizing a new voter coalition around opposition to migration, human rights and globalized trade.

Looking back, what's remarkable is how quickly the dominoes fell. In 2014, the Hindu nationalist BJP took power in India. Two years later, an alliance of right-wing Conservatives and UKIP affiliates persuaded Britain to leave the European Union. Then American voters put Trump into the White House. In 2017 the Austrian conservative leader, Sebastian Kurz, broke with decades of centrist government and formed a coalition with the right-wing populist Freedom Party. In 2018, Jair Bolsonaro won the Brazilian presidency. In the same year the Five Star/Lega coalition took power in Italy, making the right-wing populist leader Matteo Salvini deputy prime minister. In 2019, as UKIP members flooded into the Conservative Party, Boris Johnson purged his party of liberals and globalists to install a de facto coalition of right-wing populists and authoritarians.

Trump's victory in 2016 was the turning point. It confirmed that there is a massive constituency in the United States for economic nationalism and isolationism, and forced all other countries to accept deglobalization as a strategic reality. In a reversal of America's traditional post-war role, in setting rules and standards for global behaviour, Trump gave permission for other leaders to break them. He abandoned any pretence of domestic political cooperation between liberalism and conservatism and promoted a global culture war. And, through a network of aides and allies, he put rocket boosters under the extreme right, not just in America but everywhere.

Though its effects were shattering, the 2008 crisis could not, on its own, have triggered the revival of far-right ideas on the scale witnessed in the 2010s. Indeed, the disruption we're living through is primarily ideological, not economic.

Like all social systems, the free-market model needed an ideology to justify who gets rich and who doesn't – and to create a basic 'common sense' about the way to live your life. The first tenet of neoliberal ideology was that *the market corrects itself*. It does not need a state to tell it what to do, and functions best when the state is small. The market is like an all-seeing machine, computing the most rational outcomes for humanity.

From that assumption flowed others, summed up in a list of policy principles known as the Washington Consensus, written in 1989. It said that taxes should be low; state intervention to save jobs should be forbidden; trade should be free; self-regulation is better than state regulation; and money should be allowed to move wherever it wants to.[10]

The second tenet of the ideology was that *nothing better can be imagined*. The collapse of communism in Russia and the marketization of China, said the US political scientist and government adviser Francis Fukuyama, signalled the 'total exhaustion of viable systematic alternatives to Western liberalism'. The victory of liberal democracy and free-market economics, claimed Fukuyama, meant 'the end point of mankind's ideological evolution'. Liberal democracy was the 'final form of human government'. We were at the 'end of history'.[11]

The problem is not that some billionaires and professors believed this; millions of ordinary people came to believe it too. They adapted their behaviour, expectations – even their thought-patterns and personalities – to the neoliberal reality. You borrow, you spend, you rack up debt. You buy shares and property on the assumption that their value will always rise.

While my parents' generation defined themselves through work, from Generation X onwards people began to define themselves through everything *except* work: the brands they wore, the shares they traded, their sports team or some niche cultural lifestyle, ranging from BDSM to gardening. Though there was plenty of work, for many people it became meaningless. The mass unemployment of the 1980s was replaced by 'bullshit jobs' – low-paid, insecure work in the coffee bars, fulfilment depots and call centres that proliferated where the factories used to be.[12]

To cope with this new reality we created, each one of us, a 'neoliberal self'. I can remember how I did this: I adapted my outlook to fit the new world of insecurity, selfishness and cheap credit. I learned to expect all strikes to be defeated, all jobs to be temporary, all appointments to be cancelled, all promises to be broken. But for people born after 1989 there was no need to adapt. This new reality was all they'd ever known.

People pushed the logic of a self-correcting market deep into their own psyches. They became increasingly competitive, atomized, prone to calculating their worth financially, and fatalistic. They were convinced that change was impossible, that there was no other way to live. The more you learned to obey the market, the happier you would feel.

When the economic model failed, this neoliberal logic fell apart. Suddenly the story people held in their heads about how the world worked sounded like nonsense. As a result, for the past decade, we've been living through a *crisis of the neoliberal self*: a search for coherence and meaning by people who could no longer go on framing the world through the lens of the market alone.

Large numbers of people experienced the years after 2008 not just as economic dislocation but as a crisis of identity. They asked: if I am no longer a consumer, or an atomized individual in a competitive marketplace, defined by the brands I wear, the car I own and the credit card in my wallet, *who am I*? If my fate is not to be decided by the market, then by what?

While the political centre clung on to this busted neoliberal ideology, three alternative answers emerged to the question: 'who am I?'

Millions of young, networked and university-educated people said: I'm a human being, with an interest shared with everyone on the planet to halt climate change, reduce inequalities of gender, race and class, and build a more sustainable economy.

Others, survivors from the left-wing labour movements that were destroyed in the 1980s, answered: I'm a worker, with an interest shared in common with other workers, in regaining what we lost, boosting our wages, and healing our communities.

For a third group, which spans both young and old, all they had left was their ethnicity, their religion, their specific local culture and, above all, their nation – which had once been 'great' and could therefore be made 'great again', if only the cross-border movement of goods and people, which they wrongly identified as the cause of their misfortune, could be restrained.

From a unified explanation of the world, constructed around an elegant, logical statement about the market, politics now shattered into rival explanations based on people's specific experience and cultural values. No single doctrine was capable of creating a new common sense: in fact, as we discover at every family gathering, the alternative worldviews are necessarily at war with each other.

Once it failed, globalization – which had looked like a win/win arrangement – triggered a competitive scramble between countries over what's left of economic growth, a scramble in which economic nationalism seemed to be the only way to get ahead.

When, in 2016, McKinsey conducted its survey of the winners and the losers from the financial crash, the results could have been predicted by anyone who has sat on a barstool in a former factory town. The bleaker your own future looks, the more likely you are to agree that 'immigrants are ruining our culture', 'imported goods are destroying our jobs', and 'cheap labour abroad is creating unfair competition'.[13]

Anyone who has studied the rise of fascism could see where this might lead. But in the immediate aftermath of 2008 the far-right groups were small. Most G7 governments had liberal positions on race and gender. A few populist parties stood on the fringes, scooping up 'protest votes', but mainstream parties were still committed to the multilateral global order. Democracy looked safe.

What we failed to understand is the exponential power of networks.

THE WALL OF TECHNOLOGICAL POWER

In the 1990s the silicon chip inside an average PC contained three million digital switches. The chip that runs my iPhone contains 8.5 *billion* switches and is around half the size.[14] A desktop computer in the 1990s could emulate a typewriter and play Solitaire. An iPhone 12 can recognize my face, understand my voice, let me shoot and edit a video, guide me to a destination – and improve its own performance in real time, unaided by a human being.[15] As a result, people alive today have more knowledge of their surroundings, and potentially more power over them, than any previous generation.

All this happened because digital technologies are *exponential*: their capacity doubles regularly over time. To get your head around the idea of exponential change, imagine taking thirty paces down the street. Now imagine that, with each pace, you double the length of your stride. Thirty equal paces take you thirty metres; thirty exponential paces would take you twenty-six times around the earth.[16]

Information technology has injected an exponential character into our current crisis. It is accelerating the disintegration of ideologies, party loyalties, business models and established systems of government – because each of them originates in the world of 'thirty equal paces'. And it has created a vast imbalance of power between people, corporations and states.

For the first twelve years of the internet era (1995–2007), power was distributed downwards. By ending the stranglehold over the broadcast of information, formerly held by states and corporations, the internet famously 'changed everything'.

It was built on relatively open systems. HTML, the language used to write web pages, was free and universal; humanity's digital store of knowledge was accessible through basic search engines, and was structured transparently, with the home page of every website acting like a contents list. Media firms that tried to create 'walled gardens' of content, available only through subscription, always failed – because the whole point to being online was freedom. The blue hyperlinks that suddenly twinkled across every computer screen were an invitation to go on a random journey. Free music and videos were everywhere. And if you wanted to be anonymous you could be.

The rise of smart devices, alongside the monopolization of social media by giant corporations and the strict enforcement of copyright laws, reversed this trend, returning power over information back to the hands of corporations and states.

Today, the internet has become a closed, monopolized and commercialized world based around the App. This happened so stealthily, between 2008 and 2013, that – as the information scientist Zeynep Tufecki reports – the first people to notice it were Middle Eastern bloggers coming out of jail. They'd gone to prison for stuff they'd written on obscure, self-managed web pages. On their release there was only one web page that mattered: Facebook.[17]

The App system allowed corporations to re-create their monopoly over the dissemination of information, while both states and shadowy non-state agencies stood ready to exploit that monopoly. Thanks to the

App system, and the creation of powerful databases that log and analyse our behaviour, everything we do generates information we cannot own or control. On Instagram and Facebook we click on likes, not hyperlinks: that's like taking a vote, not going on a journey. If you want to publish something original, free and transgressive you have to do it outside the duopoly of Apple and Google. If you want to remain unfindable by the state, you have to smash your smartphone and throw it in the sea.

The addition of hi-res digital cameras to devices has changed the kind of information we produce. Until around 2008 the internet was mainly for writing; now it's for pictures and video. We are communicating less through words and reason, more through images and emotion – which, as we will explore below, are the precise region of human interaction where the fascist mythology is easiest to transmit.

Our behaviour generates a treasure trove of information for corporations: in turn, the algorithms deployed by Amazon, Apple, Google and Facebook are designed to influence our behaviour. In response, some people have tried to keep their communications private – but the tech monopolies have a solution for that too. Through WhatsApp, Telegram and Signal, the global conversation has retreated into controlled private spaces. The internet's original character as a searchable public forum and knowledge store is disintegrating.

In short, we have swapped our early digital freedoms for a technological prison. And it was not created spontaneously. The switch from open to closed systems, from words to pictures, from public to private conversations happened because, for one brief moment, people gathered up all the dreams, plans and connections they had assembled online, and took them into the streets.

In Egypt and throughout the Arab world in 2011, Facebook became a mobilizing tool for the Arab Spring. Networked activism produced interconnected occupation movements in Athens, Madrid, New York, London, Quebec and Tel Aviv, as young people copied the Egyptian tactics of camping in a square and mounting leaderless resistance. By 2013 the protests had spread from the core to the periphery: Turkey, Brazil and Ukraine.[18] Not only did these movements exploit information technology, they relied on new, networked forms of thinking, fluid relationships between the organizers and the masses and, above all, new ideas about freedom.

The networked revolutions of 2011–13 were so brief, and so unlike anything before in history that, once they were defeated, people quickly forgot how terrified the global elite had been. As a journalist, I was immersed in those revolts.[19] When I think of them now, I remember the young people dancing amid clouds of tear gas in central Athens, the quiet arguments in occupied squares, the eloquent speeches made by working-class women who had lived their lives in political silence. I remember the words of my TV producer: 'You can taste freedom.'

Looking back, it's obvious that, for the elite, those networked protest movements were a *glimpse of how capitalism dies*. It dies when people eject it from their everyday lives, from their brains, throw corporate deference and hierarchies into the trash can and start living as if nature and human happiness – and not corporate profit – were the main priority.

For the orthodox left the revolts of 2011–13 were a disappointment, because their model for a revolution is Russia in 1917. They see the destruction of capitalism as a cataclysmic moment, involving the seizure of state power by people organized at work. There were few glimpses of that possibility in the tent camps.

But for the elites – the 'one per cent', as they became known – the occupation of the squares, the fall of the regimes in Egypt and Tunisia, and the political revolutions in Ukraine, Brazil and Greece, felt like a near-death experience.

Their response was to erect the wall of technological control that now surrounds us. First they tried switching off the Internet. Then they tried creating a closed, online echo-chamber for their supporters only. Finally, they remembered that the best way to sabotage an information system is to flood it with 'noise', in this case consisting of disinformation, trolls, doxxing, threats, depictions of sexual violence and hate speech.

In the space of ten years, a global infosphere that once nurtured solidarity and optimism has become a machine for disseminating lies, suspicion and depression. That's not due to some intrinsic trait of human nature. It happened because specific groups of people made it happen: right-wing conservative politicians, their backers in the billionaire-owned media, the tech monopolies, dictatorships, regulators in the pockets of corporations . . . and a small army of online fascists.

The tech giants built deliberate vulnerabilities into the critical platforms – Facebook, YouTube and Twitter – allowing people to spread disinformation and boost it at the expense of verified, professional news. They did so for the simple reason that it generated traffic, and therefore cash. Under the cover of anonymity, they allowed a mixture of fanatics, paid internet armies and fictitious 'bots' to game their algorithms. They took advertising from obscure sources, allowing those with the biggest cheque books to boost 'noise' over information. And thanks to commercial secrecy these algorithms cannot be scrutinized or regulated by governments or society.[20] Sure, when the results get too outrageous, they change the algorithm. But there is no public record of what it did. In fact, the algorithms that drive social media traffic are the first major technology in history for which *there is no history*.

Though each one of these vulnerabilities helped Trump win power in 2016, and was subject to widespread public criticism, that did not stop the giant tech companies. Quite the reverse. According to the US non-partisan think tank the German Marshall Fund, between 2016 and the 2020 election campaign, traffic to known US disinformation websites grew by 100 per cent, while traffic to those amplifying the false content – primarily *Fox News*, *The Daily Wire* and *Breitbart* – rose by close to 300 per cent.[21]

The short-term winners were right-wing populist leaders like Trump and the shareholders of major tech companies; the strategic beneficiary is fascism.

A large part of the far right's power is generated by the asymmetries built into networked systems: an anonymous person can threaten you with murder, spread lies, post your address and mug shot, and influence the people around you in the voting booth, with no accountability. But since both the liberal and left political projects rely on truth, restraint, non-violence and the rule of law, the political playing field is massively slanted towards the right.

This deadly combination – the sudden ideological collapse of neoliberalism and the rapid concentration of online power into the hands of the far right – has produced a third kind of trouble: a loss of faith in democracy and the erosion of its quality.

DEMOCRACY IS DECAYING

Does capitalism need democracy? It is beyond doubt that capitalism *produced* democracy as we know it. A system based on market transactions needs a state, standing above and outside the marketplace, and a constitution that forces the state to obey the law. It needs a way of prioritizing the general interest of business over that of individual businesses, for example through taxation and regulation. It needs a mechanism for settling the disputes that arise as companies compete. And since it relies on the voluntary participation of workers and consumers, not slaves and bonded labourers, it needs their consent – which in turn means it has to set limits on what the state can do to its citizens.

It was these practical imperatives that spurred the rising class of industrialists in the eighteenth and nineteenth centuries to stage democratic revolutions and develop the liberal concept of democracy. But most of the key elements we associate with democracy today – free elections, universal suffrage, human rights, freedom of speech, an impartial legal system and the right to hold meetings and form political parties – were at some point resisted by capitalists in the name of protecting capitalism.

The right to vote was only reluctantly extended to women, people of colour and the working class, after they fought for it. Citizenship (and even human status) was denied completely to slaves and colonial subjects. Yet the clamour for democracy was so great, and the extra-parliamentary struggles so riotous, that the general direction of travel was positive.

But does capitalism *have to* produce democracy? The best way to answer that is historically: certain models of capitalism produce certain types of democracy. The model of capitalism that produced the most stable, deeply rooted democracy – though in the developed world only – was the state-run social welfare capitalism that emerged after 1945. It emerged because liberalism had been faced for the first time with its real nemesis, which was not socialism but fascism. For all their flaws and failings, many of the regimes constructed after 1945 were *anti-fascist* democracies.

Inspired by the writings of the liberal political scientist Karl

Loewenstein, who called for a 'militant democracy' to suppress fascism, the Allies designed the German, Austrian and Japanese constitutions to prevent its re-emergence.[22] Numerous other post-war constitutions were altered to avoid the fate that had befallen the Weimar Republic, with rules banning violent political parties and militias, restricting hate speech, and enshrining the state's monopoly of coercive force.[23]

During the post-war boom, political resilience lay in the party system. Indeed, the very definition of democracy after 1945 came to revolve around parties. Democracy, said the influential thinker Joseph Schumpeter, is a 'competitive struggle for the people's vote' by professionally run parties, committed to the constitution.[24] By allowing a genuine battle of ideas, this system institutionalized the class struggle: conservative, liberal, socialist and communist parties could coexist, and they were all – formally at least – seen as legitimate.

The neoliberal era, by contrast, eviscerated party democracy. Though it delivered advances in human rights and the rule of law, in practical terms it attacked the 'power to decide by competition' through two methods: the inner-party purge and the international treaty.

Margaret Thatcher once said that her greatest achievement was 'Tony Blair and New Labour: we forced our opponents to change their minds'.[25] In Britain and elsewhere, from the 1970s onwards, the elite used statecraft to purge all political parties of those who resisted the free-market revolution. Corporate money, media propaganda, organized witch-hunts and the secret state were deployed to marginalize neoliberalism's critics.

The second attack on competitive democracy came via transnational laws and obligations, which limited what national parliaments could decide. The building blocks of globalization were the European Single Market in 1986 and NAFTA in 1993, which placed supranational limits on economic policy across Europe and North America. Added to this were the Basel Accords(1988), which imposed global rules on financial markets. The TRIPS treaty (1994) forced the world to obey US law on intellectual property. The formation of the World Trade Organization in 1995, which made socialist economic policies illegal, completed the system. Out of these treaties, neoliberalism built a wall protecting itself from democratic challenge.

There was, however, an upside. Once anti-capitalism was impossible, issues such as gay rights, women's rights and the rights of ethnic minorities – which had been championed by the left – could be handled as non-systemic challenges. So, both in law and in fact, the democratic rights of citizens were extended. Britain, for example, got a Human Rights Act and a Supreme Court; the actions of its state security apparatus became challengeable; the police were forced by new regulations to stop beating confessions out of suspects. The BBC ceased to veto job applications formally on grounds of subversive leanings, and numerous historic injustices were reversed in court.

Neoliberalism, while it worked, produced a 'thin' democracy – with expanded rights for individuals, a party system devoid of real alternatives, parliaments constrained by economic treaty obligations and a police force that, though better regulated, was increasingly militarized to cope with civil unrest.

But what kind of democracy does a *broken* neoliberalism produce? What kind of democracy emerges in a system where the central bank is the dynamo of growth, not the market; where digital networks have become machines for behavioural control and where giant tech monopolies can flout regulations at will? Does that kind of capitalism need democracy at all?

In the 2020s that question is being asked worldwide, and it's easy to see why: the country that has prospered most since the 2008 crisis is the least democratic. China has no parties independent of the state; no independent labour movement; no independent judiciary; no free press; no right of association; and its ruling party rejects the very concept of universal human rights. Like Carl Schmitt, its rulers are the unapologetic enemies of liberal democracy. Meanwhile, the country that has driven the disintegration process – both of democratic culture and the multilateral global order – is the oldest democratic republic on earth, the USA.

I want us to save liberal democracy, in spite of all its defects and deceits. Not only does it allow workers and oppressed people the space to organize in but we, the people, actually helped create it, through two centuries of struggle. If we can save it, we can improve it. But it faces its starkest challenge since the 1930s.

When the authoritarian nationalists – Trump, Orbán, Modi, Bolsonaro, Erdoğan and Johnson – broke with the globalist consensus in the 2010s, they logically had to deepen the attack on democracy that neoliberalism had begun: to manipulate electoral systems, politicize the judiciary and de-legitimize their opponents. They began to redefine democracy in explicitly populist terms – as the 'will of the people', which should be allowed to override the checks and balances of the constitutional state. Even though Trump is gone, his four-year term of office has written the playbook for politicians who want to operate in the grey zone between populism and fascism, and it is certain that others will use it in future.

Liberalism's response was to treat these developments as a temporary dysfunction. The terms 'backsliding', 'abuse', 'democratic decay' and 'erosion' entered legal scholarship.[26] Though they accurately describe the regression, they do not fully acknowledge its material roots. Having erected liberal democracy as the norm, and assumed humanity was on a one-way (if bumpy) journey towards it, liberal political philosophers treated the emergence of 'illiberal democracy' as a fault in the machine.

Their remedy is to tinker with the machine. US legal scholars Tom Ginsburg and Aziz Huq propose a series of 'subconstitutional' reforms, which would involve edging democracies towards the parliamentary model and reducing presidential powers, strengthening the judiciary or adopting international treaties on human rights in order to bind the executive power.[27]

Harvard professors Steven Levitsky and Daniel Zitblatt identify the breakdown of democracy in the erosion of 'norms'; they complain that rival politicians who once clinked beer tankards together at the country club now call each other terrorists live on TV. Their solution is for politicians to revert to the old norms, exercising restraint both in rhetoric and governance.

Yascha Mounk, a German-American political scientist, has a more radical proposal: to defend universal rights and multi-ethnic concepts of citizenship by redistributing wealth, regulating social media, and restoring some national autonomy to states whose economic policies have been chained by trade treaties.[28]

Faced with this flurry of liberal blueprints for saving democracy we are left asking: how? Redistribute wealth? Sure. But the power-grab by neoliberal nationalists was designed specifically to prevent wealth redistribution. Micro-level tweaks to the constitution? The authoritarian right has become expert at manipulating constitutional law and gerrymandering electoral boundaries to entrench their power. Trump's appointment of 300+ right-wing judges is one example, the judicial coup that toppled Dilma Rousseff in Brazil another; so too, in Turkey, Erdoğan's mass dismissal of judges, his jailing of human rights advocates and his ban on the left-wing opposition party the HDP.

As for a return to the norms of democratic consensus and restraint, these behaviours were only 'normal' because there was nothing fundamental to argue about. With a split in the elites of many countries between a liberal, globalist wing and an authoritarian nationalist wing, existential values are at stake. Under Trump, for example, the Republican Party has radicalized at every level in the direction of extreme rhetoric, open vote-rigging and lawbreaking. That is unlikely to be easily reversed without a major split.

What's striking about the 'defence of democracy' literature coming out of current legal scholarship is its failure to acknowledge the economic and technological roots of the crisis. Nor does it advocate any realistic form of struggle to achieve the reforms it desires. Indeed, in the case of Levitsky and Zitblatt, they actively caution against it. Liberalism, in this time of acute crisis, has become a production line for good ideas about what to do once the crisis goes away.

The illiberal democracies in Turkey, Russia, Hungary, India, Israel and Brazil will survive without Trump. Each of these regimes holds power because people elected them, tolerated them and shrugged their shoulders at the misery and injustice they inflicted. As they face a democratic challenge in the 2020s, they will certainly resort to the tactics Trump adopted between his election defeat and the Capitol Hill riot.

The emergence of illiberal democracy in many countries at once is not a glitch. It is a feature of a broken economic system. It is part of capitalism's attempt to mutate and survive in the face of strategic threats. And the most existential threat of all is climate change.

THE PLANET IS BURNING

The nature of the climate threat is clear. As a result of rising carbon emissions, the atmosphere is now around one degree warmer than its pre-industrial average. This has triggered severe weather events, bushfires of record intensity and is rapidly shrinking the Arctic ice cap. If we do nothing, emissions will go on rising until 2050, and by the end of the century temperatures will rise by three degrees or more above the baseline. Long before 2100 unpredictable climate feedback loops will begin – in which storms, fires, melting ice caps, deforestation, species extinctions and mass migrations begin to interact with each other, making it impossible to live on some parts of the planet, massively disrupting the rest of it.

But if we reduce carbon emissions from their current 55 gigatons a year to net zero by 2050, we can limit the rise in temperature to 1.5 degrees above its pre-industrial norm, and the socio-economic damage might be containable.[29]

The baseline we start from is bleak. Thanks to the 1997 Kyoto Protocol, by 2010 the world's most advanced countries had managed to reduce their emissions by 12 per cent against a 1990 baseline. However, the rapid development of China and the global south ensured that, over the same period, total carbon emissions actually rose by 32 per cent.[30] Whenever people tell you how brilliant the upswing of neoliberalism felt, remember that this will be its legacy to the rest of human history.

Since the Copenhagen Accord in 2009, emissions have risen more slowly. But we needed them to fall, not rise. According to the United Nations Environment Programme, 'there has been no real change in the global emissions pathway in the last decade. The effects of climate policies have been too small to offset the impact of key drivers of emissions such as economic growth and population growth.'[31]

Why did we fail? Because we relied on market mechanisms to solve the problem. We took a four billion-year-old planet, disrupted its ecosystem through 250 years of industrial development, and assumed that an economic doctrine invented yesterday would solve the problem. It has not done so.

As a result, according to the International Energy Agency, we need much faster actions in the next thirty years, and critically in the next ten. The energy used globally in passenger flights will need to halve by 2030; half of all new cars sold in Europe will have to be totally electric by the same date; and 75 per cent of power generation will have to come from a mixture of solar, wave, wind and nuclear.[32]

Before the resurgence of the far right, the big question was: can liberal capitalism deliver zero net carbon? There was already strong evidence to the contrary. Today the question is starker: even if we can convince governments to speed up the transition, will the far right summon mass movements of resistance to decarbonization? Its record during the Covid-19 pandemic shows how it might.

Right-wing populist governments have already been catastrophic for the mitigation of climate change. Bolsonaro's foreign minister called climate change a 'globalist tactic' designed to 'justify the increasing power of states over the economy and the power of international institutions over the nations and their populations'.[33] Meanwhile, Trump pulled the USA out of the Paris Climate Accord (although the Biden administration has since rejoined it) and mobilized 70 million Americans to vote for fracking and Big Oil. From now until the Republican Party is reclaimed by the conservative centre, it will – in every four-year electoral cycle – pose a major threat to global decarbonization efforts.

The type of capitalism needed to decarbonize the world is one where human need, and not the market, regulates economic life – and where we expand the global commons instead of relentlessly commercializing them. It will need profound changes in behaviour, from the food we eat, to the distances we travel and the kind of homes we live in. The state will need to ensure that profit comes second to well-being; that sustainability is prioritized over growth; and that the micro-logic of the market is superseded by the macro-logic of what humans need. There would still be a private sector, profits, a stock market and global trade – but each of these institutions, which look central to capitalism now, would play a secondary role in allocating resources. *In short, we need a form of capitalism that is unacceptable to today's capitalists.*

This inescapable choice – between planetary survival and capitalism as it currently exists – has become a major impetus for the far right. But it has produced two contradictory responses: aggressive climate science denial and, more recently, 'ecofascism'.

Until the Kyoto Accord, the populist right showed little interest in climate denial. Parties such as the BNP in Britain, the Sweden Democrats and the Front National in France had inherited a form of super-nostalgic environmental politics from their fascist predecessors, often calling for a 'return' to traditional farming or venerating some aspect of nature – forests, soil or a predator species – as the embodiment of racial and national identity.

In response to Kyoto, parts of the fossil fuel industry funded a climate science denial industry consisting of think tanks, research groups and lobbyists. By the time of the Obama presidency, it had 'generated near-hegemonic acceptance of denial among staunch political conservatives – especially elites and activists – as well as widespread scepticism within the US public'.[34] To mobilize voters against the IPCC's emissions targets, climate deniers claim that they are a threat to economic growth, the free-market system, individual rights, specific national 'ways of life' or to Western civilization itself. One of their most powerful techniques is to create doubt about the science, and about media outlets that accurately report the science – and thus about truth in general.

Once the money began flowing from the corporate lobbyists, many of the right-wing populist parties picked up climate denial and ran with it. In Sweden, for example, after industry pressure groups began a campaign against the Copenhagen Accord, it was the Sweden Democrats that took the issue into parliament.[35] In Germany the AfD has campaigned to 'save diesel' – a slogan that resonated widely with its elderly rural voters in eastern Germany – arguing that climate science is 'degenerate' and a pretence invented by the elite to give the state more control.[36]

The populist right brought two of its own obsessions into the climate denial movement: the defence of male lifestyles shaped around the coal, oil, fracking and forestry sectors; and the defence of 'national sovereignty' against the requirements of climate treaties. In Finland, for example, the Finns Party, a right-wing populist party with 17 per cent electoral support, managed to combine both these themes. In a campaign against wind turbines, launched in 2016, it claimed the turbines had been 'imposed' on rural areas; that they didn't work; that they were a threat to the rural lifestyle of logging and manliness; and – on top of this – were causing people to contract a mystery illness and bats to 'explode' in mid-air.[37]

In short, though there is nothing about populist ethno-nationalism that says you have to be a climate denier, the one ideology moulds

readily onto the other. Climate denial remains one of the most important crossover points between conservative corporate interest,
xenophobic populism and fascism itself. The reasons are obvious
once we remember that fascism is, at its root, the fear of freedom,
triggered by a glimpse of freedom. For if the 2011–13 revolutions
allowed people to imagine *how* capitalism might end, the facts of climate change are forcing us to imagine *why*.

Just as in the 1920s, some people can't face the social upheaval
needed to escape the crisis we're in; and actually fear living in a society that has freed itself from dependency on fossil fuels, automobiles
and the lifestyles moulded around them. And the far right stands
ready to defend the present.

However, as the alt-right movement solidified during the 2010s,
and began exerting a new and authentic fascist influence on the right-
wing populist parties, a second – diametrically opposite – response
gained traction, labelled 'ecofascism'. Its advocates *accept* scientific
predictions of a climate catastrophe, and accept that it is man-made.
But they see this as a further justification of their existing policies – of
economic nationalism, zero inward migration and, ultimately, the
likely trigger for a global, ethnic civil war.

Ecofascism, in its modern form, is spread by numerous anonymous
groups and figures. But it has been coherently advocated for years by
the late Finnish writer Pentti Linkola. Linkola believed that humans
are the cause of the earth's problems; specifically, humans of the
global south, whose demand for development has spurred the destruction of the natural environment. Like the Traditionalists discussed in
Chapter 2, Linkola wanted to destroy 'everything we have developed
over the last 100 years'.[38] He advocated eugenics, not only to 'cull the
weak' but to reduce the earth's population to around half a billion, if
necessary through a genocidal civil war. And, of course, his proposed
political form was dictatorship.

But Linkola, and the small legion of 'anons' currently posting ecofascist messages online, are only the latest products of a long ecological
tradition built into Nazism and nineteenth-century white suprema-
cism before that. If you are opposed to historical progress, and the
self-liberation of human beings, you are left only with 'nature' as the

framework for your ideas. 'Nature', as Brunel University professor Mark Neocleous points out, was one of the core concepts of twentieth-century fascism. Just as fascism tried to replace class with nationalism, and revolution with endless war, it also 'obliterates history from politics and fills the space with nature'.[39]

For Hitler, human society was imperfect wherever it did not operate like nature, with the strong eliminating the weak. This, in itself, was an idea borrowed from the original 'ecologist', the late-nineteenth-century anti-Semite Ernst Haeckel.[40] For the environmental mystics within the 'green wing' of the Nazi Party, the sacredness of the earth became the rationale for purging it of problematic humans, which were the 'lower' races – specifically Jews and Slavs.

So it is logical that, presented with the new fact of catastrophic climate change, one wing of the far right has co-opted it as an excuse for the project of ethnic civil war. This bifurcation within the far right, between climate denial and ecofascism, is sometimes presented either as an accident, or the result of different national traditions. For me it's a matter of progression.

As the populist right reaches the limits of what it can mobilize electorally through climate denial, and as populism is back-filled with fascist theory, we should expect this deeper, more authentic ecofascist strand of the far right to grow, and outright climate denial to be left behind. The fact is that both views lead their followers to oppose globally mandated decarbonization targets.

The deniers are happy to go on burning fossil fuels; the ecofascists accept that climate chaos is coming, but not that we need to abandon the carbon lifestyle. Rather, they dream of murdering migrants at the borders of Europe and America as they flee the climate chaos.

In 1945 Goebbels told journalists that, if the Nazis were defeated, 'the whole German people will go under with us, and so gloriously that, even after a thousand years, the heroic downfall of the Germans is in the first place in world history'.[41] This time around, fascism has an even bigger downfall in mind. Destroying the conditions for human life on the planet would be the ultimate achievement for today's Hitler fanboys – and entirely in keeping with the tradition of anti-humanism they have sprung from.

COVID-19 AS A PRESSURE COOKER

The fifth kind of trouble is the Covid-19 pandemic. At time of writing (March 2021) it has killed 2.8 million people worldwide, plunged the advanced world into its deepest slump since 1921 and boosted the debt-to-GDP ratios of major countries to wartime levels. The long-term economic and geopolitical effects will take a decade to unfold.[42]

However badly they performed, most governments tried to stop the spread of the disease – and for a good reason. Capitalism is built on the foundation of human labour. If there is no workforce, there is no profit. If there are no consumers, there is no spending and no borrowing. Equally important: without popular consent there is no government. In March 2020, public health officials told politicians in many countries that they were weeks away from the collapse of their hospital systems. Whatever else you can hide in an eviscerated democracy, you cannot hide that.

No matter how many waves the pandemic generates, nor how effective the vaccines are, the economic results of 2020 are certain to accelerate all the other crises listed above.

First, because the debts incurred, and money created to finance all the bailouts and furlough schemes, are not quickly reversible. They will linger on the balance sheets of states, companies and central banks into the middle of the century. This will limit governments' room for manoeuvre in the face of the future, purely economic shocks thrown up by a decaying capitalism. It will accentuate the tendency towards secular (long-term) stagnation and exacerbate the tendency for states to seek national, rather than multilateral, routes to growth.

Second, because the pandemic hiked the dissonance between neo-liberal ideology and reality to a new level. As governments imposed lockdowns, and economic activity slumped, a distinction emerged that was foreign to neoliberal thinking: between businesses that should be saved and those that were allowed to go to the wall. After years of wage stagnation and the erosion of welfare systems, governments everywhere began to provide incomes directly out of taxation. They began to requisition goods on a wartime basis: personal protective equipment (PPE), ventilators, medicines, food and the means to transport them all. Entire sectors were bailed out; in Britain that included the train-operating companies, large airlines, the London transport body and the private healthcare system.

Who in their right mind can now claim that 'the market self-corrects'? Yes, the sudden demand for a vaccine stimulated parallel and competitive research projects by Big Pharma and university research labs. But in most cases – through the lifting of regulatory barriers and through direct coordination – it was the state that made it possible.

Third, the pandemic shows that the crisis of human security on the planet is not simply about the climate, but about a wider process of environmental destruction. The eradication of smallpox in 1977 had encouraged immunologists to believe that all infectious diseases could be suppressed or eradicated. But the past fifty years have seen the growth of 'zoonotic' viruses that cross from bird and mammal populations to humans: HIV-1, SARS, MERS, Bird Flu, Ebola and now Covid-19.

The factors driving the rise of these new infectious diseases, say scientists, are primarily socio-economic: 'industrialization, intensive farming, urbanisation, rapid transportation and climate change'.[43] In summary, they are an effect of neoliberal globalization. Around three quarters of all newly discovered human diseases are zoonotic – and the rate of increase is accelerating.[44] Even once Covid-19 is defeated, it is very likely that a development model based on deforestation, chaotic urbanization and the privatization of public services will produce new, deadly crossover viruses.

All of this, yet again, forces our collective imagination to think beyond capitalism. Faced with the increased virus risk, experts at the intergovernmental body on bio-diversity in 2019 called for:

> a fundamental, system-wide reorganization across technological, economic and social factors, including paradigms, goals and values, promoting social and environmental responsibilities across all sectors.[45]

As with climate change, it is possible to imagine a kind of capitalism that achieves this goal, but not *this* capitalism. And in response – again as with climate change – it forces the authoritarians, populists and fascists to converge on a strategy of untruth.

The first year of the Covid-19 pandemic proved a golden oppor-tunity for both right-wing populism and fascism. Far-right activists quickly colonized the pandemic denial movements ('it's a hoax'), the anti-mask movements ('it's the state limiting our freedom') and the anti-vaxx ideology. It was no surprise to see people pulled from these starting points into the stronger vortex of QAnon, and from there into the far right itself.

Because, fundamentally, we are dealing with what the psychiatrist Wilhelm Reich once called 'people in trouble': people whose existing ideology has been shattered, and who are pushed by every new shock inflicted on them into the search for a coherent alternative worldview. And while the effects may be temporary, there is no shock greater than being forced to leave your workplace, cease your social life and wear a mask over your face. We may be dealing with Covid-19 as a virus for years; we will probably have to deal with the residual polit-ical traumas for even longer.

THE CRISES ARE INTERACTING

In 1930 the Italian communist writer Antonio Gramsci wrote his now-celebrated summary of the events that had defeated the Italian left, and that were about to bring Hitler to power:

> The crisis consists precisely in the fact that the old is dying and the new cannot be born; in this interregnum a great variety of morbid symp-toms appear.[46]

As liberalism surveyed the electoral carnage of the late 2010s, Gramsci's metaphor of the interregnum crossed over to the political mainstream. In 2019 the *Munich Security Report*, a prestigious annual summary written for the world's defence ministers, quoted Gramsci's words as 'an apt description of the world order today'.[47] In 2020 even the right-wing Tory minister Michael Gove quoted Gramsci in order to justify his government's break with globalism: 'Our age is not the 1930s. But it is an age of morbid symptoms. The model that the current generation of political leaders inherited has been crumbling.'[48]

But the interregnum parallel is inexact. Gramsci could not know it, but fascism would be defeated by an alliance of democratic capitalist countries and the Soviet Union. The 'interregnum' he hoped might end by producing socialism in fact ended with the triumph of liberal capitalism in 1945.

Gramsci's interregnum model may have worked in the two-dimensional space of class struggle and national rivalries. But in our era the crises of technological control, bio-security and climate change have added new dimensions.

Climate change and the Covid-19 pandemic look to policymakers like 'exogenous shocks': the proverbial asteroid hitting the planet. But they are each a long-term product of capitalism, and their emergence signals that we are dealing with a crisis of a different order from the 1930s.

Analysts in the sphere of geopolitics, climate and economics use relatively crude models of crisis. They can see (and lament) the breakup of an international order; they can read carbon emission scenarios and compare them to geopolitical ones; they can recognize the secular stagnation of Western economies. But because they cannot accept *capitalism* as a time-limited system, with a beginning, a middle and an end, they have no way of modelling the whole chaotic reality. As a result, the official predictions continually underestimate the destructive potential of a crisis. That was true of the Iraq War and the insurgency that followed; it was true of 2008 and again true as American liberalism tried to cope with Trump.

If we stand back, and try to comprehend the situation as a *totality*, then the combined crises outlined here look like products of a deeper problem: capitalism is reaching the limits of its ability to adapt and self-replicate.

In periods of general crisis, cause and effect become difficult to follow. There seem to be many causes but only one effect – the crisis itself. Philosophers call this 'overdetermination' – and the word was borrowed by Gramsci's followers to analyse periods like ours. When several crises at once try to push their way through the bottleneck of a single social reality, we should expect them to interact, and in unpredictable ways.

Orienting ourselves will be much easier if we expect the extreme right to exploit these destructive crossovers, and stop telling ourselves lies like 'populism has run out of steam' or 'to ignore the fascists and they'll go away', or to 'concentrate on the economic issues and ignore cultural divisions'. Because, unlike Gramsci's era, our interregnum contains a ticking clock.

In the twentieth century all wings of progressive politics had a relaxed attitude to historical time. The social democrats were committed to a long-term, peaceful process of change: capitalism would 'grow over' into socialism, and in the meantime the working class would learn the skills needed to run a post-capitalist society. Revolutionaries, by contrast, wanted to force the pace of history – but they were confident that, even if they were defeated, defeats were just stepping stones to victory. Liberals, who had no overall goal, were happy to let progress work at its own pace.

But climate change has introduced a deadline. If, amid the chaos of rising temperatures and repeated pandemics, we allow the new fascism to reach a stage where it can challenge for power, or simply block effective action on decarbonization, the price we pay will be higher than the one paid in the 1930s.

Let's outline a reasonable worst-case scenario. The Western economies, heavily indebted and impaired as a result of Covid-19, remain stagnant and become more unequal; the quality of democracy goes on declining, as does the enthusiasm of law-enforcement agencies to sustain the rule of law. In the democratic world that would leave big tech, not governments, to hold the line against the extreme right and its online armies, which is not going to happen. As the scale of the change required to decarbonize finally dawns on people, and the compressed timescale needed to achieve it, many begin to reject it as a goal. 'The worst effects will happen after I am dead,' they reason, or to people living closer to the equator. Better to deploy razor-wire fences and patrol boats at the nation's borders.

And Covid-19 has already refocused the attention of major powers onto domestic security and supply, not maintaining the global system.

On its own this scenario increases the opportunities for fascism, but only incrementally. The step-change happens if one or more countries experience a moment of fragility, as Germany did in 1929. As we'll see in Chapter 6, the Wall Street Crash on its own didn't kill German democracy, but it did make large numbers of people realize, almost literally overnight, that the old solutions would not work any more. All it took then was for the elites to carry on as normal, doubling down on policies everyone knew would fail – which then laid the basis for the Nazi breakthrough. We should expect such moments of fragility to emerge repeatedly during this multilayered crisis.

The most obvious dangers, at time of writing, are a victory for the far right in France in 2022, a breakthrough for the Italian far right before 2023, the return of a Trump-like Republican president in 2024, a military coup in Brazil to stop Lula and the left regaining power, and a further swing by Modi's BJP towards the exclusion of India's Muslims. In addition, though the German conservative establishment (and constitution) looks like a strong bulwark against collaboration with the far right, that could change if the CDU/CSU were forced out of power by a Green/left alliance.

But we should remember: if these crises happen, their outcome is never decided in advance.

In 1936, clutching an antique rifle near the Spanish city of Huesca, the anti-fascist poet John Cornford summed up a way to think positively about a situation like ours. 'History's not plasticine,' he wrote, 'but roaring sands, yet we must swing it to its final course.'[49]

Cornford went to the Spanish Civil War as a convinced Marxist, certain of final victory. But the experience of war – fighting with an anarchist unit which refused to obey or issue orders, and which had no chance of achieving victory – showed him the complexities of the world.

In the poem 'Full Moon at Tierz', Cornford warns us that, to grasp the complexity of times like ours, you have to start from the big picture and expect sudden change. You cannot mould history like clay; it hits you as a complex, thermodynamic flow, like an avalanche of sand in the desert. You can't stop the flow, but you can put something in its path and divert it. In Cornford's case that 'something' was his own body and, on the day of his death, a jammed machine gun.

There are moments, Cornford wrote, when the long, slow process of change in history reaches a breaking point and solid things shatter, like at the edge of a glacier. In such moments there is no end point preordained by what went before – by the traditions of liberal democracy, or by the constitutions and treaties already written. He calls this moment 'the dialectic's point of change'.

In the 2020s it is possible that the rules-based global order will survive, even if a few, isolated right-wing populist regimes persist. But it is more likely that the world order will break, that we will end up with competing power blocs using trade, technology, diplomatic rivalry and even hostile debt write-offs to force their way out of the globalization that prevailed between 1989 and 2008. They won't need fascism to achieve that, though it will be their willing helper.

It is also possible that the calculations of the authoritarians go wrong, and that revolts of workers, minorities, women, LGBTQ+ people and the global poor inject their own unyielding complexity into the situation, bringing to power transformative governments of the left and centre left. History tells us that this is the moment when the elite becomes open to the appeal of fascism.

If so, for progressive people who want to think in terms of decades rather than tomorrow's headlines, the task is pretty clear: *to save ourselves from climate change we need to stop fascism and defend democracy. But how?*

Fascism triumphed in the twentieth century in three phases. First, irrationalism, mysticism and racism became strongly imbued into the culture of the middle class. Next, a few visionary people codified the fascist ideology – replacing class, history and revolution with race, nature and war – and then built a new form of organization around it. Then, capitalism collapsed, and with it the world order. If you are certain this can never happen again, because the interwar period was so different from ours, I hope Part Two of this book will convince you otherwise.

For now, it remains to sum up the dangers outlined in Part One. Fascism is back, in the form of movements perpetrating symbolic violence against the left, minorities and democratic institutions. Instead of forming a firewall against it, right-wing populism is being consumed by it, and parts of mainstream conservatism have become its willing host. The breakthrough, so far, is at the level of ideas, where fascism's thought-architecture has become influential. Faced with economic crisis, democratic decay, extreme technological power inequalities, climate chaos and the tensions fuelled by Covid-19, there is a non-negligible risk of a fascist breakthrough.

Hannah Arendt called fascism the 'temporary alliance of the elite and the mob'. The only thing that's ever beaten it was *an alliance of the centre and the left*. But as we will now explore, that lesson was learned at the cost of losing most of Europe's democracies – and millions of lives.

PART TWO

History

4

Destroy Everything

The Origins of Fascism

'When I observe how they silently cut lanes through the tangles of barbed wire,' wrote Ernst Jünger, of his fellow soldiers in the First World War, 'I am overcome with recognition: this is the new man, the storm pioneer, the elite of Central Europe. A whole new race, smart, strong and filled with will.'

Jünger had spent the war in frontline combat, whose horrors, almost unaccountably, he relished. Demobbed at the age of twenty-three, he wanted more. 'The war is not the end but the prelude to violence,' he wrote in his memoir *Storm of Steel*. 'The war is a great school and the new man will bear our stamp.'[1]

Jünger's words illustrate the first thing we need to know about the origins of fascism. Its earliest followers were men who had been exhilarated by the war but traumatized by the peace that followed. Whichever side they had fought on, they had 'lost' the war as a lived experience and were determined to refind it. Everywhere it appeared, fascism preyed on a mismatch between the thrill of war fighting and the drabness of post-war reality.

Jünger, whose writing glorified the pain and obedience he had seen in the trenches, hoped that in the future humans would learn not just to obey orders but also to obey the rhythm of machines, and even think of themselves as machine-like 'objects'.[2] In the future, he wrote, 'technology will be our uniform'.

And that's the second thing we need to know about the origins of fascism. It was born out of a desire among large numbers of people to become *less human*; to have less freedom and autonomy; to obey.

Understanding the roots of that desire is the key to understanding fascism.

However, in the immediate aftermath of the First World War millions of people were *refusing* to obey. Between 1917 and 1920 the political agenda was shaped not by men like Jünger, but by the organized working class. Far from learning to think like machines, towards the end of the war workers in almost every major country had learned how to switch them off.

Fascism emerged politically as a reaction to three revolutionary events that shattered the confidence of Europe's elites.

In November 1917 the far-left Bolshevik Party seized power in Russia and handed it to a congress of *soviets* – councils elected by workers and soldiers. The Bolsheviks disbanded the army and pulled Russia out of the war. They gave women the right to vote, with full legal equality, established divorce rights and legalized abortion.[3] They nationalized the banks, gave land to the peasants and cancelled the country's foreign debts.[4] Within days of coming to power they issued a call for workers all over the world to do the same: to put down their rifles, stop the war and finish off capitalism.

A year later it was Germany's turn. In November 1918, with the country days away from defeat, a naval mutiny at the Baltic port of Kiel spiralled into a full-blown insurrection. Army units rebelled, left the front line and surged into the cities, where they too set up workers' and soldiers' councils. One detachment even tried to seize a radio tower, in order to communicate directly with Russian sailors in the Baltic. Only by persuading the Kaiser to abdicate, declaring Germany a republic, and allowing moderate socialists to form a government did the elite prevent a Russian-style revolution.[5]

Then in Italy, in the spring of 1919, as demobbed peasant soldiers returned to their farms, half a million of them seized control of the fields from their landlords and set up local price-control committees, some of which they labelled *soviets*. Meanwhile, more than a million Italian workers were involved in a near-continuous wave of strikes.[6]

There were other revolts in 1919: a short-lived workers' revolution in Hungary, a general strike in Seattle, the Mexican revolution and the May Fourth uprising in Shanghai. But it was the worker and

peasant uprisings in Russia, Germany and Italy – led by Marxist parties that had opposed the war or urged an early end to it – that
triggered a new form of violent, ultra-nationalist, right-wing politics.

Within twelve months of the November 1918 Armistice, far-right
movements emerged in Italy, Germany, Romania and Hungary, each
with a recognizably similar project: to smash Bolshevism using a new
political force. Half party, half militia, this force would be just as well
organized as the left, using language just as modern, and even echoing
some of the left's demands. Though its aim was to roll back progress,
its language would focus on the future, not the past.

To counter the threat of far-left revolution, this new force would
stage a far-right revolution. In response to the revolutionary worker
and rebellious soldier, it would create a 'New Man', both obedient
and violent. The New Man's partner would be the newly subjugated
woman, rolling back the effects of factory work during the war, feminist ideas, and birth control – a baby machine to supply soldiers for
the next war.

This new force was fascism. To understand why it exploded in several countries at once we need to see Russia as the detonator, and
middle-class European culture as the explosive mass.

RUSSIA: 'WORLD WAR 1.5'

To destroy the Bolshevik regime, Britain, France and the USA backed
three so-called 'White' (anti-Bolshevik) Russian armies, their ranks
swelled by Western European volunteers, in a simultaneous invasion of
the new Soviet state, starting a civil war that lasted from 1918 through
to 1922. Both sides resorted to what they openly labelled 'terror': executions, torture, reprisals, detention camps, the destruction of infrastructure
and starvation tactics. This classic 'dirty war' killed 1.5 million people in
combat and an estimated 12 million from famine and disease.

There were few cameras, few journalists present, and both sides
had an interest in covering up what troops did in their name. As a
result, for much of the twentieth century the Russian Civil War was
something of a historical blank page, lying between the much better
documented carnage of the 1914–18 war and the rise of fascism.

Today, with better information, we can see this four-year conflict – which stretched from Helsinki to Baku and from Warsaw to Vladivostok – as a kind of 'World War 1.5' – and a vital phase in the emergence of fascism. First, because it normalized genocidal violence against Jews. Second, because it taught tens of thousands of Europeans the art of killing Marxists with impunity. Third, because it created an early model for the fascist regime.

Pogroms against the Jewish communities of Russia and Eastern Europe were a feature of pre-war life. In response to the failed workers' revolution in 1905, the Russian monarchist right had organized the so-called 'Black Hundred', a uniformed and militarized far-right movement that, under the cover of stamping out revolutionaries, perpetrated murderous attacks on Jewish communities and published anti-Semitic propaganda.[7]

The outbreak of the Russian Civil War gave them an opportunity to carry out another wave of pogroms. From December 1918 onwards the White armies operating in what are now Poland, Belarus and Ukraine systematically identified Jews with their Bolshevik enemies and routinely massacred them. In the twelve months to December 1919, around 60,000 Jews were killed by General Anton Denikin's White Army and its auxiliaries in Ukraine, in 1,300 separate attacks.[8]

Though it was convenient for the White Army to stigmatize Jews, it is also true that Jews, in return, supported the Bolshevik regime and enthusiastically took part in its new state structures. 'To many ordinary people,' writes the historian Piotr Wróbel, 'the sudden appearance of the Jews in governmental positions previously reserved for non-Jews explained why the entire world turned upside down.'[9]

The myth of the 'Judeo-Bolshevik conspiracy', which became a central justification for the Holocaust and remains an important theme for today's far right, was established in the rules-free environment of the Russian Civil War. At its heart, it expresses the basic impulse of fascism: fear of freedom triggered by the sight of people achieving freedom who were not supposed to.

Within the Russian Civil War, it is important to separate the systematic slaughter from the chaotic; both sides did the latter, but the systematic slaughter was largely a White affair. In Finland, in response to a Bolshevik uprising that took control of the country's southern half in January 1918, the White Army issued a 'shoot on the spot' order, legalizing the execution of their left-wing political opponents. Of the 35,000 people killed (more than 1 per cent of the Finnish population), 7,263 died in authorized executions outside combat.[10]

In Ukraine, Denikin passed laws stipulating the death penalty as punishment for an escalating series of political offences. They started with execution for membership of the Bolshevik party, then spread to anyone who had participated in a *soviet*, and finally anyone guilty of 'anarchistic tendencies, speculation, thievery, corruption, desertion and other mortal sins'.[11] Though the Western journalists and diplomats attached to the White armies were shocked by this strategy of legalized mass murder, some of its most enthusiastic perpetrators were German, Austrian, Czech and Italian volunteers, who would carry both the idea and the experience of 'killing Marxism' back to their own troubled democracies.

In addition to anti-Semitic violence and mass executions of the left, the Russian Civil War gave a third impetus to fascism, in the form of a model state. The White regime in Siberia took the form of a military dictatorship, led by Alexander Kolchak, a former admiral, and self-proclaimed 'Supreme Leader' of the Russian people. Kolchak massacred the entire male populations of Red villages and issued propaganda depicting Jews and socialists as alien to the Russian nation. But this, as we have seen, was not unusual for a White Army.

What makes Kolchak's regime significant in the genesis of fascism is the presence of right-wing intellectuals in his government, who argued for a new, international movement to suppress Bolshevism, and a new kind of state. Instead of a return to tsarism, he advocated the modernization of the Russian state; only a state that could defeat Bolshevism was worth defending, he said, and that's what he tried to create.

Kolchak adopted parts of the socialist programme – the eight-hour day, sickness benefits for workers and pensions for the elderly. This combination of social reform, state modernization and charismatic leadership led one of his generals to claim that, in Siberia:

> The White movement in its very essence was the first manifestation of fascism. The White movement was not even a forerunner, but a pure manifestation of it.[12]

Kolchak's army was defeated in November 1919 and he was executed by his captors two months later. But survivors from White Siberia travelled across Europe and the Far East spreading the news: Bolshevism could be beaten by waging a rules-free war, led by a charismatic dictator offering state modernization and social reform. During the 1920s, thousands of White Army veterans, now based in Western Europe, China and the USA, would create something that still exists: an international solidarity network for the far-right, aiding each other by any means necessary.

While Russian fascism was, like all fascisms, nationalist, its exile status made it functionally transnational. It became a core component of the cross-border networks that would spread fascist ideas after the initial breakthrough.

GERMANY: FROM THE *FREIKORPS* TO THE NAZIS

In Germany fascism grew out of the same impulse that drove the White regimes: fear of a workers' revolution and disgust at the sudden collapse of traditional hierarchies. Though the declaration of a republic had delayed a full-blown revolution, in January 1919 the newly formed German Communist Party (KPD) staged a military confrontation with the authorities in Berlin, the Spartacist Revolt. It was triggered by the sacking of a left-wing police chief, and drew the KPD and the politically inexperienced young soldiers who supported them into street fighting with the socialist government.

To put the insurrection down, the socialist-led government was forced to call on paramilitary groups, called *Freikorps* (Free Corps), formed in December 1918 by demobbed soldiers based in decommissioned army camps. During the Berlin uprising, the ruling Social-Democratic Party (SPD) did call on its own members to join the *Freikorps* – but they were overwhelmingly composed of, and led by, right-wing nationalists and war fanatics. More than 150 people were killed as the *Freikorps* put down the Spartacist rising, murdering the KPD's leaders Rosa Luxemburg and Karl Liebknecht in cold blood.

In February 1919, the *Freikorps* deployed themselves eastwards, as volunteers in the unfolding Russian Civil War, where the fledgling Baltic states were resisting the Red Army. On taking Riga they killed 3,000 Latvian leftists. When recalled by the German government, up to 20,000 of them rebelled and joined the White Russian forces.[13] When they were eventually forced to retreat through Latvia, wrote one, they unloaded all their despair in one wild 'power blow', torching villages and killing civilians randomly:

> We kindled a funeral pyre – there burned our hopes, longings, bourgeois codes, the laws and values of the civilised world; there burned everything.[14]

In Munich, Bavaria, where the left established a short-lived workers' republic in April 1919, the *Freikorps* again proved crucial in restoring order, executing around 1,000 people as they retook the city.

Though not all *Freikorps* soldiers became Nazis, many leading Nazis began their post-war careers in these units. They would bring to the Nazi movement both money and connections – to big businessmen like the steel magnate Fritz Thyssen, or to exiled survivors of the tsarist aristocracy and to senior military figures.[15]

The *Freikorps* established one of the most persistent tactics in the fascist toolkit: the creation of paramilitary groups, ostensibly formed to 'support' the government, but in fact designed to wage war against the left while undermining the state's monopoly of armed force.

Overt fascist politics, meanwhile, emerged in the form of competing far-right organizations, veterans' movements and anti-Semitic cultural groups. Once the Munich revolt was crushed, Bavaria became the far right's epicentre: a magnet for militaristic nationalists who wanted to rid the country of its democratic constitution.

It was there that a machine-fitter called Anton Drexler formed a ten-member group called – optimistically given its size – the German Workers' Party (DAP). It was dedicated to anti-communism, state ownership, authoritarian government and anti-Semitism. In September 1919, the DAP issued their fifty-fifth membership card to an army intelligence man who had been sent to monitor them. His name was Adolf Hitler.

By early 1920, the DAP was ready to go public with a twenty-five-point programme. Though it was heavy on the obsessions of German nationalism – restore the army, repudiate the Versailles peace treaty and strip Jews of their citizenship – as under Kolchak, the demands were mixed with elements of the socialist programme, for example the expansion of state pensions and the nationalization of major industries.[16]

At a 2,000-strong meeting in a Munich beer hall on 24 February 1920, Hitler – by now the party's star orator – launched the new programme amid an atmosphere of hate and violence. He spoke in short, unpolished sentences, railing against 'Jews and profiteers', and channelled the anger of the crowd against the socialists who'd come to heckle him.

At this point the party added the words 'National Socialist' to its title, becoming the National Socialist German Workers' Party (NSDAP). Nazism would be sold initially to the masses as a nationalist revolt against capitalism, as opposed to the class-based revolution that had been put down. It had fewer than a thousand members, 90 per cent of them living in Bavaria, 90 per cent of them male and just one in five of them actually a worker.[17]

ITALY: FASCISTS OF THE FIRST HOUR

If the formative ideas and tactics of fascism were already circulating in the post-war chaos of Germany and Russia, it was in Italy that fascism found a name, an ideology and its first successful leader: Benito Mussolini.

Before the First World War Mussolini had been a prominent figure on the revolutionary wing of the Italian Socialist Party (PSI) and the editor of its biggest newspaper. But the war's outbreak turned Mussolini into an equally revolutionary nationalist, demanding that Italy enter the war on the side of Britain and France. Expelled from the PSI, in 1915 he formed a new movement, the *Fascio d'Azione Revolutionaria* (Revolutionary Action Group). His supporters, drawing on the Italian word for group, or league, began to call themselves *fascisti*: fascists.

Mussolini believed that the war would speed up the modernization of society and blow away the liberal establishment. In 1917, after the

Italian Army's shattering defeat at the Battle of Caporetto, that process began. To motivate the troops, officers were ordered to tell their peasant soldiers that they would be given land if they won the war: 'Save Italy and she's yours' was the slogan. Meanwhile, the Italian Army formed new commando units – known as *Arditi* (The Daring) and clad in black – feeding the same kind of war euphoria that Ernst Jünger was to describe among shock troops on the German side.

When the war ended, though Italy was technically on the winning side together with Britain, France and the USA, it 'lost the peace'. The British had promised Italy control over what is now Slovenia and the Croatian coast, plus parts of Greece, Albania and Turkey. But the USA vetoed the plan, leaving Italian nationalists nurturing a betrayal complex just as corrosive as the one that was eating up the German right. 'When I came back from the war,' wrote Italo Balbo, the former army captain who would organize Mussolini's March on Rome in 1922, 'like so many, I hated politics and politicians. Better to deny everything, to destroy everything, so as to rebuild everything from scratch.'[18]

By 23 March 1919, the forces Mussolini needed to form the fascist movement had been assembled. Demobbed members of the *Arditi*, still wearing their black shirts; artists and intellectuals from the Futurist movement, who believed that 'war is the earth's form of hygiene'; and revolutionary nationalists such as Mussolini himself, drawn from the fringes of socialism and anarchism.[19] They named themselves the *Fasci Italiani di Combattimento* (Italian Combat Groups) making it clear who the combat was going to be against: 'We declare war against socialism ... because it is opposed to nationalism,' said their first pronouncement.[20]

Their first violent action came a month later, when a squad of around 300 fascists attacked a socialist trade union meeting in Milan, killing three and hospitalizing thirty-seven. Their first manifesto, in June 1919, called for the eight-hour day, a minimum wage and a progressive tax system to 'partially expropriate' the factory owners. By November 1919 they were, so they thought, ready to stand in their first election.

In fact, they were electorally demolished. Out of 270,000 votes cast in Milan, the fascists got fewer than 5,000. To the shock of the liberal establishment, it was the socialists who got the biggest share of the vote. To celebrate, socialist activists carried a coffin past Mussolini's house, representing the death of his political career.

The man himself was in despair. Hiding in his office, with a drawer full of hand grenades for protection, he contemplated emigration to the USA. When he was arrested for inciting a bomb attack against a socialist parade, the authorities let him go on the grounds that he was already a 'relic'.[21]

Let's hit the pause button there. It's February 1920. Kolchak has been executed, Hitler is working the beer hall circuit, and Mussolini is reduced to writing angry newspaper columns, his fascist movement in disarray.

'What can we do to stop these maniacs?' would have been the wrong question. They had stopped themselves. From Milan to Manchuria the fascist movements were, by early 1920, either dwarfed, sidelined or contained by their sworn enemies: the Marxist-led parties of the working class.

Yet by October 1922, less than three years later, Mussolini would take power. And by January 1933 Hitler was chancellor of Germany. Their strategy for power was, as we will examine below, essentially to exploit the breakdown process at work in the societies around them – which was not just economic but ideological.

However, none of this would have been possible without the existence of a mass, popular ideology already implanted in the collective identity of the middle class, which made people susceptible to fascist arguments once the crisis hit. It consisted of three basic components: irrationalism, scientific racism and the glorification of violence. We have seen already how central these ideas are to the modern far right. Now we need to explore their philosophical roots in the pre-1914 world. Because, just as today, fascism's initial audience was people whose everyday ideology had fallen apart.

MYTH, RACE AND INTUITION

Tracing the intellectual roots of fascism can feel like a futile exercise. Hitler knew the operas of Richard Wagner so well he could whistle the tunes from memory, but thousands of other Wagner fans did not become Nazis. Mussolini was fascinated by the ideas of the anarchist Georges Sorel, but so were many people on the left. Because of this, in the twentieth century, historians tended to focus on the *actions* of fascist movements, not their ideas. What's the point of studying an ideology, they asked, if it's only a series of negative prejudices with no logical coherence?

For us, tracing fascism to its philosophical source is important. Because, though today's far right looks very different from that of the interwar years, its intellectual sources are exactly the same. The modern fascist ideology is not a hangover from the 1930s; it is a kind of 'second growth' from the same philosophical rootstock that produced the first.

And because we live in an information society, ideas can function much more directly as weapons for today's far right. Few of those who perpetrated political murders in the 1930s, for example, would have bothered publishing a theoretical tract on the day of the killing. Today, almost every fascist lone-shooter has done so.[22]

By the end of the nineteenth century, the developed world could look back on 100 years of scientific, technological and social progress. Science had made huge advances, from thermodynamics to Darwin's theory of evolution; citizens had gained new democratic rights and new access to education; aeroplanes, motor cars and moving pictures were about to transform what it felt like to be alive.

However, three groups of people wanted more: workers, women and the peoples of the colonial world. By the 1890s the working class in many countries had formed mass trade unions and political parties, either led by Marxists or strongly influenced by them. Meanwhile, women, who in most countries had no legal status separate from their husbands, were agitating for the right to vote, and in 1893 in New Zealand they won it. Likewise, the peoples of the colonial empires were beginning to fight for national self-determination and human rights. They demanded to know why they were being denied parliaments, constitutions and nationhood.

You can deal with such problems with police truncheons and machine guns – and that's what the imperialist elites did. But you can't shoot an idea. To resist progress, you need an ideological justification, a counter-narrative. So from the 1890s onwards, intellectuals who detested the advance of socialism, feminism, anti-imperialism and democracy adopted the philosophy of irrationalism.

Science is unavoidably materialist: it believes in a real and knowable world, which we can observe and test, making sense of it through logic and analysis. For the nineteenth-century elites this was fine so long as you were only trying to understand nature and design better machines. But once the working class adopted Marxism, using materialism to understand society as well as nature, and to design a better future, a movement began to repudiate materialism.

Its overt target was 'positivism' – the idea that society operates according to laws just as fundamental and observable as those in nature. But as H. Stuart Hughes notes in his major study of the movement, for reactionary intellectuals in the 1890s, positivism was a word interchangeable with materialism.[23] Many educated people, above all creative people, became convinced that it was impossible to understand society through the empirical data of sociologists and economists alone, which obscured the intuitive, creative and unconscious factors that drive events.

Though it originated in the books and lectures of little-known intellectuals, irrationalism would, by the eve of the First World War, become a kind of alternative religion for the middle class. The foundations were laid by the German philosopher Friedrich Nietzsche.

Nietzsche today is praised in universities as a rebel, an atheist, the forerunner of post-modernism, a subtle analyst of power structures, a lyrical writer and the inspiration for several generations of doomy novelists. He was all these things. But in essence he was a racist, misogynist pro-imperialist who *hated the working class*. His genius lay in his ability to turn this set of prejudices into a coherent system of anti-rational thought.

Nietzsche insisted that all knowledge is merely the product of the individual's point of view. There are, as in his famous aphorism, 'no facts, only interpretations' – and none of the interpretations should be trusted either. In summary: 'there is no truth'.[24]

What shapes our interpretation of the world is our 'will to power'. All moral systems, said Nietzsche, are just hypocritical constructs around self-interest, and therefore equally invalid. Faced with a moral choice, those with power should do what they please. In turn, the human 'will to power' is just an expression of the driving force behind all nature, which Nietzsche attributed to animals, plants and even cells.

Nietzsche despised and feared the organized working class. It was, he said, inevitable that the masses would defeat the elite, because they were more numerous and 'shrewd'. But if you could transform the elite into a caste of ruthless warriors, you could avoid this fate. The problem I am posing, he wrote, is, 'what type of man must be *bred*, must be *willed*, as being the most valuable, the most worthy of life, the most secure guarantee of the future'.[25]

This is Nietzsche's famous Superman (*Übermensch*) doctrine, the inspiration for Jünger and his 'New Man' and – as we have seen – an idea clearly present in the writings of twenty-first-century fascists. Create a new race of tough, amoral heroes – 'blond beasts', as Nietzsche called them – and, since there is no morality, they can then use violence to maintain the natural division between the elite and the masses.

To the challenge of women's liberation Nietzsche advanced a theory that will sound boringly familiar to anyone with an internet connection:

> Two different things wanteth the true man: danger and diversion. Therefore wanteth he woman, as the most dangerous plaything. Man shall be trained for war, and woman for the recreation of the warrior: all else is folly.[26]

Men who found themselves 'defeated' by womanly guile, he said, should remain celibate. A woman's role was to produce as many Supermen as possible.

To the challenge of historical progress, Nietzsche had an equally sweeping answer: it does not exist. There is, he said, no progress, only the 'eternal recurrence of the same', an endless cycle of development and destruction. Every movement for social justice is followed by the triumph of the elite, making progressive social movements pointless. All attempts to improve humanity – from Christianity to the Enlightenment to the French Revolution and socialism – should be abandoned. The key attribute of a Superman, he said, was to accept the ultimate meaninglessness of life and history, and to learn to love the destructive phase of history.

There are still people who think it was a complete accident that the Nazis doted on Nietzsche, or that Hitler patronized the archive kept by Nietzsche's sister, or that *Mein Kampf* and Mussolini's writings are full of the same language.[27] Nietzsche's defenders are correct to say that his sister, a fanatical anti-Semite, doctored his works and methodically created a cult around them while Nietzsche was mentally ill, during the 1890s.

But Nietzsche's thought constitutes the most comprehensive statement of irrationalism ever written. It says there is no truth; no progress; no meaning to history; no basis for women's equality, or socialism, or for opposing colonialism; and that some humans are subhuman. Its recurrent conclusion is that *elite violence is justified*.

Vilfredo Pareto, an Italian economist who would later sympathize with fascism, summarized what Nietzsche meant to the generation that idolized him before 1914. The working class were continually saying they wanted to 'destroy' the bourgeoisie. No one until Nietzsche had dared to say: 'Come on then. It's us that will destroy you.'[28]

There should be no mystery about why the Nietzsche cult appeared during the 1890s, or about the wider irrationalist moment it was a part of. It was a response to the emergence of mass, Marxist parties who justified their project of socialism as the end point of historical progress, using rationalism and materialism.

In 1893, for example, in an introduction to Nietzsche for French readers, one conservative literary editor complained that, in the face of parliamentary socialism, 'we are all cowards':

> Humanity should be like nature, pitiless to the weak. The important thing is that the strong display their strength and that the strongest people project into the firmament an exact image of their extreme power.[29]

A society based on Nietzschean principles, he continued prophetically, would be 'the most unstable of all, destined to flame up like a fire and disappear'. Better this than hand power to semi-literate factory workers, or votes to women.

Nietzsche's death in 1900 coincided with a wave of irrationalist art, literature and non-academic philosophy. Its general theme was that a rich and educated people should not allow themselves to be reined in by democracy and the masses. In 1908, for example, in a preface to Nietzsche's writings, the American conservative H. L. Mencken wrote that the contents would mainly be of interest to the 'successful man ... they justify that man's success as Christianity justifies the failure of the man below'. There was no need to 'convert the many who serve and wait, but only the few who rule'.[30]

By this point, a whole community of irrationalist thinkers had emerged, and their ideas had started to filter into middle-class culture. To tell their story properly would fill an entire book with portraits of upper-class, male writers expounding on their terror of women, black people and the working class, in Tolkien-length books. Since there is no space for all that, I will briefly trace the way four formative ideas crossed over from irrationalist philosophy into popular culture and eventually into fascism.

The first is 'life philosophy', also known as 'vitalism', the idea that alongside the physical world studied by science, there is an invisible vital force that causes change – both in nature, through evolution, and society, through human action. Promoted by the French writer Henri Bergson in a series of hugely popular public lectures, vitalism claims that while science and logic are OK for producing a static picture of reality, they are useless when it comes to describing change through time. For this, we should rely on instinct and intuition.

Bergson was so popular that, when he gave his first lecture in New York, he caused the first traffic jam on Broadway. You can understand why vitalism resonated, even among the free-spirited and bohemian left. Who today has not had their horoscope read, or played with Tarot cards, believed in ghosts or read a New Age self-help book? Back then, among the artists, composers and novelists struggling to throw off bourgeois morality and produce work that was resonant with feeling, Nietzsche and Bergson were eagerly adopted.

One of the most influential applications of vitalism was Oswald Spengler's book *The Decline of the West*, conceived in the pre-war period but published only in 1918. Spengler rejected the idea of history as a process of advance, from classical antiquity to feudalism and then capitalism. Instead, he argued, history was an endless cycle, characterized by the rise and fall of major cultures. Western culture was in its own phase of decline and would soon produce a figure like Julius Caesar. 'The coming of Caesarism,' he wrote, 'breaks the dictature of money and its political weapon, democracy.' There is no cause and effect for Spengler, only the endless repetition of patterns. Instead of searching for material and economic drivers in history, 'the artist, the genuine historian intuits how something comes about'. 'Life,' he said, 'has no system, no programme, no rationality.'[31]

But the driving force of human history, according to Spengler, was 'race'. Races were rooted in the nature around them, inseparable from the soil, and the living expression of an unconscious will contained in their blood. Successful races were the ones that followed their destiny, remained 'vigorous' and rooted in the soil. Any attempt at 'world improvement' or 'world peace', he warned, would lead the race to subjugation. Spengler was not an anti-Semite; he ridiculed the scientific racism of the skull measurers. Nor would he go along with Nazism as it emerged. But his book transmitted the main themes of vitalism – cyclical history, intuition over scholarship – to the traumatized post-war middle class, and added to them the idea of racial hierarchy and racial conflict. His book would sell 100,000 copies in the first three years after its publication.

Other writers, however, did use irrationalist philosophy to justify turning scientific racism into a political strategy – above all the British-born, naturalized German writer Houston Stewart Chamberlain. Chamberlain did not invent 'race science': it was more than 100 years old by the time he published *The Foundations of the Nineteenth Century*. Nor did he invent Social Darwinism, the idea that races are in competition for the 'survival of the fittest' and need to be 'purified' by eugenic breeding strategies.

Chamberlain's grisly achievement was to use these ideas to formulate a combat strategy for the 'Aryan race' – that is, the peoples of India and Europe – against the Jews. Once again, the basis of the theory was irrationalism and intuition: 'What is the use of detailed scientific investigations as to whether there are distinguishable races?'

asked Chamberlain. 'We turn the tables and say: it is evident that there are such races.'[32] If you feel Aryan, he believed, you are Aryan.

The Jews' strength, alleged Chamberlain, lay in the purity of their bloodline. They had rushed into Europe 'like an enemy, stormed all positions and planted the flag of [their], to us, alien nature . . .'[33] Since Judaism forbade intermarriage, the 'race mixing' of Jews and non-Europeans through immigration would, he warned, leave Jews as the only 'pure' race in Europe. The rest would constitute 'a herd of pseudo-Hebraic *mestizos* [mixed-race], a people beyond all doubt degenerate physically, mentally and morally'.

This, in embryo, is what became today's Great Replacement Theory (see Chapter 2). Chamberlain's ideas helped shape Nazism because they made anti-Semitism into an issue of race, not religion. And though he proposed the supremacy of 'Indo-European' peoples, he designated the German-speaking group as the highest representatives of the Aryan race, awarding them the right to invade anywhere on earth.

Unlike Spengler, moreover, Chamberlain did not just sit in a library and write. He put his ideas into action: as an active confidant of Kaiser Wilhelm in the run-up to the First World War, he became a relentless propagandist for the combined programme of anti-Semitism, imperialism and war.

A third pathway from irrationalism to fascism lies in the way it was used to justify the elite manipulation of mass movements. In 1895 the French polymath Gustave Le Bon published *The Crowd: A Study of the Popular Mind*. In it Le Bon – who despised the left and was fully subscribed to 'life philosophy' – argued that even moderate socialist parties and trade unions were an existential challenge to capitalism. Their demands for higher wages and shorter hours, he said, 'are becoming more and more sharply defined, and amount to nothing less than a determination to utterly destroy society as it now exists, with a view to making it hark back to that primitive communism which was the normal condition of all human groups before the dawn of civilisation'.[34]

To meet this challenge, he argued, mainstream politicians had to stop trying to stand aloof from mass politics. Instead, they should grasp the dynamics of mass unrest, and channel its energies. Le Bon pointed out that, contrary to appearance, there was nothing intrinsically revolutionary about crowds. On the contrary, they were easily led, fundamentally authoritarian, and conservative. They 'think' only in images, said Le Bon, and because one image can be used to conjure up another image – irrespective of any logical connection – they can be easily hypnotized, especially when tired.

The Crowd became a bestseller. Among its many fans was Georges Sorel, a retired French civil servant turned anarchist whose writings were to have a strong influence on Mussolini. It is Sorel who provides a fourth and most direct channel from irrationalism to fascism: via the mythologization of violence.

It is important to remember that, right through the pre-1914 period there were figures on the left, as well as the right, who wanted to insert the irrational and intuitive into socialism. Sorel was one of them. He despised the reformist politics of the French socialist party and argued that the left should start manipulating crowds as recommended by Le Bon.

Instead of a dry theory of history, Sorel argued, Marxism should turn itself into a mythology, or a form of 'social poetry'.[35] When, in the early 1900s, French workers staged a wave of mass strikes, Sorel discovered the myth he was looking for. Mass strikes inevitably escalate into violence, he wrote. Rather than trying to restrain such violence, the labour movement's leaders should romanticize and mythologize it.

When we use the word 'myth' today, we generally mean 'a fantasy that explains the world'. But Sorel, inspired by Bergson, used it in a wider sense. For Sorel, a social myth is one that arises when masses of people *take action guided by their intuition*, not some political theory or programme. If you live your life according to the myth, you can experience a little chunk of the future in the present moment. Sorel noticed that, for the French working class, the mass strike had come to play a mythical role: they believed it was both the weapon that could bring socialism, and a small foretaste of socialism itself.

The general strike, Sorel said, is the 'myth in which socialism is wholly comprised, i.e. a body of images capable of evoking instinctively ... the war undertaken by socialism against modern society'. By propagating the myth of the general strike, said Sorel, 'we thus obtain that intuition of socialism which language cannot give us'.[36] Instead of painstaking self-education, organization and adherence to science, the working class, he said, should embrace irrationalism, myth and violent action.

In his *Reflections on Violence*, which actually suggested lynching members of the elite, Sorel urged the left to become subrational: 'As long as socialism remains a doctrine expressed entirely in words, it is very easy to deflect it towards this happy medium; but this transformation is obviously impossible when the myth of the general strike is introduced, as this implies an absolute revolution.'[37]

Though French socialist newspapers refused to print Sorel's articles, they were published in the Italian anarchist press. If it had ended there, he might have been an interesting footnote in history. But with the rivalry between imperial powers growing, and war looming, Sorel and his Italian supporters moved rapidly towards nationalism and violent anti-Semitism. Since the working class was clearly committed to reform, pacifism and democracy, Sorel looked for a new 'vital force' to carry out the destruction of the system – and found it in French monarchism. In 1910, four years before Mussolini, Sorel flipped direct from anarchism to far-right nationalism and began writing for the proto-fascist newspaper *Action Française*, urging unity between all opponents of democracy, left and right.

Le Bon, less surprisingly, meanwhile, authored a manual for right-wing politicians and factory owners, on how to deal with crowds. It advocated 'persuasive gestures', repetition, the creation of what we would now call AstroTurf groups – i.e. fake campaigns – and the decapitation of mass movements through sudden arrests.

So, by the time Mussolini was ready to follow his anarchist collaborators on the journey from socialism to nationalism in 1914, they had in Sorel a ready-made theory of subrational politics and violent action and, in Le Bon, a handbook for how to mesmerize large crowds. Sorel failed to transform Marxism into a doctrine based on myths and intuitions. Instead, his writings convinced Mussolini that, in order to start a revolution, you had to ditch Marx completely and embrace the full menu of irrationalism and nationalism. Asked in 1927 which thinker had exerted the greatest influence on him, Mussolini answered: 'Sorel has been my master.'[38]

*

We cannot 'blame' Nietzsche, Spengler or Bergson for fascism. It sprang more fundamentally from the wider culture of colonialism, nationalism and militarism that flourished among conservative-minded people before the First World War. But the irrationalist movement gave reactionary politics a fashionable, rebellious edge – allowing men like Mussolini and Sorel to move swiftly from the far left to the far right, where numerous monarchist, imperialist and anti-Semitic movements were coalescing.

By 1913, wrote the fascist thinker Pierre Drieu La Rochelle,

certain elements of the fascist atmosphere had already come together in France. There were young men from all classes of society, fired by a love of heroism and violence, who dreamed of fighting what they termed the evil on two fronts – capitalism and parliamentary socialism – while culling from each of them what to them seemed good.[39]

If nobody paid much attention to Hitler at first, wrote the leading historian of fascism Zeev Sternhell, it was because 'the author of *Mein Kampf* had nothing to say which had not already been said, and not by men of the lunatic fringe, but rather by the ranking intellectuals of the day'.[40]

Fascism moved forward after its setbacks in 1919 because the themes of irrationalism, scientific racism and the celebration of elite violence had been woven into middle-class political culture before and during the war. All fascism needed was for liberal self-belief to disintegrate, for economic growth to collapse and for Marxism to fail. In each respect, Italy would be its laboratory.

5

Stopping Mussolini

A Game in Five Moves

On Ferrara's main street, half hidden behind parked scooters and recycling bins, stands the Palazzo Cavalieri. It's a museum now, storing local memorabilia from the First World War. On its website, an inscription promises 'to preserve memory, to revive memory, to make memory tangible'. One memory, however, is absent.

It was behind these walls and shutters that, on 10 November 1920, Ferrara's fascists set up their first HQ. After a month of quiet recruitment, they had 150 members and a base to operate from. 'To the fascists we owe both honour and duty,' said the local newspaper. 'Only they who love youth and strength can stop the wave of madness that has arisen over Italy.'[1]

A city of medieval alleyways set amid the rich farmland of Emilia-Romagna, Ferrara was about to become the epicentre of Italian fascism. By April 1921 the men from the Palazzo Cavalieri had destroyed the socialist movement in the surrounding countryside. By May 1922 they were able to mobilize tens of thousands of unemployed peasants to occupy the city. By October 1922 their commander, Italo Balbo, would organize the fascist overthrow of Italy's elected government.

The story of how this happened should be required reading – not just for anti-fascists and democrats, but for any police officer, lawyer or civil servant determined to uphold the rule of law today. The facts are available online and in school textbooks. But to understand *why* it happened, and how easily it could happen again, we need to take a deeper dive, asking ourselves: who could have stopped Mussolini and how?

A REVOLUTION IN CONTROL

It's often claimed that Italian fascism was a reaction to the 'threat' of revolution. In fact, there *was* a revolution – though not the type of political insurrection anticipated by the left. Between the spring of 1919 and the autumn of 1920 Italy experienced a revolution in popular control, where social power passed to the workers and peasants, even while political power remained in the hands of the elite.

It began with the demobilization of the army, which by March 1919 had sent 2 million peasants home. Before the war, generations of peasants had never left their villages; now the demobbed soldiers returned to their communities with valuable knowledge of the low value the elite placed on a peasant life, and the high value of organization in conflict.

Faced with spiralling inflation and high unemployment, thousands of former soldiers – often wearing their medals – seized unused land and began farming it without permission. No party called on them to do it. But because they'd heard of the Russian Revolution, and that the Italian Socialist Party (PSI) supported it, they joined the socialist peasants' league, *Federterra*, boosting its numbers from 250,000 to 1.2 million. The league set up hiring halls, social centres, co-operatives and union offices which, by their very presence, began to assert control over rural life.

By June 1919 in the town of Forlì, for example, there was, said the local paper, a 'new power':

Men with red armbands and red scarves, officials of a newborn local *soviet*, regulate the economic life of the region; they stop the peasants' carts, dictate their prices and destinations and settle all arguments with summary justice.[2]

In the factories, meanwhile, strikes proliferated – with workers forming the kind of factory councils that Russian workers had set up two years before.

That was the background to the socialists' shock election victory of November 1919. Before the war, with the electorate limited to just

3 million, power had simply alternated between the progressive and conservative wings of liberalism. Now, with something close to universal male suffrage, the socialists won 32 per cent of the vote. It was, declared the socialist newspaper *La Giustizia* (Justice), 'The Grandiose, Formidable Victory of the Socialist Proletariat'.[3]

Adding to the political turmoil, the brand-new Popular Party (PPI) came second. Formed in 1918 by a left-wing Catholic priest, the PPI was the Vatican's attempt to counter socialism in the countryside. Its support for land seizures and mass peasant membership nonetheless made it 'subversive' in the eyes of mainstream liberals.

With 156 MPs, the socialists now had the biggest group in parliament. But they couldn't form a government on their own, and they didn't want to be in a coalition. They believed – fatally, as we will see – in their own unstoppable progress. Even so, their advance changed Italian politics profoundly. Men in red armbands running a small town you can deal with. Losing the ability to form a stable government, to a party whose logo is a hammer, a sickle and a book, was a shock the Italian elite never got over.

The liberals' response was to bring the PPI into a coalition government – to which the party agreed – and shower the working class with concessions. But instead of dissipating, the struggle for control intensified. In February 1920, workers in the shipyards of north-east Italy occupied their workplaces. In April, automobile workers paralysed Turin with an eleven-day strike over their right to control the production line. And on the land an age-old social order was being dismantled.

The term 'peasant' covered a layer-cake of exploitation. At the top of the system were the landowners; beneath them managers and bailiffs; in the middle, tenant farmers, who were granted the right to keep 50 per cent of their crops by an age-old verbal contract. At the bottom were day labourers, with no land and no security. The whole system was underpinned by the landlord's social power.

A peasant could not marry without the landlord's permission. If a peasant was in debt he could be forced to work for free; his family had to do the master's laundry, chop his wood and pay for the use of his horses, seeds and tools. There was even a rule that the master was entitled to one leg from every pig slaughtered. Break the rules and you could be evicted instantly.

In the summer of 1920 peasants across northern and central Italy blew away every single one of these rules by going on strike until the crops rotted in the ground. The discipline they'd learned in the trenches was applied to their revolt: anyone who tried to break the strike was blacklisted; shops that sold food to them were boycotted. In one region after another, they forced landlords to sign contracts handing control of their estates to the peasants. In the seven-point contract announced in Forlì, item one guaranteed 'co-management of the farm', while item seven guaranteed the peasant's right to all four legs of their own pig.[4]

Legally, the landlords could still hire, fire and evict whoever they wanted. In practical terms they could now do nothing without the permission of *Federterra*.

The account of the anarchist schoolteacher Luigi Fabbri gives a sense of the mass psychological effect of this turbulent period. On the streets and in the trams, he wrote, workers would continually hurl 'barbed remarks, innuendo, insults and vague threats' at anyone who looked middle class. The atmosphere was characterized by the 'drip, drip of vague, impersonal, unfathomable hostilities that could not be squared with one another', and which never led anywhere. The labour movement, though increasingly powerful, was surrounded on all sides by 'an irritated climate; a seething, weary public opinion'.

Fabbri was no moderate. He'd been in and out of jail since the age of sixteen for revolutionary agitation. But he saw what the socialist leaders could not: that endless minor strikes, frictions and face-to-face confrontations were creating a backlash among middle-class people, which would dissipate only if the workers actually did something lasting and successful.[5]

The factory occupations of September 1920 were the chance to do just that. For eighteen days 400,000 skilled workers in Turin, Milan and Bologna sat inside their factories, formed councils, patrolled with rifles and – in an astonishing social experiment – tried to keep production going without their managers. Women staffed communal kitchens; in the textile industry, the largely female workforce formed their own armed guards. City-level committees tried to coordinate production between different factories, and railway workers took control of moving raw materials and components from one occupied factory to the next.[6]

Everyone knew that if Italy's workers wanted to stage a Russian-style revolution the time was now. But they didn't want to. Italy's union federations organized a ballot, asking: do we tell the Socialist Party to seize power and abolish capitalism, or do we stick with workers' control over production? Some 1.1 million votes were cast – and they broke 60–40 against the seizure of power. As the historian Paolo Spriano put it, 'the revolution was rejected by majority vote'.[7]

Within days, the government brokered a compromise. The strikes ended, and though management struggled to reimpose control, it was clear that the moment for a revolution had passed. But the peasants had one more shock to inflict.

In the local elections of October–November 1920, peasant voters put the Socialist Party in control of a quarter of Italy's 8,000 district councils, known as communes. In Emilia-Romagna the socialists took control of 65 per cent of all communes and of the regional capital, Bologna. In Ferrara they won in every single district.

On the face of it the communes had little power. Though they could raise taxes to fund firefighters and sanitation, for example, they could always be dissolved by the regional prefect if they went too far. But control of the communes was central to the landlords' economic, social and political power. They were outraged and alarmed to see red flags flying over the tiled and polished offices of the commune, and its leather furniture sat on by men who worked barefoot.

The events of 1919–20, considered as a whole, constitute the seizure of social control by a section of the population that had been passive and deferential for centuries. Just as with the US Civil Rights Movement in the 1960s, and with Black Lives Matter today, it triggered a deep psychological disturbance among the people whose power was undermined. As the landlords fretted and schemed in their cafés and private clubs, one remembered, 'machine guns were often the preferred topic'.[8]

And that is what starts the fascist march to power. As they set up shop in the Palazzo Cavalieri, Ferrara's fascists were not alone. From October 1920, across large parts of Italy, the landowning class effectively 'adopted' fascism; not as a political ideology, but as a technique of social warfare. But Ferrara would be the test bed.

PHASE 1: *SQUADRISMO*

Mussolini's followers, though few, had not been idle. In July 1920 they carried out a brutal ethnic-cleansing campaign in the Adriatic city of Trieste. Mussolini's men ran riot, burning and looting to force the minority Slovene population, who were mainly left-wing workers, across the border. But this was a liminal space: just as today on America's southern border or the Greece–Turkey fence line, far-right activists could do in Trieste what they were not allowed to do at home.

In response to the socialist election victories of autumn 1920, the landlords decided to use these methods in their own backyard. The first major fascist action was the attack on Bologna's city hall, on 21 November 1920, as a crowd of around 2,000 people gathered peacefully to witness the inauguration of the socialist-led council. Around 100 fascists – including sixteen from the Ferrara squad – tried to storm the building, firing revolvers as they advanced. In a panic the socialists hurled hand grenades out of the window into the crowd, while some people started firing blindly into the council chamber itself. Ten people were killed – nine socialists and one popular local lawyer – while sixty were injured. The attack gave the government the excuse it needed to dissolve the council.[9] But that was only the start.

In the wake of the Bologna attack, fascist forces grew rapidly in the city, recruiting white-collar workers, journalists and professionals.[10] By December 1920 there were 80,476 fascists organized in eighty-eight groups, mainly across northern Italy.[11] They were formed as a private army for the landlords, who knew exactly what to do with them.

At the height of the peasant movement you could live your life in an informal welfare state composed of hiring halls, co-operatives, social centres and libraries – all overseen by the socialists. From late November 1920, fascist squads fanned out from the cities of Ferrara, Bologna and Modena to rip up these micro-organizations by their roots. Over the next four months they would torch 17 print shops, 59 Socialist Party offices, 119 labour exchanges, 107 co-operatives and 83 union offices. They broke up union meetings and hunted down councillors and union officials. Activists were whipped, tarred, left naked in the streets, force-fed castor oil to induce diarrhoea and otherwise humiliated.[12]

The average squad expedition involved over 100 men; their premises and equipment were paid for through levies raised by the landowners. Initially they had no physical infrastructure outside the cities. But they had money, guns, telephones and trucks, they had the police on their side and they attacked by night. In the village of Aguscello, an eight-minute drive from the outskirts of Ferrara, on 21 January 1920:

> Four trucks full of fascists and two cars of the [landowners], escorted by trucks full of carabinieri, did the shooting. They invaded the head-quarters of the league and trashed or looted all the furniture. The carabinieri then arrested fourteen socialists and charged them with resisting the invasion with their hunting rifles.[13]

Between January and April 1921, the fascists killed more than 100 people in these raids. Hundreds of newly elected socialist councillors were forced to resign at gunpoint. Many were given a few days' notice to leave villages they had been born in. The result was the total disintegration of the left's political infrastructure in the countryside.

Fascism, in this second iteration, was not really a political party but a template for action, labelled *squadrismo*. Mussolini, in his Milan publishing office, had no direct command over the squads themselves.

Each squad was run by a local boss, with the foot soldiers drawn from two groups still recognizable among today's alt-right: combat veterans and teenagers who wished they were combat veterans. In Bologna, 44 per cent of squad members surveyed by historian Roberta Suzzi Valli were too young to have served in the war. Some 16 per cent identified themselves as upper class, and 79 per cent as from the professional or commercial middle class, while just 6 per cent were working class.[14]

In Forlì, where in 1919 the peasants had dictated prices to the shopkeepers, a fascist described how he was able to disperse a left-wing demonstration numbering thousands:

There were a little less than a dozen of us in two cars. One drove towards the centre of the square carrying three men: one who was to give an improvised speech, and the others holding pistols. Silence fell as suddenly as in church. And then, with pale faces – nobody knows whether because of the speaker or the pistols – they ran for the exits.[15]

The squad campaign of 1921 was soon eclipsed by bigger outrages: even in academic histories of fascism it usually accounts for a chapter at most. That is in part because the source material is thin. Few journalists bothered to interview the villagers who'd been attacked, and left-wing historians saw the squads as mere 'agents' of the landowners and the factory bosses.

But we, today, faced with the emergence of far-right paramilitary violence, need to study these events closely, asking: what conditions were needed for *squadrismo* to work? First, the breakdown of the rule of law at local level: the refusal of the police to arrest the fascist squads, investigate their crimes and confiscate their weapons. Second, access to money and technology (a column of trucks bumping along an unmade road may not look hi-tech to us now, but it did to the victims).

The third condition was that a small, determined group of men knew what they were supposed to do. The squads operated just as the *Arditi* had done in the end phase of the war: through a 'war of manoeuvre' – constantly on the move, using violence and arson for shock effect. They knew that violence carried out symbolically can have far more impact than simple force. One squad leader from Pisa walked into a small-town café, pushed a random socialist against the wall, and shot him through the head – later persuading a local newspaper to print the headline: 'A William Tell prank gone wrong'.[16] At dinner parties, the perpetrator would announce himself: 'Sandro Carosi, fifteen political murders.'[17]

A fourth condition was that they had a coherent ideology. Their Marxist opponents wanted to believe the squads were full of confused, inconsequential nobodies, the puppets of the industrial bourgeoisie. Yet like Ernst Jünger in Germany, Mussolini's followers were driven by a philosophy of violence, what the historian Nino Valeri called 'violence elevated to the status of an ethical rule'.[18] As we have seen, this remains central to fascism in all its forms today.

The workers and peasants, meanwhile – though they fought back – continuously relied on the authorities to intervene. Their political culture was defensive, based around the village, estate or factory. 'Do not despair, brothers,' wrote the PSI's leader Filippo Turati, 'do not provide them with pretexts ... Be good, be patient, be holy. Be tolerant. Be compassionate. Even forgive ...'[19]

The fifth condition is the most chilling: having destroyed the left's informal welfare state, the fascists quickly created their own. In Ferrara they set up a 'land office', to which local landowners allocated about 10 per cent of the region's land: this was to be handed to day labourers and farmed under fascist supervision. They set up a rival peasant union, and by March 1921 they had 23,000 members signed up – together with a consortium of thirty-two food cooperatives which flipped from the socialists under threat of destruction.[20]

Though many were forced to join at gunpoint, others did so willingly. What the peasants had found in *Federterra* was both a welfare state and a powerful arbitrator between themselves and the landowners. Now that the fascists were doing the arbitrating, there was a straight choice: resist and get beaten, or keep quiet and join the grassroots infrastructure of fascism.

Since the whole enterprise was funded by the landowners, the outcome was inevitable. The peasants were given the poorest land; the fascist co-ops ceased to challenge the landowners' pricing power; the strikes and occupations ended, agricultural real wages halved, and soon the tenant farmers were back to doing the master's chores for free.

If we zoom out, and see *squadrismo* as a single 'beat' of the action, it can be summarized as: *symbolic violence forces the state to surrender its monopoly of coercive force.*

From May 1921 onwards, both the peasants and the workers became psychologically convinced of their defeat – even as the Marxist theories in their heads assured them of eventual victory. Scanning the archives of the left-wing press, which continued to churn out lists of future election candidates, it is clear that even as they saw their friends being humiliated, beaten, confined to their homes or run out of town, the core of labour movement activists sank into denial.

If, in the twenty-first century, fascism moves towards the seizure of power, we should expect the turning point to be something like *squad-rismo*. It would not need to replicate the exact tactics but would seek the same *effects*: to paralyse the left, demoralize its opponents through low-level violence, force the state to surrender its monopoly of armed force, substitute its own fake welfare system for the real one, and induce a general sense of despair and denial among its victims.

What would be the result? The result in Italy was that, having allowed his followers to create chaos, the establishment turned to Mussolini to restore order.

PHASE 2: FASCISM GOES MAINSTREAM

At the general election of May 1921, the liberals invited Mussolini's candidates to join their electoral coalition, known as the National Bloc, facilitating the entry of thirty-five fascists into parliament, including the man himself.

The election was marred by violent voter suppression. In Ferrara, a left-wing newspaper reported that 'during the night of 13–14 April, dozens of comrades were kidnapped from their beds, to the horror of the families, transported by truck for several hundred kilometres and threatened with death if they came back before the election'.[21]

Back in 1919 the socialists had taken Ferrara with 43,000 votes; in 1921, they polled just 17,000.[22] Though the left's vote held up in the bigger cities, giving it 25 per cent nationally, that barely mattered. An alliance of liberals and fascists had stolen the election using illegal armed force – and nobody beyond the left seemed to care.

The fascist movement, meanwhile, doubled in size – from 98,900 members in April 1921 to 187,000 the following month – and was now mainly based in towns and villages, not the cities. A survey reports that 15 per cent were workers and another 24 per cent peasants, but a solid 57 per cent of the members were from the middle class, and overwhelmingly male.

With the job done in the countryside, Mussolini's attention turned to parliament. His MPs immediately went into opposition against the liberal centrists who had backed them, and used parliament as a stage to amplify their incendiary rhetoric. Their first notable act was to physically attack a left-wing MP on the floor of the chamber.

At this point, workers in the big cities, who had been focused on a rearguard struggle in their factories, began to realize the danger.

In the veterans' associations there were many opposed to fascism, both workers and former officers, including some who'd been in the commando units. In late June 1921, Argo Secondari, a 25-year-old former officer from a well-off family, led a split from the veterans' association in Rome, announcing the formation of a new anti-fascist group, the *Arditi del Popolo* (AdP), which roughly translates as the 'People's Commandos'.

By mid-July the AdP had 20,000 members, organized in fifty-four battalions across Italy. The recruits were a mixture: many were drawn from the more left-wing veterans' groups; some had been Red Guards in the factory occupations; others came from the security detachments now obligatory at socialist, communist and anarchist meetings. On 6 July, in uniforms and marching order, 3,000 *Arditi* staged a demonstration through Rome, armed – like the fascists – with batons and knives.

Secondari's genius lay in grasping two key points: that fascism had to be contested ideologically, on the territory of the middle classes; and that it could be stopped by an equally determined, organized and armed force. For this, it needed to recruit war veterans, not just dedicated leftists. And to do that, there needed to be a specifically *anti-fascist* – as opposed to socialist or communist – movement.

Nowhere was Secondari's cultural counteroffensive better demonstrated than in the songs the AdP sang, which – like the fascist anthems – were set to tunes that had been popular in the trenches. One, transcribed in the police files in Pisa, went:

> We are of the people; our ranks invincible; the black flame at our collar, we are moved by a strong and sacred feeling: Death to Death! Death to Pain! We defend the workers from outrage and defeat; the *Arditi* fight today for the happiness of all![23]

Up to this point, the rhetoric of 'the people' was alien to the Italian left. Theirs was a strictly 'class' politics characterized, as we have seen, by cultural hostility to flag waving and patriotism. So was the idea of reclaiming militarist iconography, for example the 'black flame' badge worn by the commandos in the war, and the idea of a wartime marching song itself. But it worked. Suddenly, people who wanted to fight fascism but did not consider themselves socialists had something to join, and a cause whose iconography was patriotic, not leftist.

The *Arditi del Popolo* paired their cultural combat with effective military counterattacks. When a fascist squad arrived to invade the coastal city of Sarzana, the AdP, by preparing openly to defend it with barricades and guns, forced the police to arrest the fascists to avoid a confrontation. When other fascists arrived, demanding their release, they walked into a gun-battle with the police and then, as they fled, were hunted down in the fields by the AdP. Since it was harvest time, and their scythes were sharpened, the peasants joined in. Eighteen fascists were killed and thirty wounded.[24]

The right-wing newspapers went wild. They had reported fascist violence mainly in the crime sections, or as student high jinks; now, however, they vilified defensive violence by the AdP as mass murder. Many local authorities summarily banned the organization. In Turin, the prefect arrested eight of the AdP's leaders on subversion charges, and carried out stringent stop-and-search operations to prevent it meeting. Asked why he had done none of these things to stop the fascists, the prefect replied that the AdP had committed 'the offence of criminal association', whereas the fascist squad 'aims at strengthening the nation'.[25]

As for the left-wing parties, their attitude to the AdP ranged from suspicion to hostility. The socialists, whose leaders had urged passivity, denounced it. The communists, wary of Secondari's upper-class background and of losing control, refused to support it, despite orders from Moscow to do so. Nonetheless, in several towns the AdP succeeded in creating a united front between anarchist, communist, socialist and even republican veterans.[26]

But the whole initiative was killed off by Mussolini's next masterstroke. On 3 August 1921 he proposed a 'pact of pacification' between the fascist squads, the socialists and the left-wing trade unions: each promised not to use violence and to respect each other's right to organize. The pact not only legitimized local crackdowns against the AdP but required the socialist parties to denounce Secondari, which they did because they were desperate to return the situation to normal. To round off the betrayal the communists, though they had refused to sign the peace pact, sent out an order threatening severe disciplinary action against any member liaising with the AdP.[27]

By September 1921, in most cities, Italy's first anti-fascist militia was finished. The left parties and unions retained their own defence groups, based in the tenements of major cities – but these, as we will see, could do little to stem the political advance of fascism.

On the fascist side, the peace pact triggered a revolt among the squad leaders. In Ferrara, posters were put up around the city denouncing Mussolini as a traitor. The squad's commander there, Italo Balbo, ridiculed the pact by marching 3,000 men to the coastal city of Ravenna, occupying it for three days and inflicting random violence along the way. This mid-1921 'crisis of fascism' is seen by some historians as a sideshow. But it was real. It prefigured similar fissures within Nazism, and finds a clear parallel in the debate over 'optics' among today's far right – with some determined to win through violence alone, and others seeing violence as a tactic in a wider political game.

For the hardline squadrists, fascism was simply a revolution, which would overthrow the Italian state by armed force. And how could they give up violence when it had become the main source of their prestige? 'Each night before going into action,' says the hero of the squadrist novel *Bagliori*, 'it totally took over my life. It made me unprejudiced and decisive in action ... I forgot everything else. I developed a will of iron which gave significance and purpose to my every move.'[28]

The violence, with its ritual and even ironic forms, allowed the squads to become the directors of their own gruesome theatre. When the police in Ferrara briefly banned the carrying of clubs, for instance, Balbo's men raided a fishmongers' co-op and, for a few days, marched around the city attacking people with metre-long salted fish.[29]

Suzzi Valli, a historian who studied fiction written by former squadrists, says violence was central to their sense of self. Their combat experience and visits to brothels were what made them feel 'manly', she writes, but it is 'only with *squadrismo* ... that they acquire a sense of the religious nature of their existence. This devotion to a superior goal (also a masculine quality) becomes the most important value in their lives and transforms manly traits into virtues.'[30]

For Mussolini, however, virtue meant achieving political power. A superb judge of social dynamics, he realized the workers' movement was already ideologically defeated. His pitch now was to the capitalist elite, and his message: that capitalism no longer needs democracy. Instead of being reliant on the masses, he promised, under fascism the focus would be on the individual:

> Anonymous, grey, democratic egalitarianism, which has washed-out every colour and flattened every personality, is about to die. New aristocracies are coming, now that it has been shown that the masses cannot be the protagonists of history, but are the instruments of history.[31]

While the squad members wanted a revolution against the liberal elite, Mussolini wanted to win the elite over. He thought that, through these classic appeals to the liberal principles of meritocracy, individualism and the free market, he could convince them to abandon democracy and choose fascism. And rising fascist membership figures, at 217,072 people in 1,311 local branches by October 1921, proved his point.

At a national congress in November 1921, Mussolini renounced the peace pact barely four months after it had been made. He turned his movement, until now still labelled the *Fasci Italiani di Combattimento*, into the National Fascist Party (PNF) and transformed its squads into a centrally controlled militia, with a top-down command structure and an official uniform.[32] At the same time, he abandoned all remnants of the quasi-socialist economic programme he had started out with, committing the party to free-market policies. From now on, the squad attacks would be focused on the cities, and the audience for their performative violence would be the urban elite.

PHASE 3: THE COLLAPSE OF LIBERAL LOGIC

Mussolini could not have come to power, nor used that power to abolish democracy, without the ideological disintegration of Italian liberalism. Today the words 'liberal elite' are used as an insult by right-wing populists against progressive, tolerant, university-educated people. But in Italy they meant something more specific.

'Liberal' was the term given to the dominant political culture through which, in the late nineteenth and early twentieth centuries, the rising class of industrialists and commercial farmers expressed their interests. To picture them, think of any male character in a Puccini opera: secular-minded 'men of the world', habitual clients of sex workers, obsessed with money, automobiles and technological progress.

As for the word 'elite', it had been popularized by the Italian economist Vilfredo Pareto, who – inspired by Nietzsche – argued that elites were necessary and inevitable, and democracy a sham to justify their rule. The term 'liberal elite' was, by 1921, not an insult but a self-declared fact. Its policy was state support for big business and technological modernization.[33] Its strategy was to absorb the socialist movement through concessions and reforms, without ever giving up real power.

That strategy emerged from the war in ruins. First, the establishment were humiliated by the USA in the peace negotiations. Then, as Italian nationalist paramilitaries seized the disputed Croatian port of Fiume in September 1919, they were shown how fragile their grasp on power was. The story of Gabriele d'Annunzio, and the turmoil the poet created with his land-grab on the Croatian coast, is ultimately tangential to a history as brief as this. The relevant facts are that, by setting up a riotous, militarized, racist mini-state, he created a template for defying the rule of law that Mussolini would follow.

Adding to the instability, the socialist election victory in November 1919 robbed the liberal elite of a reliable parliamentary majority. And in 1920, after years of war profits, they were suddenly faced with the effects of a global economic slump. Each of these crises caused liberalism to fragment into breakaway liberal, democratic and even 'social-democratic' parties, each with their own leader and agenda.

After the general election of May 1921, the clearest problem for the elite was parliamentary arithmetic. Despite their reversals the Socialist Party and the peasant-led PPI, together with a newly formed Communist Party, still held 45 per cent of the seats in parliament.[34] The liberal-led National Bloc had just 20 per cent – and nearly a third of the MPs in the Bloc were fascists. To govern at all, a liberal prime minister would have to scrape together all the various fragments to his right and left, and keep the PPI in the cabinet. Over the next eighteen months, four attempts to make these numbers add up to a government ended in failure.

In a functioning democracy the solution would have been to get the socialists to join a liberal-led coalition. But nobody in the elite wanted it, and neither did the socialists. After all, the ultimate point of all the liberals' social reforms had been to keep the socialists out of office.

If we condense the twelve months after the election of May 1921 into a single phase, it can be summarized as *the collapse of liberalism's inner logic*. Large numbers of people, especially among the urban middle class, began to accept Mussolini's framing: that this was no ordinary crisis but a 'Crisis of the Liberal State'. The man who would deliver the killer blow was Ferrara's squad leader, Italo Balbo.

Mussolini's PNF was now a significant social movement. If you were too squeamish to carry a gun or murder someone, you could at least wear a uniform and take part in a parade. At mass rallies, thousands of polite and educated middle-class men and women would sing the anthem *Me Ne Frego* – a phrase from the trenches equivalent to 'I don't give a shit'.[35]

But the heavy lifting was still done by the squads. On the night of 11 May 1922, Balbo staged a mass occupation of Ferrara, demanding the city council hand central government money allocated to a public works scheme directly to the fascist unions.[36] For three weeks his men had toured the surrounding countryside telling villagers that anyone who did not turn up would be branded a 'traitor' and would never work again, or worse.

The next morning up to 65,000 peasants, hungry and shoeless, crowded around the castle that dominates the main square. The fascists cut the telephone wires and posted armed guards around the city's walls. They moved through the crowd waving pistols and telling the peasants: 'If you move, you're dead!' Then Balbo strode across the castle drawbridge, leading the chant: 'Down with the government! Long live Italy!'

The government in Rome caved in immediately, leaving the

socialist-controlled city council with no effective power. The next city in line for the occupation tactic, two weeks later, was Bologna. Here the prefect, a tough liberal democrat, ordered the police to disperse the fascists. The government responded by sacking the prefect.[37]

After the occupation of Bologna all factions within liberalism understood that the attempt to neutralize fascism by smothering it within the parliamentary system had failed. Either they had to put Mussolini into the cabinet with significant power, or form a coalition with the detested socialists and the PPI that could reimpose the rule of law.

The socialists, meanwhile, realized that the tactic of refusing coalition government had brought them to the brink of a civil war, which they were going to lose. On 1 June 1922 they decided to support a liberal government to 'guarantee the restoration of peace and freedom'.[38] Under pressure from the Vatican, the PPI squashed the idea of socialists in the cabinet, but throughout June and July negotiations to form a democratic, lawful coalition continued.

Mussolini's response was a masterpiece of political rhetoric. Until the formation of the AdP in July 1921, Mussolini had barely used the word 'anti-fascist'; when he did, it was usually to describe his opponents in parliament. After the formation of the AdP he alleged in almost every speech that the liberals and the left were about to form a 'violent anti-fascist government'. If that sounds familiar, it should do. It was Mussolini, not Donald Trump, who first invented the myth of 'antifa' – and to the same end.

In a remarkable article entitled *State, Anti-state and Fascism*, published in June 1922, Mussolini began an open process of negotiation with Italy's business elite. 'Fascism,' he wrote, 'does not deny the State.' But the solution, he argued, was not putting fascist ministers into government, it was a fascist state.

Unlike the liberal state, whose welfare system and price controls made it 'semi-socialist', a fascist state would, he promised, let market forces rip. Unlike the liberal state, whose courts upheld the rule of law, fascism would impose their own order. Either we come to power peacefully, Mussolini warned, or we will do it with the 'shoulder charge of insurrection'.[39]

That was the signal for an intense cycle of violent provocation and political negotiation. In the northern city of Cremona, when the government sacked the police chief for colluding with the fascists, thousands of squad members appeared overnight. They burned left-wing newspaper offices, a labour exchange, several co-operative stores and the apartment of a PPI MP, rounding off the day by occupying the Prefecture.

This, in turn, triggered a new parliamentary crisis. The PPI moved a motion of no confidence in the government; half the socialists backed it, and so – in a cynical manoeuvre – did Mussolini. On 19 July, in his final speech as a backbench MP, Mussolini confronted the progressives with the point-blank question: are you going to form an anti-fascist government or not? He warned:

> If, through misadventure, a government of violent anti-fascist reaction should emerge, take note, ladies and gentlemen, that we will react with the utmost energy and with the greatest inflexibility . . . We will respond by rising.[40]

Faced with an open threat of insurrection, and with the wrecks of government buildings smouldering in several cities, any democratic government would be entitled to use the police, the army and the courts to suppress it. But despite weeks of coalition talks, no stable government could be formed, and police chiefs privately dismissed the idea that their men would obey orders to suppress the PNF.

So Mussolini upped the ante once again, despatching Balbo on the so-called 'march of fire'. Massing his forces in the city of Ravenna, Balbo threatened to burn every house belonging to a socialist family unless the police handed over trucks and petrol. With the trucks and petrol duly supplied, the fascist squads attacked every town within an eighty-kilometre radius, leaving the sky acrid with columns of smoke and flames.

PHASE 4: THE CRUNCH

In a movie script there is always a point of maximum jeopardy, where the plans of every character hang in the balance and tension rises to a level impossible to sustain. So it was in Italy in the summer of 1922.

From mid-July, in the northern industrial provinces of Lombardy and Piedmont, spontaneous general strikes broke out in protest against the fascist attacks. For days the socialist leaders tried to ignore them, still intent on negotiating a coalition.

But the strikes were unstoppable, and on 28 July a joint committee of the anarchist and socialist trade unions called an official general strike in defence of the rule of law. Scheduled for 31 July, this was to be a 'legalist' strike: passive, no violence, no wage demands, but solely in defence of 'political and trade union freedoms'.[41]

In response, Mussolini ordered a general fascist mobilization to break the strike. If the government would not stop it by deploying the army, the squads – by now tens of thousands-strong – would occupy all provincial capitals, seize road junctions and take 'sudden and ruthless reprisals' against the unions.

The union leaders called the strike as a symbolic act to influence the formation of a government. The fascists turned it into an armed showdown. Though the work stoppage was widely observed, it barely mattered.

For the first eight days of August, fascist squads relentlessly attacked the urban strongholds of the Italian working class. In Genoa, where dockworkers had controlled all recruitment on the waterfront since before the war, the shipping owners donated the equivalent of a million dollars in today's money for the fascists to organize a takeover by strike-breakers. It was no easy task, because the dockers were no longer fighting for an ideal, but for their jobs and homes. After three days of conflict, the army went in with machine guns and armoured cars to clear the strikers' barricades.

And it was no longer violence done in darkness, with plausible deniability. On 5 August, as the fighting continued, Mussolini published an official inventory of the damage his men had done across thirty-five towns and cities.

Only in Parma did the fascist offensive fail – and the reasons for its failure are instructive. Balbo arrived with 20,000 blackshirts, but this was one of the few cities where the AdP had left a legacy of independent, underground, cross-party defence groups. From the first day, more or less the entire working population of the city joined the resistance. Though they had only 200 vintage rifles between them, they held the western half of the city for six days. The MP Guido Picelli, a moderate socialist who commanded them, left a startling account:

> Everybody had an absolute 'belief' – no one had the slightest doubt. Bombs were prepared in houses, along with clubs studded with razor blades, knives and nails, as well as acid bombs. A 17-year-old girl waved an axe from the windows of her hovel and shouted to her comrades in the street, 'If they come I'm ready for them!' … No quarter would be shown – inflammable material would be thrown at the fascists, and our positions would be burned and totally destroyed.[42]

After a week of infantry assaults and sniping by both sides, Balbo's army suffered so many casualties that it began to disintegrate. From the city walls Picelli saw blackshirts, 'roaming about in all directions in a great rush … jumping onto trains that were leaving, onto lorries, bicycles, or going on foot. This wasn't a retreat, but the scattering of large groups of men who clambered aboard any means of transport they found, or who ran through the streets, or into the countryside, as if they were frightened of being chased.'[43]

Across the rest of Italy, however, the labour movement was substantially destroyed. The socialist city council in Milan was forced to resign, the city hall a wreck. Genoa's port was in the hands of fascist unions. In Ferrara the fascists toured the city's alleyways armed with clubs, dragging striking workers from their homes and marching them back to work.[44]

The strike was officially called off at noon on the third day. The stunned editors of the socialist paper *La Giustizia* told their readers: 'We must face facts. The fascists are the masters of the field.'[45]

The 'legalist general strike' would become a source of controversy. The left argued that it had come too late and its objectives had been too limited; the moderates argued that it should never have been called at all. Either way, the labour movement had staked everything on the general strike and lost. The peasants, sensing which way the world was turning, joined the fascist unions in large numbers, boosting their membership to 700,000.

But the crucial problem, during this fourth, decisive phase, was that the majority of the Italian people remained passive and largely neutral. They watched a civil war break out in their own, hitherto democratic country and shrugged their shoulders.

PHASE 5: THE 'MARCH ON ROME'

The period from the defeat of the general strike in early August 1922 to the so-called 'March on Rome' in late October of that year is one of the most heavily contested by historians of Italian fascism. The central question is: did Mussolini achieve power by accident or design?

The facts are that the Liberals formed a powerless minority cabinet with the PPI and began secret negotiations with Mussolini to bring in fascist ministers. Their only dilemma was to decide how many, and with what portfolios.

Meanwhile, as early as 11 August, Mussolini began warning of a 'March on Rome' – but he kept the phrase metaphorical. Either through negotiation or violence, the fascists would take power and – so he reminded the professors, journalists and civil servants – that meant 'a new political class is in the process of being formed'. The message was clear: if you want a job, the earlier you sign up the better.[46]

There are certainly elements of farce in the run-up to the event itself. Some liberals thought they could use Gabriele d'Annunzio, the nationalist demagogue who had led the paramilitary occupation of Fiume, to outflank Mussolini by holding a rally of his own, which might reunite the nation. But they never had a chance to test this idea, because the poet mysteriously fell out of a window during a drunken soirée and was severely injured.[47]

Yet the final events of the March on Rome can't be described as 'accidental'. On 3 October, Italo Balbo published new regulations for the fascist militia, which pledged to 'serve Italy' but made no mention of either the king or the existing state. This amounted to the forma- tion of a private army. On 18 October the militia's leadership met in secret, at the upmarket northern Italian resort of Bordighera, to plan a timetable for the insurrection. This meeting was – again almost unbelievably – interrupted by an invitation to lunch with the queen mother, who was on holiday there, and whispered to one of them after dessert: 'May all your plans be fulfilled.'[48]

On 24 October, at the PNF's national conference in Naples, Mussolini held a 40,000-strong rally, ridiculing the offers and counter-offers that various liberal spokesmen had been making to him. Balbo, moving from the platform to the crowd, began the chant of 'Rome! Rome!', and that night Mussolini gave the go-ahead for the rising.

Installed at a hotel in the Umbrian city of Perugia, 150 kilometres or so north of Rome, Balbo ordered the seizure of railway stations, telephone exchanges, post offices, prefectures and barracks across Italy. On 27 October the cabinet resigned, to give the prime minister the freedom to hand Mussolini some ministerial positions. But as news of the rising spread, they were forced to meet again and proclaim martial law.

As Mussolini had always predicted, there was no enthusiasm among the high command for shooting fascists. The barriers between the state and the fascist militia crumbled overnight, with high levels of fraternization, and even the handover of weapons. Meanwhile, Italy's business associations sent telegrams urging the king to bestow power on Mussolini.[49]

On 28 October the cabinet's martial law decree was taken to the king – who twice refused to sign it, asking instead for Mussolini to be given an important ministry in a new coalition. Mussolini refused, demanding a telegram from the king to make him prime minister there and then.

Having received the telegram, Mussolini boarded an overnight train to Rome, arriving on the morning of 30 October. He had publicly promised to meet the king in 'street-fighting garb', but on the way he decided to put on a bourgeois tailcoat over his black shirt. His followers arrived a day later, again mainly by train, celebrating their seizure of power by attacking anybody they could find with connections to the left. Among their victims was Argo Secondari, the war veteran who had founded the AdP. He suffered brain injuries so severe that he spent the rest of his life incapacitated.

And that was the March on Rome. Once in power, Mussolini mythologized the event as a violent insurrection, which only his genius could have steered to a peaceful conclusion. In reality it was the voluntary handover of power by a disintegrating liberal democracy, an army that would not fight and a monarch who preferred fascism over democracy. This was not yet a dictatorship but the fascist seizure of power was complete.

WHO COULD HAVE STOPPED MUSSOLINI?

Could Mussolini have been stopped? To answer that we must turn to conflict theory. The 'matrix game' is a technique used in business schools, military academies, disaster relief organizations and political consultancies to assess the likely outcome of crises. Unlike the game theories used in economics, it does not assume all actors are rational, or that the outcomes are therefore predictable using statistics.[50]

The rules are simple. Each player presents an 'argument' about how they're going to win. An umpire guides the players through a debate about whether the argument is convincing, and rolls dice to simulate uncertainty.

If 'Stopping Mussolini' were its own matrix game, the scenario would have six players, representing the landowners, the industrialists, the working class and the peasantry – plus Mussolini and the Marxist left, who were the only forces that showed any kind of autonomy and vigour during the crisis.

The Marxist left of the PSI had led the factory councils in 1919–20, then split from them to launch the Communist Party (PCI) in January 1921. Its concept of victory was a workers' revolution along Russian lines. Its 'argument' – in game terms – might be expressed along these lines: we win by going beyond control of the factories, by persuading the workers to arm themselves and seize power.

The workers, as expressed through their actions, wanted control, not power. Their 'argument' goes something like this: we will win by educating ourselves, voting for the Socialist Party, going on strike and gaining control over production; if the fascists try to destroy our organizations we will call a general strike.

The peasants, meanwhile, wanted relief from poverty and a strong external force to arbitrate in their daily conflicts with the landowners. In the game, their opening argument might be: we've seized the land, taken control of the communes and built our own welfare state; we win by defending what we have, through strikes and voting.

Both the landowners and the industrialists, by contrast, start from a position of nostalgia. Each group wants things to go back to the way they were: to the pre-war world of respect, hierarchy, steady profits, rapid economic development and a box at the opera house.

So the liberal-voting industrialists might argue: we win by running a rigged democracy, in which the left can't hold power, and by absorbing both the socialists and the fascists into the system as subordinates.

The landowners, however, needed change more urgently. They wanted a sharp reversal in the social dynamics of the countryside. We win, they might argue, by destroying the peasants' social power, and forcing them back into a position of subservience.

As for the fascists – even if we accept that Mussolini had no initial master plan – his game position in retrospect looks simple and compelling: *we win by creating facts through violence*.

We win, Mussolini might have argued, through acting at a tempo that no other faction can sustain. We win because we have no wider coalition of party factions and industry groups to hold together; because we need no ballots to decide our strategy; and because large numbers of people – including the police and armed forces – secretly want to do what we are doing. We win because all the other forces are looking backwards and are committed to defensive strategies, whereas our war experience has educated us in the value of shock, manoeuvre, symbolism, audacity and technology. And we win because the writings of Sorel, Bergson, Nietzsche and the rest have seeded the cultural atmosphere in our favour, and taught us how to manipulate irrationality and crowds.

If we consider the five phases that brought Mussolini to power – workers' revolt, *squadrismo*, the liberal crisis, the summer of violence and the March on Rome – there are only three moments at which the other players can stop the fascists coming to power.

The first is during the workers' revolt, in the trade union ballot of September 1920, when the socialists voted 60–40 against the seizure of power. It would have needed just 100,000 out of 1 million votes to tip the PSI into a strategy of taking power. Historical sources show that, had they done so, liberal politicians were prepared to negotiate the transfer of power, so it would not have needed a Russian-style insurrection. The boss of Fiat, for example, had already offered to hand the company over to a workers' co-op.[51]

The second chance comes with the formation of the *Arditi del Popolo* in July 1921. The AdP offered the workers an effective strategy against *squadrismo*, of going on the offensive instead of passively waiting to be attacked. And it contained, in men like Secondari, the seeds of an alliance between the left, progressives from the middle class and the wider war veterans' movement. In addition, as the standoff in Sarzana showed, through pre-emptive actions the AdP could persuade the police to uphold the rule of law against the fascists.

The third chance comes in the summer of 1922 when, facing disaster, both the Socialist Party and the PPI offered to enter a coalition government with the Liberals. But the closer they came to success, the more fragmented liberalism became in its response.

For any of these three chances to be taken, the bourgeoisie – via the industrial associations, the liberal parties, the prefects and judiciary – would have to *want* to stop Mussolini. But, as it turned out, they never did. At no stage did the police, army or judiciary or monarchy ever seriously try to suppress fascist violence.

Mussolini's victory was not inevitable – but he understood the game better than the other players. By building a new, offensive movement, he obtained the greatest freedom of action. Angelo Tasca, a communist who had known Mussolini before the First World War, summed this up succinctly in the 1930s:

> The immense confusion of passions and motives which formed the essence of the Italian situation, and which, even today, is hard to straighten out, underwent an extraordinary simplification in the mind of Mussolini, while it simply befogged his opponents. The latter ... groped about encumbered by outworn beliefs and plans.[52]

The Marxist left, who understood the danger and had gained their own freedom of action by forming the Communist Party, could find no way to take the workers with them at the tempo dictated by events, and – as we will see in Chapter 6 – their own analysis of fascism contributed significantly to their defeat.

*

In the 2020s, we may be forced to play this game for real. Substitute Italian liberalism in 1922 for today's centrist political establishment and the similarities are stark: from Spain to Austria to the USA, some centrist parties and politicians will hold fast against collaboration with the far right, but others will crumble.

The twenty-first-century business elite is faced with the collapse of a reality it had assumed was permanent. Free-market globalization has failed, but parts of the elite remain convinced they can make it work. They, too, are gripped with nostalgia for better times.

In the mass social movements – #MeToo, Black Lives Matter and Fridays for the Future – we are seeing, just as with the Italian peasants, *the demand for freedom exercised by people who are not supposed to be free.* This demand is so shocking to the authoritarian conservative sections of society that they respond with the fantasies of violence that now fill their Facebook pages, Telegram channels and WhatsApp groups: a digital echo of the conversations in the landlords' clubs of 1920.

Today, there is no left-wing proletariat of the kind that terrified the Italian elite. But among the wider, educated and salaried workforce who vote for liberal and social-democratic parties, there is the same belief in inevitable progress, and the same complacency. If you read the pages of the *Guardian*, *Libération*, *El País* or the *New York Times* there is the same assumption that the normality which surrounds us – academic freedom, an independent judiciary and a police force operating under the rule of law – is unassailable.

Today we have a left which still, by and large, views liberalism as its main enemy, even though the fascist threat is plain. And, as we saw in Chapter 1, there is a resurgent fascist culture, already gaining from its synergies with authoritarian conservatives and right-wing populists.

Today the word 'antifa' has been thoroughly stigmatized and even criminalized by Trump and his media supporters, in much the same way the establishment stigmatized Argo Secondari and the AdP. Guido Picelli, whose revolt in Parma came the closest to producing tactics that could have defeated Mussolini, and who would die fighting in Spain, drew stark lessons from it.

The physical resistance to fascism, he wrote, can win only if it enjoys broad support, and for that you need to go beyond the traditional politics of the left. The socialists never seriously tried to attract the wider mass support of the middle class, or war veterans; the communists boycotted the AdP; and nobody had thought in advance about what to do if – even against their will – a civil war broke out.[53]

Though today's forces are different, the weaknesses of the progressive side of politics are similar. And the threat is real – so we need to learn lessons from the events described here.

If we reject fatalism, and cling to the belief that Mussolini, together with Hitler, Franco and their imitators, could have been beaten, we have to admit that the fascists' greatest weapon was the *confused ideas in the heads of their opponents.*

That's why we cannot swerve around the problem of the left's theories of fascism, no matter how niche and distant they appear today. Put to the test in interwar Germany, they would lead to catastrophe.

Italy 1922

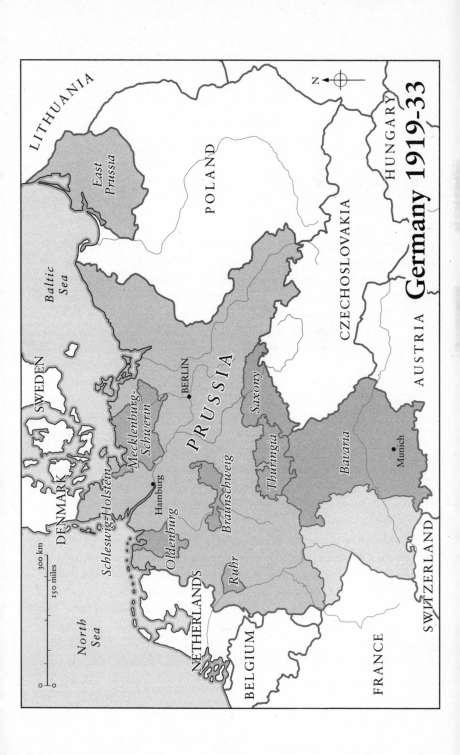

Germany 1919–33

6

'I Am Dazed'

Why Didn't the Left Stop Hitler?

'The compartment smells of sweat and stale smoke. People sit on the benches with sleepy faces. Some hang their heads . . . We give everyone a leaflet. I am dazed. It's all so different from what I expected. Nobody talks, there's no excitement. They take the leaflets silently. Some read it, most of them put it straight away.'

That was how Jan Petersen experienced 31 January 1933, the morning after Hitler came to power. A 26-year-old communist factory worker, Petersen had spent the night defending his Berlin neighbourhood against Nazi stormtroopers, a battle that left the local Nazi leader and a policeman dead. He was on the run – though that didn't stop him boarding a train at dawn, trying to persuade workers coming onto the morning shift at a nearby factory to join a general strike.

The workers were, Petersen recalled, too terrified to act: he watched them throw the leaflets into the snow as they left the train. As he headed into the streets to join thousands of other communists in a protest, he told his friends: 'This is our last demonstration.' He was right.[1]

Within six months all political parties in Germany would be banned. By the end of the year, 130,000 left-wing activists were in concentration camps and 2,500 had been murdered. The labour movement had, between its socialist and communist wings, polled 13 million votes in each of the last four elections. Now it would be destroyed – even more brutally and comprehensively than the Italian left.

Petersen turned the experience into a novel, which he smuggled out of Germany a year later. In a final act of rebellion, he describes pasting a tiny sticker across a Nazi poster, in memory of an executed friend, saying: 'The dead also speak to us.' But as a committed communist, he could not bring himself to write what the dead might say. For all the breathless narrative of Petersen's novel, it is devoid of explanations. The causes of Hitler's victory were, for Petersen's generation, the subject of an angry silence.

'Theory, dear friend, is grey . . .' says Mephistopheles in Goethe's play *Faust*, 'but green is the everlasting tree of life.'[2] But what colour is bad theory? The red of blood on the pavement? Or the blue you can still see on the walls of the gas chamber at Majdanek, caused by the chemical Zyklon B?

The fact is that Hitler's path to power was paved by the political theories of his left-wing opponents. The Nazis could have been stopped had they been properly understood.

We can forgive the left's incomprehension and panic when faced with the totally new challenge of Mussolini. But by the time Hitler began his ascent to power in 1929, the democratic world had had ample time to think about what fascism was, who it represented, where it came from and how to fight it. Understanding why they got it wrong is of deep and lasting relevance to us, even at a distance of ninety years.

The Nazi rise to power is one of the most studied events in history. In this chapter I will explore it from the viewpoint of the people who let it happen: the leaders of the German left. Many of those discussed here paid for their mistakes with their lives. But we owe it to their memory to learn the lessons they did not, and to understand – thanks to new data, research and almost a century's hindsight – the reality they could not.

We, like them, will get only one chance, because Mephistopheles was right: life always moves faster than theory. In the mid-twenty-first century, as the tide of irrationalism and prejudice rises, there may be periods in which there is no time for theorizing at all, only acting. Like Petersen, we will write 'I am dazed. It's all so different from what I expected.' Preparation is everything.

THE FIRST LEFT THEORIES
OF FASCISM

The first people who tried to make sense of fascism were its victims: the Italian socialists whose offices Mussolini's squads were trashing. Because landlords had always used gangs to intimidate peasants, and because the White armies had responded so aggressively to the Russian Revolution, many people assumed fascism was just a new form of ruling-class violence.

Giovanni Zibordi, who edited the newspaper *La Giustizia* in Emilia-Romagna (see Chapter 5), was one of the first to realize that fascism was different. In 1922, with the Italian countryside in flames, he published a book arguing that it was 'a dangerous oversimplification' to consider fascism only as a 'White Guard in the service of the bourgeoisie'. Instead, he said, fascism was a combination of three things: an elite backlash triggered by the unjustified fear of workers' revolution; a revolution of the increasingly disoriented middle classes; and a 'military revolution' – that is, an assertion of social power by large numbers of traumatized ex-soldiers.[3]

Zibordi, though a moderate socialist, was schooled in orthodox Marxism. As such, his mental picture of society consisted of four major classes: industrialists, landlords, workers and peasants, discounting intermediate social groups. The middle class, went the theory, were incapable of independent action, and destined inevitably to be absorbed into the working class. Now, however, Zibordi became one of the first to admit that the facts didn't fit the theory.

Fascism, said Zibordi, was relatively autonomous from the landlords and the factory owners, even if it ultimately served their aims. In addition – in complete contrast to the generals, bishops and aristocrats who usually led reactionary movements – it had a mass base, whose aim was a revolution against the existing order.

The word 'revolution' here was important. It implied – contrary to all accepted left-wing opinion – that the middle class in an advanced society were capable of overthrowing the existing order on their own terms.

At around the same time the thirty-year-old Turin journalist

Antonio Gramsci, a leading figure in the Italian Communist Party, came to an even more radical conclusion. Fascism, he wrote, 'can only partially be interpreted as a class phenomenon, as a movement of political forces conscious of a real aim':

> It has spread, it has broken every possible organisational framework . . .
> it has become an unchaining of elemental forces which cannot be
> restrained under the bourgeois system of economic and political gov-
> ernment. Fascism is the name of the far-reaching decomposition of
> Italian society . . . [4]

Marxism taught that class determines everything, and that all social conflicts are in the end reducible to the economic interests of those waging them. So here, too, was a theoretical challenge: how could there exist something that defied interpretation as a 'class phenomenon'? And what did it mean for historical progress?

The traditional Marxist view was that capitalism would produce the conditions for socialism. Moderates like Zibordi thought progress towards socialism would be slow and peaceful, but nonetheless that socialism was inevitable, thanks to rising levels of education and expanded democratic rights. Revolutionaries like Gramsci, on the other hand, were convinced it would be fast and violent – but equally inevitable, since the war and subsequent economic slump had plunged the system into chaos.

What nobody on the left considered until now was the possibility of a complete reversal of social progress: the cancellation of all advances in democracy, rationalism and human rights since the French Revolution. Some, in their worst nightmares, imagined capitalism's collapse into a barbaric state of war and chaos. But nobody had dreamt that this reversal could be consciously achieved by a new, autonomous movement led by people wearing high fashion and reciting Futurist poetry. Gramsci's break with orthodox Marxist assumptions began with the realization that such a reversal might be under way.

But once we categorize fascism as something new and relatively autonomous, we face a major analytical conundrum. Should we ana-lyse this new thing from within, focusing on its ideas, symbols and rituals, or should we begin by trying to understand the social conditions that produced it? Zibordi focused on the internal dynamics. Gramsci, in this first flash of insight, identified it as the product of social breakdown.

Unwittingly, they had run into the problem facing all historians of fascism, including those today: do we point the lens primarily at the movement, or at its social context? Unfortunately there was no time to explore that dilemma in the early 1920s, because the whole debate was about to be shut down.

Shortly before Mussolini's March on Rome in October 1922, the Italian communist leader Amadeo Bordiga set off on a clandestine journey to Petrograd (now St Petersburg) in Russia, to attend the Fourth Congress of the Communist International (Comintern). Bordiga's views were too extreme even for Lenin: he thought the left should abstain from all elections; that workers should not be allowed to vote on party policy; and that socialism was the 'complete negation' of democratic principles. It was Bordiga who, alongside Gramsci, led a split from the socialists to form the Italian Communist Party in 1921. And when Moscow ordered the communists to support the *Arditi del Popolo*, it was Bordiga who defied those orders (see Chapter 5).

Arriving in Petrograd five days after Mussolini's seizure of power, Bordiga assured the Comintern's delegates that Mussolini's regime would be 'liberal and democratic'. (Yes, really.) Fascism, he said, has 'added nothing to the traditional ideology and programme of bourgeois politics'. Since it represented the bourgeoisie and nothing but, it would not need to destroy any democratic institutions. 'The democratic system,' he reminded them, 'is only a collection of deceptive guarantees, behind which the ruling class conducts its battle against the proletariat.' The Socialist Party, he predicted, would 'unite with the new fascist government'.

Bordiga finished with a flourish: with the victory of fascism, he declared, it is possible that 'we will now be able to work better than was the case before'. Finally, he reminded them of Item #1 in the orthodox Marxist belief system: 'Historical development is on our side.'[5]

Here, in embryo, was the theory that would guide the European left to suicide over the next thirteen years: that fascism and liberal democracy are the same; that the left can flourish under both regimes; that historical progress is unstoppable; that the moderate socialists will inevitably side with fascism; and that fascism is just the military arm of the ruling class. There were wilder assertions yet to come, and catastrophic decisions to be made, but Bordiga had spelled out the essentials of a theory that you can still hear today in the chatrooms and podcasts of the far left: fascism is no big deal; the liberals are the main enemy.

But the Bolsheviks didn't buy it. They told Bordiga that his ultra-left theories had led to the biggest defeat for the working class in the twentieth century.[6] They ordered the Italian communists to reunify with the socialists, and advised all communist parties to seek coalition governments with socialist parties. Dismissing Bordiga's optimism about the liberalism of Mussolini, they made detailed preparations for an underground organization in Italy.[7]

But even as they did so, events were under way that would lead Bordiga's theory to be imposed on communist parties throughout the world.

In January 1923, Germany defaulted on the war reparations imposed by the Treaty of Versailles after the country's defeat in 1918. In response French troops occupied the Ruhr valley, and began seizing the coal and steel produced there. The move triggered mass civil disobedience from the Ruhr's inhabitants, which was encouraged by the German government. Soon, however, it escalated into strike action, guerrilla warfare, the formation of workers' councils and even workers' militias, terrifying the authorities on both sides.

Meanwhile, the economy went into a death spiral: output collapsed and hyperinflation kicked in. In 1918, a loaf of bread had cost less than one mark; by January 1923 it cost 250 marks; by November the same year it cost 200 billion marks! Money ceased to have meaning. Anybody with savings was ruined; anybody with property or gold was saved.

The only viable solution was to start again, with a new currency, a new government and a new deal with the French, which meant agreeing to pay reparations and calling off the civil disobedience. And in

September 1923 that is what the new chancellor, the right-wing liberal Gustav Stresemann, pledged to do. But, though it would solve the hyperinflation problem, the deal with France triggered a full-blown crisis of German democracy.

The Weimar Republic was federal: it had a president with strong powers, a national parliament (the *Reichstag*) and a second tier of regional 'free states' whose elected governments had power over their own police forces. The army, though small, was highly politicized and semi-autonomous, with a strong contingent of *Freikorps* veterans who continually dreamt of a military coup.

In the regions of Saxony and Thuringia, the ruling Social-Democratic Party (SPD) had adopted left-wing economic measures and was being actively supported in power by the Communist Party (KPD), which could call on a network of workers' councils and militias.[8] In secret, on Moscow's orders, the KPD was planning an armed insurrection if Berlin moved against these left-wing regional governments.

At the same time the nationalist right – monarchists, generals and aristocrats outraged at the government's submission to France – were scheming to topple Stresemann and seize power. Their stronghold was Bavaria, where in September 1923 the regional government declared a state of emergency and set up a three-man junta headed by the far-right monarchist Gustav von Kahr – a clear challenge to the authority of the national government and the sign of an impending coup. In response the national government declared martial law across Germany.

At the start of 1923, Hitler's NSDAP had numbered just 8,000 members, still mainly concentrated in Bavaria.[9] Hitler had equipped the party with a brown-shirted militia, the *Sturmabteilung* (SA) – literally 'storm detachment' – plus a newspaper, a youth group and the swastika flag. Now, amid the chaos and inflation of 1923, the Nazis cornered the market for extreme right-wing politics. Numerous existing groups joined *en masse*, boosting the membership to 55,000 – many of whom urged Hitler to stage a march on Berlin, modelled on Mussolini's coup.

Faced with this dual regional challenge, from the left in Saxony and the far right in Bavaria, Stresemann – backed by socialist ministers – moved first against Saxony. On 19 October the army began to deploy across the region to 'intimidate extremist elements and restore public order'.[10]

As the social-democrats wavered, the KPD leadership called off the planned national uprising. But its local leaders in Hamburg failed to get the message. They staged a three-day armed insurrection, during which KPD units fought pitched battles with a police force under socialist leadership, and were met with open hostility from the rank and file of the SPD.[11]

Meanwhile, von Kahr's junta in Bavaria was in backroom negotiations with other right-wing factions, trying to get the military in Berlin to stage a coup to remove Stresemann. In von Kahr's mind, Hitler and the SA would play an auxiliary role; he himself would be the star of the show. But as the coup plotters bickered about the details, the Nazis went ahead and took control.

On 8 November 1923, Hitler walked into a Munich beer hall, where von Kahr was rallying 3,000 of his supporters. He fired his revolver into the ceiling and shouted that a national revolution had begun. His stormtroopers dragged a machine gun into the hall while, in a side-room, Hitler forced the three-man junta at gunpoint to join his insurrection. His own supporters were massed in a different beer hall, and now moved to take over various government buildings.

Overnight, however, von Kahr got cold feet. He telegrammed the Berlin government that the junta would not support Hitler's rising and plastered the streets with posters to that effect. Furious, Hitler and his supporters took to the streets, fully armed, where they marched straight into a police roadblock. After a brief standoff, somebody opened fire. Within thirty seconds the 'Beer Hall Putsch' was over; fourteen Nazis and four policemen were killed. Hitler, his shoulder dislocated as he dived for cover, was arrested and sentenced to five years in jail.

The Bavarian police, backed by the army and made up largely of conservatives, had given the world a lesson in how to deal with fascist paramilitaries that remains valid today. But while the failure of the Beer Hall Putsch derailed Nazism for half a decade, the events in Saxony and Hamburg set the international communist movement on a course that would prove fatal.

Stresemann's cabinet was a coalition of right-wing liberals, centrists and social-democrats. But it had sent the army into Saxony, crushed a communist rising in Hamburg and now – albeit temporarily – banned the KPD completely. Even though the socialist ministers in Stresemann's government resigned in protest at this wider crackdown against the left, the Comintern concluded they were culpable.

In a formal resolution of January 1924, the Comintern announced that 'the leading strata of German social democracy are at the moment nothing but a fraction of German fascism wearing a socialist mask'.[12] Stalin, amplifying the point, argued that 'social democracy is objectively the moderate wing of fascism ... they are not antipodes [polar opposites] but twins'.[13] The attack was not limited to the moderate leaders of social democracy. 'Even more dangerous than the right-wing SPD leaders are the left,' said the resolution, because they were the 'last fig-leaves' for the counter-revolution.

Nor was their denunciation limited to the German socialists alone. 'International social-democracy has now become a wing of fascism,' claimed the Comintern's general secretary, which meant that, in a surreal turn of events, British Labour prime minister Ramsay MacDonald and the American socialist figurehead Norman Thomas both had to be labelled 'fascist'.[14]

This was Bordiga's crazy position turned into a global doctrine. Though conceived in the heat of the moment, with recriminations over the fiasco in Hamburg flying in all directions, during the next four years this rhetorical attack on moderate socialism took on a life of its own. As the world economy stabilized, the turmoil subsided and Stalin extended his control over communist parties outside Russia, what started as an insult was transformed into the fully fledged theory of 'social fascism'.

CLASS AGAINST CLASS

Put yourself in the shoes of the young communist Jan Petersen, on the eve of Hitler's breakthrough, in the Berlin of 1929. There are just four years to go until you'll be handing leaflets out on the train to a defeated and terrified workforce – but the rise of Nazism seems unimaginable. The trauma of hyperinflation is over, and you are living through a so-called 'Golden Era': there are dancehalls, movies and a riotous night-time economy. Wages are rising. The SPD has come first in a general election, with 29 per cent of the vote, and its leader heads a centre-left coalition. The Nazis, unbanned and re-formed, are polling at just 2.6 per cent. The KPD, also unbanned, has achieved 10 per cent of the vote and is recruiting hard among young people like you.

Petersen grew up in a workers' enclave surrounded by the opulent main streets of Charlottenberg, in west Berlin. A warren of mansion blocks, taverns and courtyards, 'Little Wedding' was a communist stronghold. There were organizations for everything, including the KPD's veterans' group, the Red Front-fighters' League (RFB), which had evolved into a strong paramilitary organization; plus numerous politicized football, cycling and walking clubs. Most of Petersen's neighbours were communists, as were many of the kids in the gangs that populated the backstreets.

What would Petersen hear at the KPD's meetings? By 1929 the politics of every communist party in the world were reduced to just three ideas: 'class against class', the 'Third Period' and 'social fascism'. Class against class was a euphemistic way of saying: it's the Communist Party against the world. Every union, choir or cycling club that was not allied to the communists was seen as working for the elite.

The 'Third Period' described the global situation. The 1917–23 period had witnessed revolutions; things had stabilized in the mid-1920s. But now – out of nowhere – Stalin declared that a new, 'third' period of global revolution and world war had begun. Every communist in the world was required to believe they had entered the final phase of capitalism, in which all democracies would die, and be overtaken by fascism.

The socialist parties, who had been labelled the 'twins' of fascism in 1924, were now depicted as enemy number one. The SPD – the biggest left-wing party in the world, with 937,000 members and 9 million votes – was designated as 'social fascist'.[15] Members of the KPD who said the entire theory was bullshit (and there were many) – well, they too were deemed to be under the influence of social fascism and expelled from the party. As a result, the KPD was at its lowest ebb, with 112,000 paid-up members – a third of its size in the early 1920s.[16]

How could any rational person sign up to this catalogue of

delusions? First, because it was an internally coherent theory: class against class, the Third Period and social fascism constituted a mental framework that allowed you to believe in a better future. Second, because it had the weight of the Soviet government behind it. Third, because by acting on it you could prove it to be true.

On 1 May 1929, fearing left–right violence, the socialist-controlled regional government of Prussia banned all public demonstrations, including those planned by their own followers. The KPD in Berlin defied the ban. The heavily militarized police, under the command of an SPD police chief but still mainly recruited from the right, attacked – and when the marchers retreated into two communist-held suburbs, the police switched from baton charges to bullets. This prompted two days of barricade fighting, which left more than thirty civilians dead and 200 injured. This is the incident known as *Blutmai* (Bloody May).[17]

Because both the interior minister and the police chief involved were socialists – and the SPD's newspapers backed the police action to the hilt – communists saw the event as proof that the theory of social fascism was correct. Their convictions were only reinforced as the socialist-led national government banned the RFB, the KPD's paramilitary group, and seized its assets.

As for the actual Nazis, they were at this point deemed an irrelevance by the communists. The KPD leader Ernst Thälmann told his members that Hitler was 'little more than a nuisance, whose irrational propaganda and boisterous street marches should not be allowed to detract from the real battle against the social-democrats'.[18]

But ultimately people accepted the social fascism theory because it began to play out in front of them: in October 1929 Wall Street crashed and took the stock markets of the world down with it. Within months the German economy had slumped and unemployment was rising fast. To many, this was proof that Stalin was right, and that the 'Third Period' had begun.

1929: HITLER'S BREAKTHROUGH

Just as with Italy, the Nazis' rise to power is best understood as a succession of major turning points, each of which delivers a shock that resets the expectations of individuals, parties and elites, and narrows their options.

Though sentenced to five years in prison after the Beer Hall Putsch, Hitler was pardoned just over a year later, in December 1924. Once free, he rebuilt the NSDAP around a new electoral strategy. Initially he thought he could win votes among the urban working class, but after 1928, when that failed completely, he switched his focus away from the cities, making a direct appeal to the middle class and to the countryside.

Hitler's plan was to hoover up the votes of various right-wing parties, above all the populist German National People's Party (DNVP), whose 14 per cent tally had put it second in the 1928 election. Somewhere along the line he expected the communists to launch an uprising – something their 'class against class' policy demanded – at which point Hitler's *Sturmabteilung* would come to the rescue of the elite.

The leap from obscurity began in July 1929, when Germany's creditors announced a new proposal on war reparations. Under the Young Plan, Germany's debts would be reduced, but in return Berlin would have to commit to the principle of long-term reparations. In response the DNVP launched a referendum campaign to reject the deal and invited the Nazis to participate. This was a gift to Hitler, allowing his activists to front the agitation in rural areas, using all the anti-elitist tropes and anti-Semitic rhetoric for which they were to become famous.[19]

To the farmers, the Nazi pitch was simple: their high debts and depressed prices were the fault of 'international Jewish finance capital', which had conspired to destroy German agriculture and flood the market with foreign goods. Since farmers were a minority, and the working-class majority was incurably left-wing, it was in the farmers' best interests for democracy to end. The referendum, writes the historian Timothy Taylor, allowed the NSDAP to militarize rural politics:

> It penetrated into every village and sought out every potential recruit. It saturated areas with propaganda and followed up with personal canvassing. Meetings were planned like battles . . . [20]

Though the referendum campaign ultimately failed (because of low turnout), by the time it was held in December 1929 the aftershock of the Wall Street Crash was under way. Unemployment rose rapidly, from 1.4 million before the crash to 3 million by the start of 1930.[21] Industrial production collapsed by a third. Wages, which had been rising during the good years, stalled.[22] But it was not pure hardship, or the efficiency of Nazi Party organizers, that drove a large section of voters to the extreme right in 1930; it was the self-inflicted crisis of the democratic parties.

Once the Depression began, the social compromises built into the Weimar Republic – a welfare state plus institutionalized wage bargaining – looked unaffordable to the industrialists. They needed a government with the power to impose rapid cuts to wages, pensions, welfare and public services – but the mainstream right-wing parties were too weak to achieve one. The SPD had no stomach for fronting the austerity policies that the industrialists required, so in March 1930 its ministers quit the government. The centre-left coalition was replaced – without an election – by a minority government of the right headed by Heinrich Brüning, a right-wing liberal, which the SPD kept in power through a policy of 'toleration'.

Throughout the 1920s German society had been awash with veterans' groups, 'combat leagues', youth organizations and political militias, all engaged in something we would today recognize as a culture war. Among the rich there was strong support for a so-called 'conservative revolution' – against modern art, jazz, Jews, liberated sex lives, 'cultural Bolshevism' and feminism. But the economic slump raised the stakes; as unemployment rose, people sensed the middle ground in politics was dissolving. Hitler's achievement in 1929–30 was to create a political brand that mobilized all this prejudice and panic.

In the general election of September 1930, the Nazis – who had been nowhere in 1928 – came second, scoring 18 per cent. The socialists (on 25 per cent) came first and the communists (on 13 per cent) came third. The three main parties of the German ruling class trailed at fourth, fifth and sixth, their combined votes totalling just 22 per cent, and their parliamentary groups unable to form a government.

The Nazi breakthrough was strongest in the rural areas. In Schleswig-Holstein, for example, they scored 27 per cent, taking the majority of the DNVP's voters and halving the vote of the mainstream conservatives.[23] And, as with nearly every far-right breakthrough in history, they had mobilized new voters. According to one estimate 23 per cent of those voting Nazi had never voted before.[24]

If the election breakthrough constitutes Hitler's first move in the power struggle, the resulting political paralysis prepared the way for his next. He now held a deck of cards similar to the one Mussolini had held in 1921. The elite parties could not form a majority government without support from the socialists; but the entire project of the industrialists was to keep the socialists out of power. Sooner or later, Hitler reasoned, the elite would have to put him into the cabinet – and he would dictate the terms.

By late 1930 every major economy in the world faced the same dilemma: demand was collapsing, unemployment was rising and prices were falling. The solution was obvious: the state should borrow money to fund public spending; it should build new infrastructure to create jobs. The government would need to take command of the economy and – as far as Germany was concerned – reparation payments would have to end.

Brüning, who remained in power heading a minority government, did the exact opposite: he imposed welfare cuts and wage cuts so vicious that the economy collapsed and unemployment soared. Through this senseless austerity programme, the centre-right parties managed to inflict social catastrophe on their own electoral base, the farmers and the urban middle class.

In the cities, the Nazis now adopted a strategy of confrontation. They had no chance of suppressing the labour movement Italian-style, since an SPD-controlled defence league – the *Reichsbanner* – had 1 million members, 200,000 of them trained in the use of firearms. For the KPD's part, though its uniformed fighting group was banned, it continued underground, alongside two more open communist self-defence organizations, with activists ready to defend working-class neighbourhoods street by street. Faced with such overwhelming opposition, the Nazis' approach to urban violence was symbolic.

The tavern at 20 Hebelstrasse was the headquarters of Storm 33, one of the most notorious sections of the Berlin SA. Storm 33's mission was to provoke and terrorize the area known as 'Little Wedding', where Jan Petersen lived. Surrounded by a dense network of KPD-controlled tenant groups, courtyard protection squads and meeting rooms, the Nazi HQ had to be a mixture of tavern and fortress, with shuttered windows, tight security on the door and bicycle patrols in the streets outside.

By 1930 Storm 33 had 100 members, who met daily for political discussions, followed by drinking sessions and raids into the surrounding area. Police interrogation records show their average age was twenty-five; three-quarters of them were unemployed. Their common background, according to historian Sven Reichardt, was of 'unsteadiness and decline, with frequent changes in employment and . . . a generation-determined hopeless situation'.[25] They included a trained glassblower who was now a porter, a trained bricklayer who was now a security guard and a qualified carpenter who was long-term unemployed. For these working-class men, the SA filled a vacuum, creating a world of the discipline and emotional bonding that they lacked through work.

Above all, the SA gave them agency. In November 1930, after Hitler ordered an offensive, members of Storm 33 opened fire into a crowded dancehall frequented by communists. On 1 January 1931 they knifed and maimed two socialist activists who happened to walk past their HQ. Later that month they discovered a group of communists drinking in the public area of their tavern and stabbed one of them to death. On 1 February, spotting a communist activist in a nearby ice-cream parlour, they shot him dead.

I've walked the routes between these attacks, in the quiet streets behind what is now the *Deutsche Oper* building. All took place within 300 metres of the Nazi tavern. Even amid the tennis courts and kindergartens that now occupy this urban landscape it is possible to feel the way Storm 33 must have terrorized the surrounding streets. The SA staged a deliberate surge of provocations, concentrated in time and space, designed to create an atmosphere of fear and tension.

By 1933 the Nazis had 107 such local bases in Berlin, 64 of which were sited in working-class districts and 13 – as in the case of Hebelstrasse – provocatively located inside communist strongholds.[26] Using symbolic violence, and the inevitable ritualized funerals of any

SA members killed in the clashes, their aim was to stir up anti-communist sentiment and fantasies of revenge among their base in the villages and the middle class. And it worked. At its moment of electoral breakthrough, in September 1930, the NSDAP had 129,563 members. By the start of 1932 it had grown to 450,000.[27]

WHAT COULD HAVE STOPPED HITLER?

Let's once again hit the pause button and ask, as we did with Italy: in the years before 1932, how could Hitler have been stopped? The most obvious point was after the Beer Hall Putsch. If he had been treated as a terrorist, his backers among the elite prosecuted and the SA permanently dissolved, then right-wing extremist politics in Germany might have been forced down a more containable route.

Thirteen million people voted for the SPD and KPD in the 1930 election. At 43 per cent of the vote that was not enough to form a government, but might have been enough – if united around a single project – to appeal to middle-class people who were suffering under austerity, and to those in farming communities not completely blinded by nostalgia and anti-Semitism. But the KPD's 'social fascism' theory was mirrored by an equally blinkered set of ideas among the socialist leaders.

First, they were blindly committed to legality and parliament, at a time when politics was becoming radical, violent, populist and moving to the streets. Second, decisively (and just as social-democrats in the 2015 Eurozone crisis would do) they subscribed totally to the austerity doctrine: that prices must fall before consumption can rise. They overtly rejected the solution of state-funded public works, which under the influence of John Maynard Keynes was becoming popular on the European left. Third, they were committed to defending the international order agreed in the Versailles Treaty of 1919, and thus to honouring the reparations system.

Finally, they were terminally dull. When their own experts, including a leading professional psychologist, urged the socialist leaders to focus on emotion not economics – deploying a single logo, a few key slogans, simple language and a positive vision of the future – they were dismissed: 'We shall make ourselves look ridiculous with all this nonsense,' came the reply.[28]

Though dissidents inside both parties pushed for a united front between the SPD and KPD, the effects of the crash turned ideological differences into sociological ones. In places like Little Wedding, mass unemployment meant that working-class life became detached from the workplace and focused on the streets. For KPD members like Petersen, day-to-day politics were reduced to physical confrontations with the Nazis, solidarity with those injured or arrested, and election agitation.

The KPD's leadership knew that – as both they and the Nazis were competing for the allegiance of young, unemployed men – the only way to survive was to destroy the Nazis. But they had no idea how to do so. From September 1929 the KPD's slogan had been: 'Hit the fascists wherever you meet them.'[29] In June 1930, however, they withdrew the slogan, ordering their members to engage the Nazi rank and file in political arguments, and sent speakers to Nazi meetings to hand out specially targeted leaflets and put the communist point of view.

At the same time, the KPD repeatedly tried to appeal to the Nazi base using the rhetoric of national resistance, and to out-shout the Nazis as revolutionary opponents of the system. When this strategy also failed, they launched concerted attacks on the Nazi taverns in an attempt to shut them down. In response the Nazis used their growing reserves of cash to buy up taverns used by communists.

Next, the KPD leadership called for 'mass terror' – which, stripped of its hyperbole, meant rent strikes in the tenements surrounding the Nazi taverns, and protest strikes in nearby workplaces. But the rent strikes always failed. The threat of eviction – plus the fact that the state paid unemployed people's rents direct to the landlord – meant that the rent strikes were impossible to sustain. And such protest strikes as took place had no effect on the Nazis.

For young communist street-fighters, mass terror sounded like a joke. 'We don't care for the idea,' wrote one communist youth group in Berlin to their leaders, 'that if we are murdered by SA-men a small part of the proletariat will carry out a half-hour protest strike, which only makes the SA-men laugh.'[30]

So for two years, under the twin pressure of the Third Period ideology and its members' demand for action, the KPD alternated between 'mass' and 'individual' resistance. By late 1931 it was clear that neither tactic was working. The more the KPD tried to out-shout the Nazis with anti-systemic rhetoric and tactics – culminating in a joint attempt with the Nazis to depose the socialist government of Prussia in August 1931 – the more it alienated the SPD supporters.

Meanwhile, the RFB's underground cells began to shrink, through arrests, the effects of unemployment and demoralization. At a despondent central committee meeting in February 1932, the KPD for the first time faced the possibility that 'fascism can come to power . . . without the Communist Party being able to begin a serious fight'.[31]

Thanks to a compulsory insurance scheme for SA members, we know exactly how many brownshirts were injured badly enough to miss work between 1930 and 1933: the figure is 22,813, around half of whom were attacked in the final twelve months. We rightly celebrate the bravery of the anti-fascist fighters – of the RFB, Antifascist Action, the left sports organizations and the socialist *Reichsbanner*. But their combined efforts managed to incapacitate less than 5 per cent of Hitler's private army; as for the dead, during its entire struggle for power, the SA lost just ninety-nine members.[32]

Even if the left had succeeded in inflicting greater casualties and losses on the SA, once the Nazis had broken into the suburban world of clubs and fraternities and their ideology had become embedded in middle-class life, individual acts of violent resistance alone could not have contained them. Only coercion of a mass character – general strikes, the occupation of city neighbourhoods, actual armed resistance, the expulsion of Nazis from every workplace – might have defeated the SA militarily.

But would such a strategy have dispelled the ideology of race war held by thousands of NSDAP members and sympathizers? In the parallel situation of Spain in 1936, where it did come to fighting, Falangist beliefs did not suddenly evaporate when the anti-fascists were winning battles.

To say that the strategy of street violence failed is not to argue against anti-fascist self-defence in principle. It was necessary then and is necessary now, where workers and minorities are faced with intimidation from the extreme right. But for the KPD it became a substitute for thinking clearly about political strategy. The one strategy that might have worked – unconditional unity in action with the SPD and an end to anti-systemic rhetoric – was never permitted.

As the panic mounted in response to the Nazi electoral surge, the socialist leaders were equally culpable. In support of a constitutional republic they repeatedly backed bans and restrictions on the KPD. Though the *Reichsbanner* was a large uniformed movement, the SPD's commitment to legality meant that it was never deployed in a sustained offensive to contain the SA. 'What does the Reichsbanner have to say?' wrote one KPD member bitterly, from jail. 'Sits in the tavern and carries on the fight against fascism [there], Landlord, another pint . . . '[33]

Leading SPD thinkers posed exactly the right question: why is the middle class losing its belief in democracy and how do we win them over to the left? But their orthodox Marxist mental framework, which reduced everything to economic interests and a struggle between two classes, produced entirely the wrong answer.

Theodor Geiger, a party sociologist, identified Nazi voters as coming from both an 'old' middle class – of farmers, shopkeepers and pensioners – and a 'new' middle class consisting of civil servants and white-collar workers. Since the Nazis could deliver economically to neither demographic, their vote was bound to disintegrate, he predicted, with the farmers moving back to their traditional parties and the urban middle class moving to the SPD.[34]

Geiger was challenged by numerous socialist thinkers. Alexander Schifrin, a Russian émigré, drew on the experience of Italy to argue that the rush towards fascism indicated that the middle class could act autonomously, and would not necessarily break with fascism on economic issues. 'One must stress,' he argued, 'fascism's independent existence . . . Its will to power, brutality and means of action . . . do not lie in the economic sphere.'[35]

Modernizers in the SPD knew the party needed to reach out to the middle class with a different message. But they could not persuade their members and low-level bureaucrats to change fast enough. The socialist trade unions had spent years complaining about the privileges of white-collar workers; it was easier to mock office workers as reactionaries than to engage them in arguments. Ultimately, for all its talk, the SPD made no change in its strategy until the spring of 1932, when Hitler announced he would stand for the presidency, against the incumbent conservative general Paul von Hindenburg.

1932: 'STOP IT NOW!'

'It must be made clear to the masses of German voters,' ordered the Nazi propaganda bureau in February 1932, 'that the National Socialist movement is determined to use the presidential elections to put an end to the entire system of 1919.'[36] Hitler's campaign slogan would be *Schluss Jetzt!* – literally 'Stop it now!'

Hitler's bid for the presidency was no token gesture. The Nazi vote had been growing in local elections and the economic crisis was at its deepest. By mid-1932 industrial production had halved; GDP was down by 37 per cent compared to 1929; one in three people of working age was unemployed.[37] Crime, suicide and despair dominated the headlines as Hitler zipped around Germany in an aeroplane, visiting twenty-one cities in six days.

The socialists, true to form, backed Hindenburg. The communists, again true to form, stood their own leader, Thälmann. In the second-round run-off on 10 April 1932, Hindenburg won – but Hitler had scored 37 per cent, with 13.4 million votes.

That was a massive psychological blow, both for the mainstream parties and the left: 13 million votes were more than any single party had achieved during the history of the republic, including those supporting Hindenburg. Nazism was now undeniably a mass movement and, if it kept on growing, had a serious chance of coming to power with a parliamentary majority.

Yet the two left parties were still incapable of uniting. Each formed rival 'fronts': the SPD inaugurated the 'Iron Front', bringing together its workplace self-defence groups and sports clubs with the *Reichsbanner*, while the KPD formed Antifascist Action – Antifa for short. But their objectives were incompatible.

The socialists had framed their entire project around the defence of

a republic that was on the brink of collapse, and defence of a government implementing the most ill-advised austerity programme in
history. Even the logo they chose to represent anti-fascism – three
arrows – was meant to symbolize their equal opposition to monarchy,
fascism and the KPD. Their 1932 election poster shows one of the
arrows piercing a crown, one a swastika and one the hammer and
sickle.

The communists, meanwhile, were only allowed to seek unity
'from below'. And their own voter base – which was growing at the
expense of the socialists – wanted a revolution.

In 1932 the young French leftist Daniel Guérin hiked through Germany, staying at youth hostels frequented by both KPD and Nazi
hiking clubs. He watched them face off in the common rooms, bran-
dishing rival newspapers, singing rival songs and shouting slogans at
each other after lights-out. But, as one communist youth whispered
to him:

> Occasionally we kill each other but deep down *we want the same
> thing* . . . a new world radically different from today's . . . a new system.
> But some believe adamantly that Hitler will provide this, while others
> believe it will be Stalin. That's the only difference between us.[38]

Though shocked by this, once Guérin met the SPD he began to
understand. Reaching Dresden, he was taken to the HQ of the socialist trade unions, a sleek modernist building where the elegant waiters
looked askance at his hiking boots, and elderly socialist bureaucrats
bought him beer. He wrote:

> Red in the face, bloated and dull, confined to their cushy, tiny, bureau-
> cratic and corporative world, they made me want to grab them by the
> collar and give them a good shaking. Seven or eight million German
> proletarians were dying of hunger . . . [39]

However mad and self-defeating this refusal to unite against fascism appears to us now, the socialist and communist leaders were
aligned with the sentiments of their supporters. Socialist and communist workers wanted different things, had different visions of the

future, held diametrically opposed views of democracy and, thanks to the financial crash, lived increasingly in different social worlds.

There were splits and opposition groups of course, but party discipline on both sides made them easy to marginalize. The biggest splinter group from the SPD had around 30,000 members and a daily newspaper, but come election time it was squeezed into insignificance. Another dissident group, which included both SPD and KPD members trying to create a single working-class party, had to work in complete secrecy because of the danger of expulsion, through a system of codenames and safe-houses. This, paradoxically, allowed them to survive as a resistance movement under the Nazis until 1935. But at the critical moment the wider public knew nothing of their existence.[40]

Only a strategic rethink by the leaders of both parties early in the process could have stopped the Nazi breakthrough between 1930 and 1932. But it didn't happen.

1932: THE GROUND-RUSH

As in the last twenty metres of a parachute jump, the ground now rushed up towards the German left at disorienting speed. On 14 April 1932, reeling from the size of the Nazi vote in the presidential election, the SPD persuaded Brüning to ban the *Sturmabteilung*. But it was his last throw of the dice. The right-wing parties were now determined to form a cabinet including Hitler, to suspend parliamentary government and to launch an army crackdown on the political chaos that the Nazis had played such a key role in fuelling.

On 2 June Hindenburg sacked Brüning and appointed the reactionary Catholic aristocrat Franz von Papen as chancellor. Papen's first act was to dissolve parliament, triggering elections for 31 July. His second was to lift the ban on the SA. The third was to launch a military coup against the socialist regional government of Prussia, marching its elected ministers out of their offices at gunpoint.

In the July 1932 election campaign, the SPD leaders finally did what their members had been calling for: they staged hundreds of mass rallies; they used populist slogans; and the *Reichsbanner* attacked and sometimes beat the SA in street fights. But despite the pleading of activists and union leaders, the socialists still refused to demand a state-funded programme of public investment. Instead, it was the Nazis who made the public works programme their signature policy.

There was now pressure from below within both left parties for a united campaign against the Nazis. Activists in five cities staged joint demonstrations during the campaign. In Berlin, activists tried to register a joint anti-fascist list of candidates. But the bureaucracy prevailed: both the KPD and SPD issued formal instructions to cease collaboration, the latter admitting in private that the push for unity was 'extraordinarily strong'.[41]

As the election results were declared on 31 July 1932, the price tag for two years of delusion and division was presented: 13.8 million people had voted Nazi. Hitler had eaten even further into the base of the mainstream parties and – to their dismay – both the socialists and the communists saw their periphery begin to flip towards the Nazis.

With 37 per cent of the vote, Hitler now had the biggest parliamentary group by far. The socialists had lost half a million votes to the KPD – paradoxically reinforcing confidence among its members that the 'social fascism' line was working. Meanwhile, the mainstream parties were finished: their remaining vote was now clustered in the Catholic provinces of southern Germany and in the Rhineland. Among the Protestant majority of the electorate it was now a straight battle between Marxism and Nazism.

Even at this late stage there was room for hope. Hitler could not form a majority government. And it was clear that, with votes for the two left parties staying largely solid, he was unlikely to make further gains. The Nazi Party's finances were also shaky. So Hindenburg rebuffed Hitler's demand to be made chancellor and Papen carried on until September, when a vote of no confidence – in which the KPD and the Nazis (again astonishingly to modern eyes) combined forces – triggered yet another election.

When the next elections were held, in November 1932, the Nazi vote slid back to 33 per cent – partly due to Hitler's support for a group of SA men convicted of a gruesome murder. The KPD vote grew to 17 per cent, mainly through disillusioned SPD voters switching to the communists. Papen was sacked and the reactionary army general Kurt von Schleicher was given the job of stopping Hitler.

Schleicher's brief term in office has become one of the most examined episodes in history. Since the onset of the crisis in 1929 he had been the main representative of the army in politics. He pushed continuously for a presidential dictatorship. But he didn't want Hitler as chancellor.

To this end, given the job himself, he explored two solutions: to tame Hitler by bringing him into the cabinet; or to create a cross-party national government that would exclude Hitler, drawing in forces as diverse as dissident Nazis and socialist trade union leaders. But neither Hitler nor the forces required for an anti-Hitler dictatorship would take the bait, and so, on 28 January 1933, unable to govern effectively, Schleicher resigned.

On the morning of 30 January, the SPD leaders met in their parliamentary office in a panic. They resolved to tell Hindenburg they would support any regime that could stop Hitler. Characteristically, they were too late. The man they sent out to make the phone call was greeted by 'wild running and shouting' in the corridors. Hindenburg had already made Adolf Hitler chancellor of Germany.

DOES 'CLASS' EXPLAIN THE NAZIS?

Three basic questions need to be answered: why did the business elite switch from opposing the Nazis to facilitating their seizure of power? Why did the middle class abandon respectable racist parties of the right to become fanatical followers of Nazism? And why didn't the workers' movement effectively resist?

Alfred Sohn-Rethel left a convincing answer to the first question. As a Marxist economist, hired unwittingly by a secretive business lobby group, he observed first-hand how two factions emerged within Germany's corporate monopolies and cartels: those reliant on international finance and trade (such as the Siemens electrical group and banks handling US money); and firms focused on the domestic market, such as the Steel Trust, the coal industry and the savings banks.

Once the economic slump began, the globally focused firms backed

Brüning; to maintain the flow of foreign investment into Germany they needed reparations payments to continue. In addition, Britain, France and the USA had the power to lock businesses like Siemens out of infrastructure projects in the developing world. Those on the other side – mainly the heavy industrial sector – had little option but to ride out the crisis.[42]

So long as both factions believed the downturn was a 'normal' economic crisis – and would sort itself out through falling wages and lower taxes – backing Brüning looked sensible. But when the slump turned into a banking crisis, in May 1931, it became clear that the programme of austerity and deflation was a dead end. The reparations system collapsed and the flow of investments across national borders ground to a halt.

Now both factions of German industry were in deep trouble. How could the home market – with wages collapsing and public investment slashed – replace the global economy, either as a source of capital or an outlet for goods? Logic pointed to a new solution: a state-driven investment model and rearmament, and the attempt to carve out new colonial markets in the Middle East, the Balkans and Eastern Europe.

This was the background to the formation of the Harzburg Front, at an ostentatious right-wing rally in the spa town of Harzburg in October 1931. The front brought together the right-wing populist DNVP, the *Stahlhelm* veterans' group, numerous monarchists and top executives from the heavy-industrial sector of German business. Hitler gave a speech at the rally – but resisted the idea of the Nazis joining a unified 'National Opposition'.

Nevertheless, Harzburg was the moment when a significant chunk of German big business came together to form a plan for economic self-sufficiency – summarized in the word 'autarky'. They would break with the global system and rebuild the German economy around highly concentrated monopolies, relying on state support, a revived weapons industry and, ultimately, territorial expansion. But the obstacles were huge: namely, a mass workers' movement, the Versailles peace treaty and the constitution of the Weimar Republic. 'What united this conglomeration of desperadoes,' wrote Sohn-Rethel in a manuscript smuggled out of Germany as he fled, 'was the demand for a dictatorial government directed against the organised working class.'[43]

But that did not have to mean Hitler. Plan A was to put von Papen in power and suspend parliamentary government. That, however, needed an army ready to stage a full-scale military coup, suppressing both the left parties and the trade unions. But the army was too small to achieve this.

Hitler's offer to the German industrial elite was never simply an alternative economic plan, it was an offer to destroy the labour movement and rid the country permanently of communists. If you imagine the Reichstag without a bloc of Nazi politicians, he once warned the industrialists, then you have to imagine those seats filled with communists. And as the KPD's vote increased, and the SPD's base radicalized in the second half of 1932, so did the attractiveness of Hitler's offer.

The ace-in-the-hole that toppled Papen and put Schleicher in power was the report of a secret war game staged by the military general staff, which showed that the army could not defeat the KPD in open battle at the same time as defending Germany's borders.[44] Hitler was handed power because all other options had been tried; he had mass support; and he was ready to do what the army couldn't – crush the working class.

It is an established fact that the social base of Nazism was the middle class. Certainly, it drew electoral support from all sections of society, but the solid backbone of its membership consisted of farmers, shopkeepers, craftsmen, civil servants, students and office workers.[45] Why did such people, usually committed to order and respectability, become fanatical enthusiasts for racist terror?

As we will explore in Chapter 8, left and liberal theorists were at such a loss to explain this phenomenon that they worked on the assumption that these were atomized loners, terrified amid the rising chaos.

More recent research, drawing on Nazi membership files, has challenged the atomization thesis. It shows that the Nazis grew most rapidly in places where there was a strong culture of civic associations: choirs, bands, gymnastic clubs and organized hiking groups. Critical to each local breakthrough was the Nazis' ability to colonize the social networks of influential people. If a Nazi recruit was a member of the local gym, dog-breeders' association or carnival float group, they would then recruit people in every one of these locations. The more clubs they were in, the more effective they were at recruiting. This translated into a higher vote share, because the Nazis' chosen campaigning method – face to face meetings and conversations – helped get out the vote.[46]

A micro-study of Nazi membership in Marburg, a university town, substantiates this: after 1930 the people who signed up to the NSDAP were 'joiners', not loners, and they joined in groups, from the same gymnastic, rifle or student clubs. 'Much of Nazi mobilisation,' writes historian Rudy Koshar, 'depended on the independent social activity of these opinion makers, string pullers and culture brokers. Responding individually to their environment, and perhaps only marginally familiar with Nazi ideology, these were the unauthorised facilitators of German Nazism.'[47]

In short, people joined because their friends did, and because it made them feel better. The Nazis built their party as a rival 'world-within-a-world' to match that of the SPD. Once you were wearing the Nazi lapel badge, or the SA uniform, you could feel part of something bigger, something that German conservatives had dreamed of, but never achieved: a 'folk community' in which inequalities came second to national solidarity. At the same time, the Nazis exploited people's rivalry and self-interest. As a Nazi takeover began to seem inevitable, many striving members of the middle class realized that they could achieve promotion and higher social status by joining up.

As we saw in Chapter 4, the deeper ideologies that Nazism drew on were already widespread among the middle class: life-philosophy, anti-rationalism, occultism and racial pseudoscience. The Nazis mobilized these prejudices around the myths of symbolic violence, national rebirth and conquest, to devastating effect.

Why didn't the workers' movement resist effectively? Why, instead, did they delude themselves with irrational theories, bureaucratic routines, false hopes and tactics that could never have stopped Hitler?

How, on the morning of defeat, could an activist like Jan Petersen write: 'I am dazed'?

For many historians this is a non-question because, at root, they don't believe working-class people are capable of independent thought and action. Marxists usually reduce the answer to 'bad leadership'. If only Stalin hadn't imposed the social fascism line; if only the SPD left had been more vocal and pushed for a break with Brüning; if only they'd listened to Trotsky, whose analysis was spot-on but who only had 600 followers in Germany.[48]

It is an explanation that flies in the face of Marxism's claim to be 'materialist' – that is, to trace social phenomena to their socio-economic roots. If 'bad leaders' are to blame for the defeat of the German labour movement, what created the bad leaders? And why did the working class so readily accept their advice? By implication, 'good leaders' could have defeated Hitler – but when they spoke out, why did people ignore them? Why did rank and file militants like Jan Petersen go along with all the purges and witch-hunts of people inside the KPD who raised objections?

The answer revolves around something the left rarely wants to consider: just as there can be a 'mass psychology of fascism', there can be a mass psychology of Marxism. Unfortunately, more than eighty years on from Hitler's seizure of power, you can still see it exerting influence on today's left.

As a writer working within the Marxist tradition I want to address the problem unflinchingly. Orthodox Marxism's signal characteristic was its inability to grasp complexity. It reduced all conflicts to their economic essence; it assumed that individuals could only be the finger-puppets of economic forces; it reduced political strategy to 'reform or revolution' – ignoring completely the intermediate elements of control and culture, and thus belittling questions of iconography, narrative or grassroots decision-making.

Where it considered the possibility of failure, it framed it around Rosa Luxemburg's famous concept of 'socialism or barbarism' – either we win or the world ends. For all wings of Marxism, history was seen as a machine producing progress, and the working class as the machine's tool. These concepts prevented activists from grasping the new and complex social dynamics at play.

The working class as it actually existed was heavily stratified by skill, income and outlook. Far from disappearing as technology developed, this stratification had been designed into the industrial system on purpose by the early practitioners of management theory, Frederick Winslow Taylor and Henry Ford. Stratification was achieved not just through the creation of new job functions such as team leader or foreman, but through organizational changes, like forcing workers to do quality control on each other's output.[49]

The middle class was not dissolving or bifurcating as predicted; it was expanding and had coalesced around fascism. The often celebrated resistance to Nazism among the Catholic middle and upper classes should have signalled why: this was not primarily about economic interest, nor even status. It was the collapse of a passive belief system that opened the Protestant middle class to the active belief system, fascism. As their doctrines of honour, respectability, reward for hard work and national pride were shot to pieces by defeat in war, the overthrow of the Kaiser, hyperinflation and then the Wall Street Crash, they embraced a new, active ideology: irrationalism, occultism, racial pseudoscience, the mythology of violence.

As for a theory of the state, on both the communist and social-democratic sides it was primitive. Communists learned that the state was the 'executive committee of the bourgeoisie', committed to maintaining a monopoly of force to prevent a workers' revolution. Social-democrats believed the opposite: that with the foundation of the Weimar Republic they had, for the first time, created a state that was neutral, and could be used to implement socialism once they had a parliamentary majority. Every time the SPD came under attack – as with the coup against its ministers in Prussia – it told its supporters to wait for the next election. Even the KPD, despite its insurrectionary rhetoric and theory, made no serious preparations for an armed uprising in the case of a Nazi victory.

At the most fundamental level, both sides of the labour movement were mesmerized by the two-class theory of reality and the fatalistic optimism that it implied. Even as critical left-wingers warned of the possibility of a 'middle-class revolution', with a dynamic of its own, the ideas in left-wing workers' heads told them it was impossible.

Class dynamics on their own cannot explain the rise of Nazism. But the over-emphasis of the left on class dynamics played its part in creating a culture of fatalism, which lasted way beyond Hitler's appointment as chancellor.

'FROM THE DEPTHS OF THE GERMAN PEOPLE'

The Nazi consolidation of power took place in stages. On 30 January 1933 Hitler appointed a cabinet dominated by the traditional right, and set 5 March as the date for new elections. All over Germany the SA launched a police-backed terror campaign aimed primarily against the KPD. Where there was resistance, as in Little Wedding, the police carried out mass arrests; the SA turned their local HQs into torture chambers.

The KPD's response was to call for a general strike, which – as Petersen reports – failed. The SPD, true to its history of legalism, refused to back the strike. Both parties concentrated instead on the election campaign; both were eliminated without a serious fight.

On 27 February the Reichstag Fire – allegedly started by a mentally ill Dutch communist – gave Hitler the excuse to suspend large parts of the constitution, ban the KPD's newspapers and arrest around 4,000 of its members. In Little Wedding the SA toured the homes of communist workers handing out swastika flags and giving them a choice: fly the flag from your window or go on a hit list.

Backed by systematic voter intimidation, Hitler scored 17 million votes in the March 1933 election. Despite mounting repression, the SPD achieved 7 million votes and the KPD almost 5 million – its highest ever score – after which it was banned and all its MPs arrested. By the end of the year half its members would be in concentration camps and 2,500 had been murdered.[50]

With stormtroopers patrolling the aisles around them, the SPD delegation in parliament stood heroically and alone to oppose Hitler's demand for the power to rule by decree. Not a single vote from any other party was cast against. On 22 June 1933 the SPD was shut down. In July the NSDAP was declared the only legal party; all other parties of the right and centre dissolved themselves voluntarily. What had taken Mussolini four years took Hitler less than six months. It was not until August 1934 that Hitler fused the positions of chancellor and president, declaring himself *Führer* (leader) – but by then the German labour movement was reduced to a precarious underground existence.

Today's left orthodoxy says that Nazism could have been beaten through a united front between the two left parties. But united around what?

As Daniel Guérin concluded, after a second tour of Germany in April 1933, the decisive battle was fought in people's heads. Fascism, he wrote,

> surged forth from the depths of the German people. It's because of its popular appeal that it was irresistible, that it swept everything else away . . . In Germany I learned that in order to defeat fascism you have to oppose it with a living example, a flesh and blood ideal . . . [51]

If you only remember one paragraph from this book, remember that one. The lesson should be: to defeat fascism, you have to win the battle of ideas, and well in advance of its electoral breakthrough. It is not the slogans you are up against – although slogans are important. It is the thought-architecture discussed in Chapter 2, the mythology fascism draws from, the self-contained logic, internally coherent but detached from facts: this is how fascism wins.

After their defeat the SPD's leadership, exiled in Prague, concluded that the Nazi victory was inevitable. The Comintern, which had authored the disastrous Third Period line, reaffirmed it in April 1933:

> The calm that has succeeded the triumph of fascism is only a transitory phenomenon. Despite fascist terror, the revolutionary surge in Germany will rise; the revolutionary resistance of the masses to fascism is bound to grow. The establishment of the open fascist dictatorship . . . is accelerating the rate of Germany's advance towards the proletarian revolution.[52]

It wasn't their failure to fight that doomed tens of thousands of workers to imprisonment, torture and death. It was their failure to understand the threat. They thought they were fighting a party, or a gang of violent thugs. In reality they were resisting a process of mass psychological conversion. And so are we.

PART THREE
Resistance

7

A Theory of Fascism

Beyond the Definition Wars

In 2020, when anti-fascists in America started a Twitter thread listing all known definitions of fascism, they came up with more than thirty. Some were a page long. Others were three-line sentences so crammed with academic jargon that they could give you a migraine. Many directly contradicted each other.[1]

It would be easy to shrug our shoulders and say: why does theory matter? You generally know a fascist when you see one. And the extreme right don't sit around constructing cute definitions of their enemies – they act.

But, as we've seen, the need for a theory is urgent. Fascism achieved power in the twentieth century because neither the liberal centre nor the Marxist left understood what they were dealing with. Today fascism, once presumed dead, has revived, fused itself with right-wing populism, and stands poised to exploit all the instabilities of the twenty-first century. Without a coherent explanation of why it has returned, we risk the same outcome.

Today, any theory of fascism has to tackle four questions:

- Why, in the 1920s, did the same kind of people start doing the same kind of things, with such devastating results for democracy?
- Why is it happening again?
- Is there a deeper cause underlying both iterations?
- How can it be stopped?

The problem is that, for much of the post-1945 period, the study of fascism was focused on the first question, and the answers were always in dispute. Though we can learn much from the historians who thought fascism was 'dead but interesting', its resurgence means any theory based on that assumption has to be revised.

In addition, a theory that works for historians may not work for us, as politically engaged participants. Many of the definitions being screengrabbed and debated by anti-fascists today were written as research hypotheses, designed to guide investigation and analysis. We, by contrast, need theory as a guide to action. We can't expect academia to produce this – though its data, case studies and insights are invaluable.

In 1930, as the German left debated how to respond to Hitler's breakthrough, the most influential debates were conducted not in a university seminar but in a *trade union theoretical journal*. These debates were read and argued over in workplaces and party meetings, and the experience of activists fed into what political theorists wrote next. Activists, in other words, shared not only a political culture but a *means of producing theory*.

For us that's a lost horizon. Today, the organized labour movement is in survival mode; to suggest running a theoretical journal would sound laughable to most union activists. Much of orthodox Marxism exists in the form of re-enactment groups, regurgitating the same theories that led to defeat the first time round. The centre-left parties, watching helplessly as their traditional voter base swings to the right and seemingly unable or unwilling to stop ceding political territory to the populists, don't appear interested in either theory or strategy.

As a result, activists in social justice movements, trapped at the bottom of the hierarchy of degrees, PhDs and publication league tables, tend to treat academia as the only reliable source of knowledge. It has become heresy for any young activist to say – as I will below – that some highly regarded experts have got it wrong.

But we can make a start. What follows is a critique of both the academic and classic Marxist theories of fascism, and the outline of a new, materialist theory of fascism, drawing on the work of Marxists in the 1930s who looked *beyond* class, and beyond the world of capitalist exploitation, in search of fascism's origins.

FROM LIBERAL DISARRAY TO 'TOTALITARIANISM'

After 1945, writers in the liberal tradition produced competing accounts of fascism that reflected the bias of their existing disciplines. Historians specializing in Germany identified Nazism as a German problem. Psychiatrists studied the 'demonic personalities' of the Nuremberg war criminals; economic historians slotted fascism into the trend towards state-controlled economies; while sociologists studied the 'fascist personality type'.[2]

The historian Roger Griffin described the result as liberal disarray: 'a sustained Babel effect that lasted over half a century, proliferating largely incompatible and sometimes mutually incomprehensible definitions of minimal use to historians and political scientists'.[3] But in 1951 the publication of Hannah Arendt's *The Origins of Totalitarianism* seemed to produce clarity. Suddenly there was a popular, sweeping and generalized account, not just of fascism but of the whole twentieth-century phenomenon of totalitarian rule.

Between 1922 and 1925 Mussolini ran what we would today call a 'managed democracy'. Critics were jailed, exiled and occasionally murdered with impunity; elections were rigged and the National Fascist Party inevitably won them by a landslide. If it sounds like Russia, Turkey or the Philippines today, that's no accident: all modern strongmen treat Mussolini's early years as a playbook.

But his opponents could see where things were headed: towards a single-party dictatorship, which would force its ideology into people's brains like a new religion. Fascism's end game, they warned, was to create a 'totalitarian' state.[4]

In response, Mussolini's *squadristi* took up the word 'totalitarian' as a badge of honour. They were entirely open about their desire for a full fascist state – and in January 1925, Mussolini began to build it. He sidelined the legislature and judiciary, concentrating power on himself. He cancelled freedom of assembly, declared all other parties illegal, placed the press under state control, introduced the death penalty for sedition, and began to round up thousands of his opponents.[5]

By 1928 Mussolini had created a 'party state'. But he was not done yet. Though he had come to power promising to liberate the private sector, after the Wall Street Crash he turned instead to outright state ownership. By the time Mussolini co-authored *The Doctrine of Fascism* in 1932, he had created the most state-dominated economy outside the Soviet Union. He decreed:

> Everything is in the state and nothing human or spiritual exists, much less has any value, outside the state. In this sense fascism is totalitarian, and the fascist state – the synthesis and unity of all values – interprets, develops and gives strength to the whole life of the people.[6]

Totalitarianism, then, was not a concept invented by Arendt, it was a term used both by fascism and its critics. But in the 1930s, after Hitler's victory and Stalin's turn to mass murder and repression, a theory emerged that claimed the whole world was turning totalitarian.

As early as 1931 Lucien Laurat, an Austrian Marxist, argued that because Italy and the Soviet Union were so similar, a new, bureaucratic form of exploitation had emerged to replace capitalism: a kind of technology-enhanced slavery. The differences between the Soviet and fascist systems, he proposed, were merely ones of degree.[7] By the end of the 1930s Laurat's 'bureaucratic collectivism' theory had become commonplace among left-wing critics of Soviet communism. But as an explanation of fascism – and indeed as a guide to action – it proved a dead end. Once fascism was destroyed, and replaced by fully functioning market democracies after 1945, it was worthless to the left. From 1951 onwards the totalitarian thesis would become the property of the Cold War right.

Arendt's description of Nazism as an alliance of 'the elite and the mob' contains important insights for us. What the two groups have in common is the same desire she observed in 1920s Germany: 'access to history even at the price of destruction'.[8] That is, the desire to derail the global order and trigger a giant historical re-set – even if it destroys the society they live in and the country they claim to love. Trump and the middle-class crowds who adulated him fit Arendt's description of 'the elite and the mob' perfectly.

Arendt's dissection of Hitler's reliance on conspiracy theories, discussed in Chapter 2, is also relevant. The Nazis, she said, had created a 'lying world of consistency which is more adequate to the needs of the human mind than reality itself'. Her words could just as easily describe the collection of QAnon believers, anti-vaxxers, climate deniers and neo-Nazis that stormed the US Capitol in January 2021:

> They do not believe in anything visible, in the reality of their own experience; they do not trust their eyes and ears but only their imaginations, which may be caught by anything that is at once universal and consistent in itself.[9]

Significant and insightful as it is, as an account of fascism's origins Arendt's work is flawed. In the first place, by creating the overarching abstraction of 'totalitarianism' to describe both the USSR and Nazi Germany, she had to exclude Italy from the category until 1938. Up to then, wrote Arendt, fascist Italy was 'not totalitarian but just an ordinary nationalist dictatorship developed logically from a multi-party democracy'.[10]

Second, because having established 'social atomisation' as the precondition for the rise of totalitarian movements, she admits it was not present in tsarist Russia, nor in the early Soviet regime, and had to be created during the 1930s using mass terror, famine, purges and intrusive surveillance.[11]

Third, Arendt's account of Hitler's rise to power is at odds with the facts. She argued that the original adherents of fascist movements were mainly 'non-joiners who for individualistic reasons always had refused to recognize social links or obligations'.[12] That's how, to her, it may have felt. But as we saw in Chapter 6, from war veterans to students, to members of shooting clubs and shopkeepers' guilds, the Nazi breakthrough happened among 'joiners', not non-joiners.

Finally, Arendt severs the link between fascism and capitalism. In no version of history did Russia's factory owners wish for Bolshevism. In all accepted histories of fascism Hitler and Mussolini had encouragement from at least a section of the ruling class, and large sections of the business elite collaborated with them once in power.

Emilio Gentile, a modern advocate of totalitarianism theory, summed up the problem with Arendt's theory. For her, he writes, totalitarianism is like a strange plant: in Russia it has no roots, but can germinate and grow; in Germany it has roots but grows slowly; in Italy it flowers despite having no roots and never germinating.[13] The theory, in short, does not stand up, despite the acuity of her insights. If you are going to use the word 'totalitarianism' today, Gentile argues, you have to strip it of the abstract character it assumes in Arendt's work.

Yet, after Arendt, totalitarianism became the signature tune of Cold War political science. Checklists were invented and the 'six key features of totalitarian states' rote-learned by undergraduates. For Friedrich and Brzezinski, who in 1956 wrote the most influential textbook on the subject, the regimes were the primary focus. Movements came a distant second, their ideologies dismissed as 'trite restatements of certain traditional ideas, arranged in an incoherent way that makes them highly exciting to weak minds'.[14]

Throughout the 1950s it became an article of faith that fascism and communism were the same thing. And then, in the 1960s, the historians intervened.

FROM GRAND THEORY TO SOCIOLOGY

Ernst Nolte's book *Fascism in its Epoch* signalled a return to the study of fascism as fascism, rather than a subcategory of something else. Published in Germany in 1963, at a time when hundreds of thousands of former Nazis were still alive, it was a cathartic moment: here was a figure from conservative academia coming to terms with the past. It also signalled a return to the study of mass movements, not just regimes in their final form; to the study of ideas as well as actions; and to seeing fascism as a product of something deeper.

Both Marxists and liberals believed that fascist ideas were an incoherent fiction and served only as a pretext for violent actions. Nolte, by contrast, insisted that fascist ideology is important: we must allow it to 'speak for itself' and understand its 'staggering logicality and consistency, even though we disagree with it'.[15] Drawing on the experiences of France, Italy and Germany, Nolte wrote the first influential definition of fascism:

Fascism is anti-Marxism which seeks to destroy the enemy by the evolvement of a radically opposed and yet related ideology and by the use of almost identical and yet typically modified methods, always, however within the unyielding framework of national self-assertion and autonomy.[16]

It's not the catchiest definition. Broken down into bullet points it means:

- Fascism is anti-Marxism: without Marxism and the Russian Revolution there is no fascism.
- Fascism's aim is to destroy Marxism as a movement and ideology, if necessary by killing millions of people.
- Fascism's ideology is the mirror image of Marxism, but with one crucial distinction: it's based on nationalism, not class.
- Fascism's methods are similar to those of revolutionary Marxist parties, but modified according to its nationalist goals.

Not content with a definition, Nolte also produced a checklist. Any movement that can be called fascist has to have six attributes: anti-Marxism, anti-liberalism, anti-conservatism, an all-powerful leader, a party army and the expressed aim of a totalitarian state.

Finally, Nolte offered an explanation of the underlying cause that had driven millions of people to embrace the far right. Fascism, he wrote, is 'the practical and violent resistance to transcendence'.[17] This, too, needs unpacking.

Nolte identified the irrationalist ideas circulating before 1914 as indispensable to the rise of fascism. The French Revolution, and the rise of capitalist industry, he said, had made progress possible. In response, throughout the nineteenth century, conservatism tried to halt this progress, or roll it backwards towards the pre-revolutionary order of peasants, priests and aristocrats.

By the late nineteenth century, however, it looked like the reactionaries had lost. If science could refute the Bible, proving humanity's origins in evolution, it could one day probably map the human brain. If music could move beyond tonality, if art could move beyond representation and machines could fly, then it was possible to imagine human freedom (what Nolte calls 'transcendence') coming soon.

Those devoted to the ideals of absolute monarchy, eternal war and social hierarchy realized that if they didn't stop human progress now, it would be too late. They began to mobilize and act. That is what Nolte means by 'practical resistance to transcendence'.

It is this fear of progress, rather than the mere loneliness and atomization produced by modern life, that for Nolte explains the emergence of mass fascist parties. Fascism is resistance to social progress, and to the idea of liberation, by a group whose social position makes them scared of the prospect. Fascism, in short, is a movement of people unwilling to think beyond the present.

Nolte ended up in a dark place. What began as an explanation of fascism became, in his work after 1968, a tacit justification for it. As German conservatism moved rightward he began to imply that the Nazi response to Marxism may have been justified; that the Bolsheviks' crime of 'class murder' was the trigger for the Nazis' 'racial murder'; and that the Holocaust was not a unique crime in history. All of which sparked a bitter debate in German politics, and outright war among historians: Nolte was ostracized for the rest of his career, though more recently celebrated by the rising stars of the AfD.[18]

Even his critics, however, admit that *Fascism in its Epoch* was a landmark text. But it was to be the last major attempt by a non-Marxist to theorize fascism as a totality. For Nolte's book now spawned the discipline of comparative fascist studies, and the definition wars began.

Over the next forty years numerous writers tried to improve on Nolte's definition and his checklist – not only in order to study the historical movements but to identify fascist tendencies within the post-war right.

In 1976 Juan Linz, a Spanish political scientist, wrote an extensive definition of fascism, taking Nolte's six points and adding to them. A party could be defined as fascist, said Linz, if it was hypernationalist, anti-parliamentary, anti-liberal, anti-communist, populist, anti-proletarian, partly anti-capitalist; aimed to integrate the whole of society in a single party; had a distinct style and rhetoric, relying on violence plus elections, with a totalitarian goal; was based on vitalistic philosophy; offered a new elite status to those not integrated into the class structure; had a deep-seated hostility to all parties, movements and religions that look international.[19]

This is only a short summary: Linz's full definition runs to nearly a page. But it doesn't explain fascism. The method of building 'ideal types' – what we today call 'models' – has been central to social science since its foundation. Models allow us to simplify reality in order to see what is general, typical and recurrent. But in an attempt to improve on Linz's abstract model, historians began a fruitless competition, in which their definitions got denser, the checklists ever longer, and their usefulness declined.

To take one example, in 1980 Stanley Payne, a historian and expert in Spanish fascism, wrote that fascism is:

> A form of revolutionary ultra-nationalism for national rebirth that is based on a primarily vitalist philosophy, is structured on extreme elitism, mass mobilisation and the *Führerprinzip* [leader principle] as end as well as means and tends to normalise war and/or the military virtues.[20]

Emilio Gentile also produced his own ten-point checklist of fascism's common features: a mass movement drawn from every class; an ideology expressed through the myths and rituals of a secular religion; an activist vision of life; a totalitarian view of politics; a public ethic based on virility, comradeship and the warrior spirit; a single, armed party; a police apparatus using organized terror; a political system focused around a charismatic leader; a state-led economy and an expansionist foreign policy.[21]

But definitions are not explanations. And checklists cannot capture cause and effect. When you produce an abstract model of anything you are necessarily stepping away from both detail and time. Detail is not such a problem because, if you're isolating the basic features of something, these can be used to highlight variations in the nature of fascism. So – if we take Payne's definition – Mussolini's 'vitalist philosophy' was drawn from Sorel and Nietzsche, while Hitler was much more fundamentally attached to the racist psychobabble of Chamberlain.

Time, however, is a big thing to ignore, because all fascisms – then and now – have a beginning, a middle and an end. And once you've discarded time, it's easy to cast aside another key question: causation.

Linz, Payne, Gentile and their co-thinkers were historians determined to remain close to the concrete, to name and identify rather than explain; their typologies are lengthy, their warnings not to over-use them loud. Their achievement was to refocus our understanding of fascism on the factors that the left had dismissed: myths of national rebirth, irrationalism and quasi-religious symbols and routines. They also showed, disturbingly for the left, how close early fascism was to anti-Marxist socialism and, in Italy, to anarchism.

But in the 1990s the definition wars – like much of social science – took a turn away from reality altogether. Some historians decided to abandon any relationship between definitions and concrete facts. According to one of them, Roger Griffin, they were 'illuminated by the realisation that fascism is not an objective "thing" to be found or defined. Rather, like all other political concepts, it is a heuristic device which can be articulated as a working definition.'[22]

Marxists had tried to explain fascism as the product of economic and social conflict; anti-Marxists like Nolte had focused on resistance to progress. Griffin and his co-thinkers would instead focus on fascist culture – and they would do so from the 'inside out'.

Fascism, Griffin said, was best studied from the point of view of the fascists themselves. This way historians could at last see fascism as 'the expression, albeit a generally propagandistic one, of deeply held beliefs and emotionally and mythically powerful ideals about what is wrong with society and what should be done to regenerate it'.[23]

This approach did work, up to a point. It allowed a new generation of social historians to listen more carefully to what fascists said and wrote, and to produce new, granular histories – such as the microstudy of the *Sturmabteilung* quoted in Chapter 6.

Griffin's definition was the most defiantly abstract and became the most influential:

Fascism is a genus of political ideology whose mythic core in its various permutations is a palingenetic [obsessed with rebirth] form of populist ultranationalism.[24]

But even at the abstract level there are huge problems with this two-line summary. First, it defines fascism wholly as an ideology; second, it removes all mention of violence; third it introduces the idea of populism – which is fine if you are trying to stretch the definition to encompass the new right parties emerging in the 1990s, but seems anachronistic if applied historically. Finally, as we have seen, most twenty-first-century fascism is focused on ethnicity, not national greatness. It wants the rebirth (and 'purification') of the white European race, or of the Hindutva, or the non-indigenous elites of Latin America.

At one level, the argument over definitions is simply an expression of the tension between history and sociology: the historian is concerned with time, causation and detail; the sociologist takes snapshots and looks for structures. But at another level it mirrors what happened to the way academics think in general, between the 1960s and today.

Nolte, though a conservative, was determined to match the breadth and totality of the Marxist explanation of fascism. Linz and his generation retreated to descriptions and the naming of parts, mirroring the emergence of 'structuralism' in social science. Griffin completes the process by detaching the concept entirely from the thing it is supposed to describe, which is the signature of post-structuralist thinking.

The result of this progression was an outpouring of primary research into the lives, crimes, fantasies and voting patterns of people caught up in fascist movements. But it moved further and further away from the study of fascism as a totality, one with a root cause and a typical trajectory.

By the time fascism actually began to re-emerge as a mass phenomenon, after 2008, the anti-Marxist camp was polarized between sterile abstractions and the study of concrete 'things'.

WHAT MARXISM GOT WRONG

Marx and Engels predicted the rise of imperialism, the expanded finance sector, monopolies and the inevitability of total war. But they failed to predict fascism. In fact, no Marxist predicted fascism. Once the fascist bid for power began, no Marxist writer was able to develop a coherent theory of it, and no Marxist-led party had a strategy to defeat it. As a result, fascism killed an entire generation of Marxists, destroyed every mass workers' party in continental Europe, and, in 1942, came within a hair's breadth of destroying the USSR.

No Marxist can regard these failures as secondary. They should haunt the mind of anyone who wants – as I do – to call themselves a Marxist today.

But they do not. Everywhere on the left you will hear activists repeat the basic flawed assumptions that led to disaster in the 1920s and 30s. Let's summarize them:

- Determined to reduce all phenomena to their economic roots, the orthodox Marxists of the Comintern were surprised by the attraction of middle-class people to a violent 'revolution against the revolution', and had no effective answer to it.
- The 'agent theory', whereby fascists were seen as the puppets of big business, blinded Marxists to the relative and prolonged autonomy of fascist parties from the business elite and to fascism's actual relationship to capitalism.
- Convinced that history was on their side, they saw their initial defeats as temporary and the 'managed democracy' phase of fascism – both in Italy and Germany – as reversible and even survivable.
- Finally, in their relentless focus on class antagonism as the driver of fascism, Marxist parties failed to realize the significance of anti-Semitism within Nazism. Leon Trotsky, who in the weeks after Kristallnacht in 1938 predicted the coming Holocaust, was among the rare exceptions.[25]

After Hitler's victory, as we will explore in Chapter 9, the Comintern's tactics changed. By forming an alliance with liberals and moderate socialists in France and Spain, the communists temporarily halted the spread of fascism. But to justify the alliance, they doubled down on the 'agent theory', albeit with a modification.

Fascism, said the Comintern leader Georgi Dimitrov in 1935, is 'the open terroristic dictatorship of the most reactionary, the most chauvinistic, the most imperialistic elements of finance capital'.[26] Since fascism was the agent of the *bad* capitalists, it was now OK to ally with the *good*, democratic capitalists. But the agent theory itself survived.

The current state of the left suggests that there is a clear danger that these errors will be repeated. On any given Sunday you can hear the 'class against class' theory expounded on left-wing Twitter, where liberals like Hillary Clinton are vilified in the same language as Trump.

Three interwar Marxist writers are often praised by today's left for their opposition to the policies of the Third Period, and for their attempts to critique the errors outlined above: Trotsky, who was assassinated in 1940; August Thalheimer, an oppositionist in the KPD, who fled Nazi Germany and died in 1948; and Antonio Gramsci, who died in prison in 1937, but whose mature work was published only after the war.[27]

Trotsky, who relentlessly criticized the 'class against class' strategy, urged German communists to make a formal united front agreement with the SPD. After Hitler's breakthrough he correctly identified the Nazis, not the centrist parties or the socialists, as the main enemy; he understood Nazism as a mass movement, rooted in the middle class, and capable of achieving power with significant autonomy from its elite backers.

Trotsky, Thalheimer and Gramsci were all fascinated by fascism's similarity to 'Caesarism' – that is, the ability, at critical moments in history, of unrepresentative factions within society to seize power. In Marx's writings, they had a case study: the seizure of power by the self-styled 'Emperor' Louis Bonaparte during the defeat of the 1848 revolution in France. Bonapartism, Marx said, was an example of the elite giving up political power to save their economic power: 'handing over the sword to save the purse'.[28] But as they mulled over the parallels between Bonapartism and fascism, the critical Marxists of the 1930s stuck to the mental framework spelled out by Engels in his introduction to Marx's famous pamphlet on Bonaparte:

> All historical struggles, whether they proceed in the political, religious, philosophical or some other ideological domain, are in fact only the more or less clear expression of struggles of social classes . . . [29]

This 'great law of motion of history', Engels claimed, had the same status for history as the second law of thermodynamics does in science.

Here, in a nutshell, lay the problem Marxists in the 1930s failed to grapple with. You can admit fascist movements are temporarily autonomous from the capitalist class; you can see the fascist state as saving capitalism as a whole through actions autonomous from individual capitalists. But ultimately you are still required to see fascism as an expression of ruling-class interest and as an 'agent' of capital.

Because they could never go beyond this 'last analysis', most dissident Marxists in the 1930s produced only a thin, tactical critique of the orthodox position. Only Gramsci, in his prison cell, began to rethink the premises of Marxist theory, not just its conclusions. He asked: if the middle class has discovered a new, historic capacity for autonomy and revolution, creating regimes that the working class cannot beat, where does that leave Marxism?

As early as 1921 Gramsci realized that fascism can 'only partially' be explained with reference to class. 'Fascism is the name for the profound decomposition of Italian society,' he wrote. That process had unchained 'elemental forces' which not even the bourgeoisie could control.[30] This was an astonishing claim for a Marxist to make; it signalled a rip in the fabric of the Marxist universe. But at this point he could explain fascism away as the outcome of Italy's underdevelopment. Mass irrationalism, Gramsci reasoned, had to be a hangover from the past, not a product of the present.

By 1926, however, he had rejected both the 'agent theory' and the comparison with Bonapartism. Fascism was not a violent reaction by the elite to the threat of revolution, he said, it was a by-product of the weakness and failure of the working class. As a result, he argued, the left would need to seek a strategic alliance with the middle class and defend democracy against fascism. It was at this moment, however, that the doors of history slammed shut.

'We must stop this brain working for twenty years,' said the prosecutor at Gramsci's trial, where he was charged with trying to undermine the Italian state.[31] But in prison Gramsci's brain continued working, despite severe physical illness and depression. What it produced was the first serious attempt to explain fascism as a phenomenon beyond class.

In his *Prison Notebooks*, Gramsci developed six concepts that remain indispensable tools for anyone trying to construct a left-wing strategy against today's fascism.

The first concept is Gramsci's demand (based on Soviet military science) for a rigorous 'analysis of situations'. In any given crisis, you have to lay down the kind of 'brutal audit' attempted in Chapter 3, to recognize the unpredictable ways multiple crises can combine to generate new social and political forces.

The second concept, flowing logically from this, is to treat politics as an 'autonomous science'. In a developed country, said Gramsci, an economic crisis doesn't automatically produce a political crisis, but once it starts, a political crisis can have dynamics that only vaguely and indirectly reflect class and economic forces. Fascism can functionally 'defend capitalism' without being an *agent* of the existing capitalist elite at all. In the process it can alter capitalism and even reshape the structure of the elite.

The third Gramscian concept is the 'passive revolution'. Some revolutions, he asserted, do not take the form of a direct attack on state power, but of a gradual erosion of the elite's legitimacy: first conquering the minds of large numbers of people, then the wider sphere of culture and institutions. The rise of Christianity in the Roman Empire, said Gramsci, was an example of passive revolution. And in a shocking departure from Marxist orthodoxy, he admitted, so was fascism. To fight it, the left would need its own, long and patient project of persuasion.

The fourth and most important concept is Gramsci's notion of *hegemony* (or dominance). It is not enough for the working class to unite and to seek tactical alliances with the middle class. In a developed country, the labour movement cannot come to power unless it exerts moral, cultural and intellectual leadership over the whole of society.

A fifth insight, linked to this, was to create a mental picture of capitalist power based on the metaphor of trench warfare. Contrary to the Leninist position, which assumes that a coercive state is all that stands between the left and power, Gramsci insisted that in a democracy the state was 'only an outer ditch, behind which there stood a powerful system of fortresses and earthworks' – namely the ideologies, religions, institutions and networks essential to the functioning of an industrialized society.[32]

From this he derived his sixth big idea: that the path to power lies through a 'war of position' – a prolonged effort to build rival ideologies, institutions, cultures and networks, similar to siege warfare, not a revolutionary coup modelled on the Russian experience.

Fascism had triumphed, Gramsci said, because it understood these rules of political science better than Marxism. At the crucial moment, when all classes begin to detach from their traditional parties, one party has to emerge that represents the nation. Fascism had done so; neither the socialists nor the communists had even grasped the problem.

If you return to Chapters 5 and 6, and run the 'how to stop fascism' scenario over again, the toolbox Gramsci developed in the *Prison Notebooks* contains a viable strategy for resistance. It would mandate formal unity between all workers' parties, an appeal to the middle class on its own terms, an end to revolutionary phraseology, fatalism and over-optimism, and an alliance with liberalism to defend the existing democracy, no matter how flawed it was.

In turn, these principles could also be the starting point for a viable anti-fascist strategy today, albeit in radically different circumstances. But even Gramsci's additions to Marxism are not enough. Because once you acknowledge there can be a fascist revolution that is not merely a reaction to a workers' revolution, but something autonomous, only one materialist conclusion is possible.

In every major crisis of capitalism there is a potential third outcome that is neither socialism nor the survival of capitalism: it is the collapse of the elite's legitimacy and its mainstream ideology and the rapid conversion of people to irrationalism, self-destruction and hate. Historical time cannot be reversed, but progress can be.

If fascism is only 'partially' a class phenomenon, we have to find out what's driving the non-class aspect and work out the relationship between the two. Fortunately, there were people in the 1930s who had been exploring exactly this.

ENTER THE SHRINKS

When sociology emerged in the early twentieth century, Marxists welcomed it as a form of inferior 'capitalist materialism': flawed by class prejudice but a worthy sparring partner in discussions about social dynamics. The emergence of modern psychiatry, however, provoked outright hostility.

Here was a *rival* materialism: equally certain that beneath the surface reality of human life is hiding a deeper, more profound dynamic; equally determined to expose that dynamic, which psychiatrists were certain lay not in the exploitation of labour but in the repression of sexuality. Since its battleground was the *chaise longue*, and Marxism's battleground was the factory, the two movements were able to keep a wary distance from each other.

But if the core of the labour movement was hostile to psychoanalysis, its edges were alive with interest. In the 1920s, key figures from the Freudian movement gravitated towards Marxism. Wilhelm Reich, one of Freud's star pupils, joined the KPD in 1930 and convinced the party to launch an association for Proletarian Sexual Politics (abbreviated to Sex-Pol), which at its height had 40,000 members.[33] Erich Fromm, another Freudian psychiatrist, joined the Institute for Social Research in Frankfurt (commonly known as the Frankfurt School) to head up a research programme into working-class attitudes to fascism.

Reich and Fromm made real-time attempts both to theorize fascism and to fight it. Both asked questions that begin at the point where Gramsci ends: exactly how does pro-capitalist ideology seep into the minds of individual people? How does it function at a subconscious level as well as at the level of conscious ideas? How does this differ between social classes, age groups and genders? And why – at certain moments – does the passive, mainstream ideology of society evaporate, leading some people to embrace fascism through a quasi-religious conversion to doctrines previously seen as transgressive?

As we today witness the emergence of far-right movements driven by conspiracy and paranoia, their work is especially relevant. Because unlike most of the theories discussed above, their findings suggest that fascism could happen again, even under radically different conditions.

Today, Wilhelm Reich is notorious for an eccentric theory of orgasmic energy developed in the late 1930s. But in his Marxist period (1927–35) he made two significant contributions to the understanding of fascism.

First, he gave an account of the emotions that fascism had mobilized. Their origins, Reich argued, lay not in the class structure of industrial capitalism but much deeper, in the patriarchy whose roots stretched back to the Stone Age – and lay specifically in the family.

His starting point was Freud's theory. In it, the repression of childhood sexuality creates all kinds of subconscious fears and urges, which are controlled by an intermediate layer (the pre-conscious), so that the conscious mind can be made aware of them only through analysis. Sexual repression, Reich said, acts like a factory for producing all other ideologies. Unlike the theft of material wealth through exploitation, most people don't even realize that their sexuality is repressed. The result is to produce – in all humans, in all class societies – a subconscious 'fear of freedom'.[34]

Long before it had to confront fascism, Reich argued, Marxism had 'failed to understand the character structure of the masses and the social effect of mysticism'.[35] The Nazis' ability to exploit people's fear of freedom lay in their willingness to use symbolism, emotion, language and sexual imagery in a way no mainstream party had ever done. This, he said, was the 'mass psychology of fascism'.

Reich illustrated his point by quoting from a pamphlet by Goebbels, in which the Nazi propagandist answers the question 'Is a Jew a Man?':

> If someone cracks a whip across your mother's face, would you say to him, Thank you! Is he a man too? One who does such a thing is not a man – he is a brute! How many worse things has the Jew inflicted upon our mother Germany and still inflicts upon her! He has debauched our race, sapped our energy, undermined our customs and broken our strength . . . [36]

To the activists who had to endure this rhetoric, in the workplace and on the doorstep, it seemed then – as it does when we hear it today – the product of pure hate and ignorance. Reich, by analysing the imagery, pleaded with the German left to understand its appeal: the Nazis were consciously using transgressive language and imagery (the mother's whipped face) to trigger people's repressed sexuality.

The left had no response to this, because they did not believe in the subconscious. But the Nazis, though no supporters of Freud, had long subscribed to the idea that intuition was more reliable than thought: that was the very basis of Bergson's vitalism. Likewise their obsession with the Sorelian techniques of myth-making and symbolism had armed them with a communicative power that their opponents could not counter. As we have seen, the ability to mesmerize people was not some spontaneous talent the fascists and Nazis happened to possess: they had studied the technique from its masters.

Reich's second contribution was to propose a new kind of activism. If fascism relies on mysticism and repressed sexuality, he reasoned, anti-fascists had to stop treating this problem like a secret. To counter it, they had to do youth social work, sex education, and provide contraceptive advice.[37] That is what the Sex-Pol movement did.

Reich issued a pamphlet aimed at working-class youth, defending masturbation and teenage sex, explaining contraception and advocating abortion on demand: 'Fight against the system,' it reasoned, 'and you will be fighting for your sexual freedom and dignity.'[38] A second pamphlet explained the basics of sex to children; a third was aimed at giving their parents the right language to describe sex. The pamphlets were massively popular, especially among those the left needed to reach: women, the young unemployed and, in one case, even a group of Hitler Youth members who circulated the material in secret.

Through Sex-Pol, the KPD was able to find supporters in unorganized workplaces and even to address Nazi voters directly. In the Ruhr, the group was so successful that, according to Reich, working-class women from both the Nazi Party and the Christian parties joined in droves and even attended its demonstrations. Soon, communist officials complained that 'sex alone was being discussed, and that interest in the questions of class struggle was decreasing'.[39] These officials could not see, Reich complained, that sexual freedom and reproductive rights were also part of the class struggle.

Despite – or rather, because of – its success, Sex-Pol's end came abruptly in December 1932 when teenage members of a suburban communist sports club, citing Reich, demanded their leaders set up a hostel where they could have sex. Fearing a scandal, the KPD shut down Sex-Pol, banned Reich's pamphlets and persuaded a doctor to issue stern medical advice, which stated that 'there are no orgasm disturbances in the proletariat' – only among the bourgeoisie.

Reich's work – as a therapist, organizer and educator – was not a substitute for his anti-fascist activism. He lived in Charlottenburg, the Berlin district terrorized by Storm 33. To the consternation of his psychoanalyst colleagues he joined the KPD's local antifa group, fighting the riot police as a defence steward on demonstrations and standing guard with milk bottles to throw from the rooftops if the Nazis attacked the tenements. But through his work as an educator, he drew conclusions that few on the German left were prepared to accept:

> The average individual was suffering from a contradiction: he wanted the world changed but the change was to be imposed upon him suddenly from above, just as the exploitation and suppression had been imposed upon him ... No leaders entertained the thought of telling them the truth, namely that they had to think and act in a responsible manner for their freedom. On the contrary, the Communists, for example, did everything in their power to make the masses subservient.[40]

Large numbers of people were trapped between the possibility of freedom and the fear of what such freedom might mean. But if the left didn't understand what Reich was trying to say, the Nazis did. They identified the Sex-Pol movement as a key component of 'cultural Bolshevism' and shortly after seizing power in 1933, attacked Reich in their newspaper, forcing him to flee the country.

You don't have to accept Freud's theory of the *id* and *ego*, or identify the family as the sole source of all neuroses, to accept Reich's wider point: a materialist theory of fascism has to explain how structures of oppression produce ideologies, how the desire for freedom and the fear of it interact, and how the subconscious mind can be seduced by a politics of emotion rather than of facts.

Erich Fromm rejected Reich's idea of 'mass psychology'. Only individuals can have neuroses, he insisted, not entire groups. Instead, he focused on studying the psychological traits of people drawn to political parties: what he called their 'social character'.

In 1929 Fromm distributed a questionnaire to 3,300 German workers, with 271 questions probing their views on culture, politics and authority.[41] Of the 1,100 forms that came back, more than half were lost when he had to escape Germany; his study – completed in exile – remained unpublished until the 1980s. But as the first real piece of quantitative research into fascism, it produced results that would have been useful then and are invaluable today.

Based on their answers, Fromm divided the respondents into three basic personality types: radical, compromiser and authoritarian. The Nazi voters fitted easily into the authoritarian type. Workers who voted SPD clustered into the space between radical and compromiser, while the communists were bunched strongly at the radical end of the scale. There was, said Fromm, 'a far-reaching accord between personality and party programme'. So far, so predictable.

But a significant number of workers *didn't* follow the pattern. In fact, only a minority had a values-based connection with their party. The numerical strength of the SPD and KPD disguised the fact that the left 'had by and large not succeeded in changing the personality structure of its adherents in a way that they could be relied upon in a critical situation'.[42]

Even more startling (at the time), a significant minority of the left voters held what Fromm called 'authoritarian radical' views. They thought Lenin was one of the greatest figures in world history, that war should be abolished by proletarian revolution, and were resolutely opposed to anti-Semitism. But their social attitudes 'betrayed the wish to submit to a strong leader and also a desire to dominate the weak':

> These people were filled with hate and anger against everyone who had money and who appeared to enjoy life. That part of the socialist platform which aimed at the overthrow of the propertied classes strongly appealed to them. On the other hand, items such as freedom and equality had not the slightest attraction for them, since they willingly obeyed every powerful authority they admired and liked to control others.[43]

Once the NSDAP emerged, said Fromm, such people 'were transformed from unreliable leftists into convinced National Socialists'. Looking back, he conjectured that this conversion took place at two critical points: the 1929–30 electoral breakthrough, and after the 1933 seizure of power.

The sample is small; the data processing methods primitive. But Fromm's survey remains the only real-time attempt by Marxist social science to analyse working-class interior life during the rise of fascism. It confirmed what Reich had tried to tell the KPD: that the 'class consciousness' evident at rallies and protests was fragile. Part of the working class was susceptible to fascism because their own leaders had never properly challenged their members' views about society and authority, and at worst replicated them.

In order to understand what created such 'authoritarian rebels', and what social conditions empowered them, Fromm dug deeper. In 1941, his bestseller *Escape from Freedom* gave the answer: the mental exhaustion created by modern life, plus war and crisis, and the defeat of the labour movement. Fromm noted that, even among fully committed leftists and liberals, a state of 'tiredness and resignation' had risen in the face of Nazism:

> They still remained members of their respective parties and, consciously, continued to believe in their political doctrines; but deep within themselves many had given up any hope in the effectiveness of political action.[44]

In contrast, those gravitating to the Nazis were active and enthusiastic. By joining the Nazis or the SA, the authoritarian rebel types could experience the hierarchical utopia they craved in the here and now. For the anti-fascist left, communism was always something a long way off, and the present always dreary.

It was not, said Fromm, the economic and political crisis that had created authoritarian rebels, susceptible to switching from far left to far right. Rather, society itself had created them. The crisis triggered and enhanced their desire for authority; and the hollowing out of belief among activists in the workers' parties destroyed their ability to resist.

Until Reich and Fromm, Marxist theory understood pro-capitalist ideology through the experience of the factory: managers are strong, workers weak; trade union struggles achieve reforms and thus the illusion grows that capitalism will eventually become 'fair'. Add a strong dose of racism and militarism, based on workers' supposed stake in colonial expansion projects, and that's what the left is up against: an ideology that says 'the capitalist world is OK, natural and unchangeable'. The Marxist remedy is class struggle and education; with enough of both, the working class learns 'class consciousness' and moves towards the project of revolution.

The genius of Reich and Fromm was to understand that ideologies of obedience could be explained in an equally materialist way, via the structure of the family, and to identify sexuality as the battleground against them. They were the first Marxists to explain what Gramsci could not: that sex, sexual repression, the family and power were the 'elemental forces' driving fascism. And that the anti-fascist struggle has to take place on a battleground of vivid imagery, emotion and instinct – which is always going to feel like playing in the away stadium in a football game, but unavoidable.

TOWARDS A MATERIALIST THEORY OF FASCISM

The Marxism in the heads of the workers who first fought fascism was clearly flawed, both as a framework for understanding the threat, and as a guide to action. But there is only one revision we need to make it work. And though it's a big one, it is not exactly rocket science: *We need to put the human being, not class or capitalism, at the centre of the picture.*

Once we remember that – as Marx taught – *humans make history*, we can understand fascism as the product of a deep human contradiction, not just class antagonism. Before it is a theory of class, Marxism is after all a theory of human beings – and it is this 'materialist conception of history' that best explains the cause of fascism and its specific relation to capitalism.

It begins with the proposal that humans possess, purely by the accident of evolution, the capacity for imagination, language, technology and teamwork. That's what makes us different from all other animals. It's our human essence; what Marx in his earliest work called our *species being*.[45]

Throughout history we have used these capacities to create not just things – such as stone tools, printed books and smartphones – but *social relationships* that allow those things to work. We are also – as far as we know – the only species on the planet that can look at our surroundings and draw them accurately; we began doing so around 50,000 years ago. It is in our DNA to be able to represent the world as well as live in it.

As a result, we have a social history: society changes and human nature changes with it. To paraphrase Marx, it is not classes, nations, 'fate', movements or religions that make history but individual human beings. We do so, however, in conditions that we cannot choose. Those conditions include the natural world; the technologies already invented; the behaviours drilled into us as children; the routines we follow and, above all, the belief systems that surround us.

But our innate abilities – to imagine something different, collaborate in the attempt to realize it and communicate the vision – mean that we are always in the process of 'breaking out' from the ideas and structures that surround us.

Once a particular kind of class hierarchy has been formed and stabilized, the ideology that justifies it works passively and pervasively. It becomes invisible, as if everyone is viewing the world through a pair of tinted spectacles which they cannot see.

One of the most useful things about the materialist approach to history is that it lets us see a Trump election rally, or a statement by Boris Johnson, in the same way as we might see the false reassurances of an Egyptian pharaoh that he will protect his subjects 'to the limits of eternity'. We can see that, in our own era, commonly held ideas, cultural norms, laws and political vocabulary serve to reflect and justify the existing power hierarchies and class divisions.

But precisely because ideologies are passive and pervasive, every new development produced by human ingenuity poses a challenge to them. Some developments can be absorbed; others threaten the existing structure and challenge the ideology's internal logic. Change happens because our power to imagine, build, communicate and cooperate never stops working.

And change is neither a smooth nor constant process. Societies like ancient Egypt can exist for centuries without breaking down, but suddenly they do. Once the established mechanism for creating and distributing wealth no longer works, and the accompanying ideology no longer explains the world, change is rapid, violent and unpredictable.

Marx did not invent the class struggle. He simply formulated what eighteenth-century historians had observed: that it drives historical progress. The biggest changes take the form of struggles between different interest groups within the hierarchy, over who gets what. When the system no longer works, the ruling class usually gets overthrown by a new, rising class whose access to new technologies, forms of organization and ideas puts them in a better position to move forward.

The take-off of industrial capitalism made many people understand that human freedom was close. It was logical to assume, said Marx, that industrial capitalism would eventually produce a) enough for everybody and b) a crisis in which the working class would overthrow the capitalists. The working class could not be a 'ruling class', since they owned no technologies or property; they would have to abolish the class system altogether.

But here's the problem, and it is highly relevant to the explanation of fascism. On the evidence of 250 years of industrial capitalism, Marx was wrong about the working class. The working class organized themselves into an influential force, but they rarely achieved political power. Nor were they really capable of holding on to it when they did.

What they achieved was control – islands of social autonomy where the rule of the factory owner and the logic of the market were absent. It was a magnificent control, exercised through the creation of deep, resilient counter-cultures, in which you could live a rich institutional life separate from the institutions of capitalist power surrounding you.

In his early writings, which were not discovered until the 1930s, Marx expressed four radical ideas at once:

- individual human beings make history – it is our human nature that makes social change happen;
- capitalism, through technological progress, creates the potential for communism, a society without class hierarchies;

- communism will bring complete liberation of every individual by ending our alienation from nature, the things we produce, from each other, and from our own human 'essence';
- the way to get there is for the workers to take power, so in this sense the working class is the 'subject' of history: it embodies the general desire of humanity for freedom.

The workers who faced the fascist threat in the 1920s and 30s knew nothing of these radical humanist foundations of Marxism. They had been taught only that the working class would overthrow the capitalists, that the middle classes would be 'proletarianized' and disappear, that all forms of oppression other than class were subordinate, and that their own victory was inevitable.

Fascism was the living refutation of the orthodox Marxist doctrine. Fascism happened above all because the hierarchies within capitalism are more complex than those created by class interests alone. Deeper than all specific class antagonisms is a human antagonism: the desire for freedom, tempered by the fear of freedom whenever it approaches.

In some people the fear of freedom is stronger than the desire for it. When they decide to defend capitalism through fascism they are not doing so as the 'agents' of capitalists, or even because they like capitalism. They are doing it because *they fear the end of class society and hierarchy in general*. They fear freedom.

Marxism acknowledged the economic role of the family as the basis for all exploitation; it recognized and fought women's oppression and it attacked the hypocrisy of nineteenth-century paternalistic morality. But it gave no account of how the oppression of women and children shapes the subconscious ideology that validates capitalism for all of us.

As a result, said Reich, while the Nazis ranted to large crowds about 'blood and soil', using symbols, clothing, imagery and desire as weapons, the communist leaders could only stand at a rival lectern, reading out the unemployment statistics to the unemployed.

For those who feared freedom, there were strong grounds for doing so. The great wave of strikes, mutinies, factory occupations, land occupations, and armed insurrections and revolutions at the end of the First World War was the biggest outbreak of freedom the capitalist world had witnessed.

Many were, inevitably, frightened by it. Middle-class people did not want to be subsumed into the working class, and they refused to abandon the important material things which gave their lives meaning, from the family motor car to the nation state itself. The long rearguard action of the nineteenth-century conservatives against liberalism, democracy and science mutated suddenly into fascism, launching a 'revolution against the revolution'. That was not in the script for orthodox Marxism. But we, experiencing this phenomenon for the second time, must write it into ours.

Until the 1970s, the Marxist understanding of ideology was unsophisticated. The general ideology justifying capitalism in people's heads was thought to be produced in two locations: passively and spontaneously through work and everyday life, while the elite's monopoly over the spread of information (through the media, universities, the church, etc.) reinforced the ideology actively, from above.

When Karl Mannheim drew a distinction, in 1929, between passive, spontaneous ideologies and active, utopian ones like fascism, and suggested that Marxism itself had become an ideology for the German working class, dozens of critical articles in the socialist press attacked his view.[46] But his insight was correct.

It is futile to try to trace the ideology of fascism to the economic position of the twentieth-century middle class, just as it would be impossible to trace the ideology of the Proud Boys or Identitarian movement to the specifics of middle-class life in the 2020s. Yes, a large number of people indicted for the Capitol Hill riot, for example, are ex-military, or small-business owners. But it would be ludicrous to try to identify that class position as the cause of their behaviour. Nor do we need, as Reich did, to look for susceptibility to fascism through the prism of the nineteenth-century family, or people with specific sexualities.

The much more basic truth is this: human society has been based on hierarchy and oppression for 40,000 years. Part of that hierarchy is based on the economics of ownership and control; another, overlapping part is based on gender, racial and sexual oppression; yet another part is socially constructed around biological and behavioural differences, like the right-wing obsession about Alpha and Beta males.

Put plainly, some people like these hierarchies. They tend to be the people who benefit from them. That's what put thousands of white working-class men into London's Parliament Square to defend a statue of Winston Churchill. It's what makes some women join the far-right 'TradWives' movement, accepting systematic gender oppression in return for status within a broader movement for white supremacy. And it's what made people storm the US Capitol.

Marxism failed in the 1920s and 30s because it didn't have concepts that could describe this emergent reality. What follows is an attempt to synthesize these insights into a theoretical summary.

FASCISM: A SUMMARY

Fascism is the product of a social disintegration process that begins when capitalism enters an acute, prolonged economic crisis, and when an ideology that is usually reproduced passively ceases to explain the world, for large numbers of people at once.

The turn to fascism is triggered when a group that is supposed to be subservient suddenly gains power and agency, and begins to revolt in ways that actually embody freedom, and show what it might look like.

Fascism mobilizes a subconscious fear of that freedom, a fear that is embedded in the deep structures of class society, through exploitation, the family, racial and even biological hierarchies.

Those most susceptible to this fear, and fascism's most likely converts, include: those with no clear, future-oriented identity; those who believe their status is reliant on stopping other people achieving freedom, for example white racists and violent misogynists; religious fundamentalists whose beliefs are entirely moulded around hierarchy; and people for whom violence and repression are already a way of life (e.g. the classic ex-serviceperson or military fantasist).

Once they sense they can no longer rely on the capitalist elite, its

state apparatus, or its passive ideology to hold the line against progress, those susceptible to fascism begin their 'revolution against the
revolution'. Though its function is to defend capitalism, its ultimate
intention (always explicit both in theory and ritual) is to go further:
to end society's reliance on rational thought, stop progress and reverse
human history back to a pre-modern, pre-Enlightenment state.

Fascists adopt methods designed to force a violent rupture, whether
in pursuit of national rebirth (as in the 1920s) or the global ethnic
civil war (as in the present). In preparation for this moment, their
actions become violent, symbolic and ritualized.

To replace the passive ideology of capitalism, fascists actively co-
create a new kind of active ideology based on racism, male dominance,
dehumanization and violence, with a strong internal logic but no
necessary connection to the facts. This ideology operates both as a
myth and an *ethos* – a code for what's right and wrong, which fascists
can be rewarded for following even before they reach their goal.

Because it is not anchored in facts, or in a single sociological class,
fascism at the movement stage is unstable. It must react to all setbacks
by bolting on new explanations, new conspiracy theories, targeting
new enemies and regaining momentum. If it cannot, then on the basis
of the failed fascisms of the 1930s – in Britain and the USA for
example – it dissolves back towards its constituent parts: authoritarian conservatism, nationalism, religious radicalism, folk-racism and
misogyny.

Where it gains power, fascism inherits the capitalist economy in its
existing form. There is no specifically fascist economic model. From
the historical evidence, fascism then has to push whichever economic
model it inherits towards a project of war and conquest. Because
dehumanization is the centrepiece of its ideology, as fascism radical-
izes and mobilizes for war, it begins to think about and prepare for
genocide, if for no other reasons than those advocated by Carl
Schmitt: it needs enemies and it cannot tolerate difference.

Fascism is neither the direct 'agent of the bourgeoisie' nor even its
autonomous proxy. Fascism's defence of capitalism serves only to
defend the bigger phenomenon of *all class society, all inequality, all
hierarchy and all forms of oppression* against the prospect of human
freedom. It is, in this sense, a movement against the potential for

self-liberation. It is, as Ernst Jünger's machine fantasies reveal, always *radically anti-humanist*.

As a result, where it fails, it will attempt to destroy everything, including itself. At all stages, from Hitler's bunker to today's lone shooters, suicide – single or mass – forms part of the logical structure of fascism. I will explore this further in the final chapter.

Fascism is compelled to attack all ideologies embraced by those fighting for freedom. Where Marxism becomes the dominant liberation theology, as in the early twentieth century, 'fascism is anti-Marxism' (Nolte). Where it cannot find Marxism, it is obliged to invent it, as in today's paranoia over 'cultural Marxism'. In both iterations it has identified and dehumanized specific social groups as 'carriers' of Marxism (Jews in Germany, 'social justice warriors', LGBTQ+ people, feminists, etc. today).

Fascism is, in summary, the fear of freedom triggered by a glimpse of freedom.

Once it gains momentum, fascism can only be defeated by state action combined with a popular mobilization by groups likely to be victimized under a fascist regime. Though liberalism and the left cannot abandon their defence of rationality and democratic institutions, they can (within limits) construct a dramatized, symbolic politics of their own.

COMPONENTS OF THE FASCIST PROCESS

In 'The Five Stages of Fascism' (1998) the historian Robert Paxton argued that rather than static, isolated definitions, academics need 'to study fascism in motion, paying more attention to processes than essences'.[47] Instead of compiling a list of similarities, he said, we should focus on the differences between fascist movements, states and ideologies.

To facilitate this, Paxton identified the five stages fascism went through in the interwar period: the creation of movements; their entry into the party political system; the ascent to power; the regime; and finally the point at which they either radicalize while in power (towards war and genocide), or collapse in the direction of 'normal' dictatorships.

Paxton is alive to the problem of abstraction. If we write down a five-stage process there is a danger that it, too, becomes an 'ideal type' – a model of fascism that never existed in reality.

The way to avoid this, he said, is through a *functional definition* of fascism: that is, by summarizing what fascism *does*, rather than what it *is*. Fascism, Paxton wrote in 2004:

> may be defined as a form of political behaviour marked by obsessive preoccupation with community decline, humiliation, or victimhood and by compensatory cults of unity, energy and purity, in which a mass-based party of committed nationalist militants, working in uneasy but effective collaboration with traditional elites, abandons democratic liberties and pursues with redemptive violence and without ethical or legal restraints, goals of internal cleansing and external expansion.[48]

It should be immediately obvious how relevant Paxton's definition is for those resisting fascism today, and how much more useful than all the others. Paxton's work stands head and shoulders above every other contribution to the 'definition wars' for this reason. It aptly describes the panoply of groups active on the American far right, the Identitarian movements in Europe and – critically – how they collaborate with traditional elites.

Paxton describes fascism not as a movement, or party, or religion, but as a kind of 'political behaviour': people can take part in such behaviour who are not fully signed up to the party, and don't wear a badge. He emphasizes the interplay between the party and its allies among the elites, rather than just the obvious conflicts. Finally, he restores something that had slipped away completely during the definition wars: the philosophy of violence.

In a prophetic summary, written more than twenty years ago, Paxton listed the questions we should ask about far-right movements:

> Are they becoming rooted as political parties that represent major interests and feelings, and wield major influence on the political scene? Is the economic or constitutional system in a state of blockage apparently

insoluble to the existing authorities? Is a rapid political mobilisation threatening to escape the control of traditional elites, to the point where they would be tempted to look for tougher helpers to stay in charge?[49]

In many countries, the answer to all of this is: 'oh shit, yes!' But the emergence of networked society poses a new question: are the fascists capable of wielding major influence without a party? And the collapse of globalization in the 2010s raises another one: is the elite itself split fundamentally over its geopolitical strategy?

In the spirit of Paxton's 'five stages' this chapter concludes with a model of the fascist process, in which Paxton's first three stages are broken down into ten smaller 'components'. They don't need to happen in the order presented, but are dependent on each other, and suggest where the process might be stopped.

1. **The Big Disruption.** To start the process that propels fascists into power, something big has to happen that disrupts the 'ordinary world', which individuals, groups and institutions have taken for granted. In Italy's case it was the First World War; it transformed the peasantry, shattered the confidence of liberalism, empowered and radicalized the working class and created a multilayered sense of loss. In Germany it was the economic slump following the Wall Street Crash.

    For us the Big Disruption is the 2008 crisis and its aftermath, combined with the scale of the social transformation needed to mitigate climate change.

2. **The Big Threat.** On top of a big event, there has to be a large, persistent and unmistakable perceived threat, around which the latent fears and prejudices of those susceptible to the fear of freedom can be mobilized. In Italy's case it was the Comintern. In Germany it was unmistakably 'the Jew' – the abstract, generalized image of an entire people. At half a million people, Germany's Jewish population constituted just 0.75 per cent of the country's citizens in 1933. But in populist right-wing culture their existence had become intertwined with broader and more significant

'threats': international finance, cultural modernity, 'mass society' and Marxism. Hitler mobilized these fears with precision when, in *Mein Kampf,* he wrote:

> Marxism is the pure essence of the Jew's attempts to eliminate the importance of character in every aspect of human life and replace it with the numerical power of the masses.[50]

In our time the perceived Big Threats driving fascism are black civil rights, migration, Islam and feminism. We will explore in the next chapter how that changes the way we need to resist.

3. **An oppressed group rises.** A third trigger for the fascist process, highly relevant for today, is that a segment of the population that is supposed to be passive has to become suddenly rebellious, overthrowing the deep-rooted hierarchies that underpinned their expected behaviour at local level. In Italy this was the peasantry. There is no exact parallel in Germany, but the emergence of a new, rebellious and subversive culture among working-class youth, and its alignment with the KPD, worked on the anxieties of right-wing voters in a similar way.

   In our time the oppressed group rising includes black people, migrants, women and young people. The #MeToo, #BlackLivesMatter and Fridays for the Future movements represent a demand for freedom by people who, in the minds of everyone to the right of mainstream conservatism, are not supposed to be free, or to possess their current level of influence and voice.

4. **The Culture War.** To the interwar left, the idea that disagreements over cultural values could divide the working class looked impossible: working-class culture was solid. Nevertheless, acute observers such as the anarchist Luigi Fabbri warned of the political cost of all the cultural hostility expressed by working-class people towards the lower middle class. In Germany, too, the moderate wing of the SPD increasingly bemoaned the hostility shown by their

largely manual (and therefore male-dominated) mass base towards the emerging class of clerical (and more often female) workers.

Today, as I will explore in Chapter 9, the working class is much more heavily divided by cultural conflict. The conclusions we should draw from the Italian and German experience are obvious: if there is a social force that represents progress, deeply attached to its own conceptions of justice, solidarity and fairness, it needs to build alliances with other social forces who do not share those conceptions, and to avoid needless cultural friction with them.

5. **A single fascist party.** To move from the periphery to power there must be an identifiable and legal fascist party, oriented to achieving political power, with some form of allied paramilitary group. Though this seems a no-brainer, it is a crucial point. If the German far right had been as fractious and incoherent as the far-right militias, Proud Boys and Boogaloos in the USA today, they could never have made the electoral breakthrough of September 1930. Keeping fascist movements divided, off-kilter and suppressed is a strategy that worked well in the countries where fascism failed, and should be pursued today. Unfortunately, however, fascism is cognizant of this weakness, and has proved capable of colonizing populist and conservative parties, as with the US Republican Party.

6. **Middle-class panic.** In both Italy and Germany, the moment when fascism began to mobilize serious numbers from the middle class was pivotal. In both cases, panic about the Big Threat/Big Other energized middle-class people to embrace a radical antidote, casting aside all reticence at being associated with a movement based on organized violence.

In the twenty-first century, where class distinctions are overlaid by cultural rivalries, the psychological traits that were once associated with the urban middle class – volatility, individualism, respect for authority and a preference for charismatic leaders – have cascaded down into the lives of working-class people and the urban poor.

An episode of middle-class panic today, parallel to the one that drove Hitler's electoral breakthrough in 1930, would look more like a 'panic of the unorganized', and might resemble the anti-mask, anti-vaxx and QAnon demos staged in 2020, though at a much more massive scale. Once such a panic becomes a mass phenomenon, that is the critical moment, and it requires all fascism's opponents to change their tactics and narrative to stop a fascist political breakthrough.

7. **The rule of law is eroded.** A critical turning point for all successful fascisms comes when a section of the elite gives up on the rule of law. In the name of defending order, the police begin to turn a blind eye to fascist violence; the newspapers blame 'both extremes'; senior politicians – having voiced their disappointment at the violence – begin expressing moral support for the fascist squads. The combination of uniformed militias, the fragmentation of the state's repressive apparatus and the politicization of the army high command were crucial to the success of both Italian fascism and Nazism. No mass movement on its own can resist this; the anti-fascists have to fight for a majority in the legislature and defend the rule of law.

8. **Progressives are paralysed.** A further condition for fascist success is that, amid rising violence and intimidation by the far right, the mass of progressive people remain inactive and on the defensive, wedded to their traditional forms of organization, clinging to ideologies that no longer explain the world, sitting on social gains they assume are irreversible.

This, unfortunately, is a condition clearly replicated today. The trade unions and social-democratic parties are weaker than in the interwar years, and the wider, cultural progressive forces – the readers of *Le Monde*, the *New York Times* and *Guardian,* plus academia and the culture industries – seem paralysed by the populist and extremist right. Even after the Capitol Hill riot, and with rising electoral support for figures such as Marine Le Pen in

France, much of liberalism is – at time of writing – in a state of denial about the seriousness of the threat.

9. **Right-wing populism fails.** Both Italy and Germany had populist right-wing forces that could have channelled people's energies away from fascism, but failed. Italy had Gabriele d'Annunzio and his blueshirt movement, fresh from the illegal occupation of Fiume; Germany had the DNVP and its leader, the rabidly nationalist newspaper magnate Alfred Hugenberg. In the machinations of mainstream politicians these populists – then as now – were supposed to act as a firewall against full-blown fascism. But just as today, the firewall caught fire. When it mattered, such parties and leaders were not the antidote to fascism but the gateway drug.

   Any idea that parties like Viktor Orbán's Fidesz, Salvini's Lega Nord or the post-Trump Republican Party can act as a reliable barrier to outright fascism has to be swiftly abandoned.

10. **The elite goes fascist.** At some stage, the most powerful people in the country – the owners of capital and the managers of major industries – have to make a conscious choice: to hand power to the fascists in order to 'contain' them and suppress the left.

    Mussolini was able to force that choice on the liberals through relentless violence. In Germany, where liberalism was chronically weak, it was more like a process of elimination: the business elite and their aristocratic allies worked their way through every possible alternative to Hitler before concluding that there was none.

    Today we are a long way from that. But the ease with which elements of Wall Street and Silicon Valley flipped to Trump, and championed Bolsonaro, or the fascist-led coup in Bolivia in 2019, can leave us with no confidence in their reaction to a future far-right upsurge. For all the MBAs they hold, and all their ostentatious giving to charity, the modern bourgeoisie contains just as many people who would put on an SS uniform, if given the chance, as the German elite did in 1933.

Faced with the first three components of the fascist process – big disruption, big threat and the rising of the oppressed – there is little that left or progressive parties can do other than stake out clear alternatives. Items 4, 5 and 6 are where strategy matters. Avoiding the culture war or fighting it intelligently, breaking up and de-platforming fascism before it coalesces into a single force, and responding to mass panic with a clear alternative narrative, are the 'middle game' in the anti-fascist struggle. Once you are reliant on the state and the elite alone to hold the line, history suggests you are close to losing.

Fascism has to be stopped at the breakthrough stage. The experience of France in the mid-1930s shows that it was done once and can be done again.

8

Militant Democracy 2.0

We Need a New Popular Front

'The country is in danger. Be ready all members and youth sections!' That's how French fascism announced its intent to overthrow the government on 6 February 1934. After a month of street violence, it looked like the far right's time had come:

> Your parliament is corrupt. Your politicians discredited. Your country dragged in the quagmire of scandal. Your security threatened. Civil War is imminent . . . [1]

If it sounds like the alt-right bulletin boards in the run-up to the Capitol Hill attack, that's because the fascist assault on the French parliament in 1934 is the closest parallel we have to what Trump's supporters were trying to do.

In Paris, by early evening, thousands of right-wing paramilitaries, students and war veterans were on the streets, determined to overthrow a centre-left government. At the Place de la Concorde, a vast public square just over the river from the French parliament, the crowd made concerted attempts to storm the bridge. Others already across the river tried to break into the chamber. The police, facing a barrage of cobblestones, lumps of asphalt and iron railings, panicked and opened fire, killing fourteen protesters.[2]

The French far right had been splintered into rival leagues and groupings; now they came together with a common cause. *Solidarité Française*, a fascist militia in blue shirts, led the storming of the bridge; large numbers were mobilized by *Croix de Feu* (Cross of Fire), a veterans' group that had morphed into a uniformed fascist movement; and a contingent from the official war veterans' association also got drawn into the fighting.

Though it failed in the attempt to storm parliament, the demo – and the rioting that spilled out across Paris that night – succeeded in its primary aim: the government resigned the next day, to be replaced by a right-wing administration. For the first time in modern history, an elected French government was brought down by street violence. Parliamentary politics were temporarily stabilized but this was a breakthrough moment for the far right. *Croix de Feu* grew from 35,000 members on the eve of the trouble to 150,000 six months later.[3]

The background to the crisis was, as in Germany, the Depression following the Wall Street Crash. Since 1932 France had been run by the Radical Party, a left-leaning liberal party. Yet its government was committed to the same programme of austerity that Brüning had inflicted on Germany, with similar results: 14 per cent unemployment, falling prices, pension cuts and a double-digit decline in real wages.[4] Like the German SPD, the Socialist Party (known by its initials SFIO) had adopted a policy of 'toleration' for this austerity programme, in order to keep the right out of power.

The spark for the 6 February riot was not poverty, however, but corruption. Numerous Radical politicians had been implicated in a financial scandal centring on the Jewish businessman Alexandre Stavisky, who committed suicide as police moved to arrest him. Amid cover-ups, sackings and rumours that Stavisky had been shot to protect the powerful, the parliamentary right and the fascist right converged around the single slogan: 'Down with the thieves!'

After the bloodbath of 6 February, the far right had a victim narrative, political momentum, a flood of new members and growing support among the French elite. The two major parties of the left – the SFIO and the French Communist Party (PCF) – were weak, and divided by the same issues that had split the German left. The scene was set, it seemed, for another European democracy to fall. Yet it didn't.

What turned the tide was the realization, by millions of people, that in order to stop fascism they needed to try something new. Not just new tactics or slogans but *a new strategy, a new political programme and a new political culture.*

One of the first to do so was an egotistical bully called Jacques Doriot, the communist mayor of the tough Parisian suburb of St Denis. As he watched the fighting on 6 February, Doriot sensed the danger: 'Those who lived through the demonstrations of Tuesday and Wednesday,' he wrote, 'will long remember the extraordinary dynamism of that crowd, its hunger for action. What a lesson for revolutionary organisations.'[5]

Ironically, Doriot would, within three years, convert to fascism himself, and would later collaborate with the Nazi occupation of France. His character fitted precisely the stereotype Fromm had found in Germany: the 'authoritarian rebel'. But in 1934 he was a dissident communist with a big mouth and a cult following. Physically imposing, 'Big Jacques' had risen through the ranks of the PCF to become its most charismatic member of parliament in the mid-1920s. But after Stalin imposed the 'social fascism' line in 1928, Doriot led a rebellion and was sidelined. Now he saw a chance to regain his place in the party hierarchy.

In defiance of the PCF leadership, Doriot formed a local 'anti-fascist vigilance committee' in St Denis, consisting of eight communists and five socialists. Through it, he mobilized for a large, illegal anti-fascist demonstration in Paris on 9 February. The police again attacked the demo, with Doriot in the thick of the fighting. Six people were killed and the political crisis escalated.[6] When the socialist trade unions called a general strike for 12 February, and scheduled a mass demonstration in Paris, it was Doriot who pressured the PCF to join the strike – though they ordered their members to stage a rival demo, separate from the official one.

Fortunately, the workers of Paris had other ideas. On the night of the 12th, as the rival communist and socialist demonstrations converged, after a brief moment of uncertainty, 'to the astonishment of the party and union leaders', they rushed into each other's arms, chanting 'Unity! Unity!'[7]

In a single moment, years of futile sectarianism were blown away – and not just in Paris. Some 346 towns staged anti-fascist protests that night; in eighty-six of them joint anti-fascist committees had been formed, fifteen with the participation of the Radical Party. And these were not talking shops. In St Denis, Doriot's committee set up local self-defence squads, installed an anti-fascist defence group in every factory, and set up an inter-factory conference to coordinate the strike.

The Comintern was outraged. This sudden outbreak of collaboration between communists and socialists was not the work of one person, but Doriot was its figurehead. He was ordered to desist, and travel to Moscow to explain himself. Sensing this might turn out to be a one-way journey, he refused, and instead published a defiant open letter to Stalin. In it, he called for a united anti-fascist movement, drawing in not only communists, socialists and the working class, but also the peasants and the urban middle class. It should, he wrote, be formed around a new programme of action, limited to basic economic reforms, in order to draw in the 'broad social layers' needed to defeat fascism.[8]

This, in its essence, was the idea that would become the Popular Front. Doriot, a one-man chaos engine, put it on the agenda. The man who turned it into a global strategy was Georgi Dimitrov.

A veteran Bulgarian communist, Dimitrov had been Stalin's representative in Berlin in the early 1930s. After Hitler's rise to power, Dimitrov was accused of starting the Reichstag Fire, and was made the subject of the first Nazi show trial. He conducted a brilliant self-defence in court, making headlines around the world by ridiculing the senior Nazis he called as witnesses, and was acquitted. On 27 February 1934 the Nazis put him on a plane to Moscow.[9]

In the weeks between Hitler's victory and the Reichstag Fire, Dimitrov had been involved in the first, tentative negotiations towards a truce between the Comintern and the world's socialist parties, grouped in the Labour and Socialist International (LSI). They'd got as far as the offer of a non-aggression pact – but there was deep mistrust on either side.

Yet by the time Dimitrov landed in Moscow, a year later, the world had changed. Not only was there a real and rising threat of fascism in France; in Austria the far-right government had declared a one-party state and launched a military crackdown against the socialists, triggering four days of armed conflict. In Spain, meanwhile, a political standoff was escalating between far-right parties and the left. It was now possible to look at a map of mainland Europe and imagine all of it under fascist or military rule.

On 4 April 1934 Dimitrov told Stalin to his face that the social fascism line was nonsense, that it had failed in Germany and would, if pursued, hand the rest of Europe over to fascism. Communists, he argued, should form an anti-fascist alliance with other left-wing parties and aim to draw in the middle classes, to defend democracy.[10]

It was a complete reversal of the strategy the Comintern had imposed in Germany. But, without offering a word of explanation or self-criticism, Stalin gave Dimitrov the green light. In May, the Soviet leadership told the French communist leader, Maurice Thorez, to request a formal electoral alliance with the SFIO and, once it was signed, ordered Thorez to begin negotiations with the Radical Party and its offshoots. In October 1934, on the eve of the Radicals' national conference, Thorez made a historic speech inviting them to join a Popular Front for 'work, freedom and peace': a comprehensive, cross-class alliance against fascism, involving a formal electoral pact between the communists, socialists and Radicals. Within a year the Popular Front would be a reality; within two it would govern France.

Moscow's political handbrake turn was driven in part by self-preservation – a re-armed fascist Europe would inevitably be hostile to the Soviet Union – and partly by the emergence of Doriot-style rebels in other communist parties. Yet it was still hesitant. Even on the eve of Thorez's appeal to the Radicals, Stalin sent a high-level delegation to ask the French leader to delay. The delegation, remembered one of its members, 'was received in an icy manner'. Thorez told them it was too late and ushered them out of the party HQ.[11]

But the emergence of the Popular Front as a mass social and cultural movement was also the product of changes within socialism and liberalism. After Hitler's victory, and the Austrian crackdown, it was clear that social-democracy had to adapt to survive. Exiled in Prague, the leadership of the German SPD were in no doubt as to the mood among their members who had stayed behind, organized in underground cells across Germany. One female activist wrote:

Here only one opinion prevails. Force can only be broken by force. And to topple the current regime in order to reinstate the democratic state of the past, for this absolutely no one can be found in Germany who would be willing to lift one finger.[12]

There would have to be a revolution against Hitler – and for that to happen, there had to be unity. From one clandestine cell after another, the party received messages calling for a tactical alliance with the communists. Some even urged the creation of a united party 'as the melting pot for all forces combating Hitler's dictatorship'. In Dortmund, activists from both parties circulated a common united front leaflet in the factories and mines.[13]

In response, the exiled SPD leadership issued a manifesto, committing the party to a revolution against Nazism and the destruction of the Nazi state. As a result, the SPD's concept of democracy also changed. The new German state would be purged of Nazis and their sympathizers, and the pro-Nazi corporations would be nationalized.[14]

'Revolutionary social-democracy' seemed a contradiction in terms, but in the mid-1930s many socialist thinkers had this same idea at once. And though in 1936 the SPD's underground networks were destroyed by mass arrests, the idea of a united democratic movement against fascism had permeated the European left. Because while the German-speaking left were discussing the revolution in theory, Spanish socialists had been preparing for one in reality.

In 1931 the military dictatorship that had ruled Spain for a decade fell apart, together with the monarchy it upheld. Though the Spanish Socialist Workers' Party (PSOE) took part in the first republican government, its activists were moving leftwards fast and agitating for more radical action. In the general election of November 1933, the right won overwhelmingly, partly because the anarchists abstained, and partly because fascist, monarchist and authoritarian groups formed a single electoral alliance, known as CEDA, to game the voting system. Though the president refused to give CEDA any ministerial posts, reserving them for the mainstream right, everyone knew it was only a matter of time before the fascists forced their way into government.

The socialists had no intention of allowing the Spanish republic to go the way of Germany. In January 1934 they formed their own united front, consisting of the PSOE, the 30,000-strong Communist Party and a left-wing youth organization. They set up a joint network of revolutionary committees and cells, following strict military discipline, and stockpiled weapons for the inevitable day of reckoning.

On 5 October 1934, when CEDA was finally invited into government, the trade unions called a general strike; the next day the PSOE launched an armed insurrection. In Barcelona, Catalan nationalists declared their own autonomous republic. But the revolt was quickly defeated. Only in the northern mining region of Asturias did the left hold out, fending off the army for two weeks – after which the army responded with executions, torture and mass arrests.

This dress rehearsal for the Spanish Civil War was a failure, but it spurred on the French socialists in their efforts to form an anti-fascist alliance. First in Austria, now in Spain, a mainstream socialist party had been forced into armed struggle against the right. The ideological walls that had divided the left were crumbling.

While the socialist parties were moving left, so too was French liberalism. In March 1934, leading thinkers formed the Anti-fascist Vigilance Committee of the Intellectuals (CVIA). Though its prime movers were from the left, its star attraction was the celebrity philosopher Émile Chartier, known by the pseudonym 'Alain'. Alain, with his signature waxed moustache, occupied a position in French society equivalent to a major YouTube influencer today. Through his lectures and newspaper columns he had single-handedly defined the politics of the Radical Party: against war, monarchy and religion, and for freedom. His concept of freedom was classically liberal, based on private property and individual rights. But his theory of democracy asserted that parliaments had to be kept in check by the legitimate threat of a popular revolution. Revolution, he said, is the great 'controller' of democratic states.[15]

Though he never attended a single CVIA meeting, Alain's support for the initiative gave it massive grassroots impetus, even as the political machinery of the parties struggled to get into gear. On 4 March 1934, in an appeal headlined *To the Workers*, the CVIA expressed both the extreme danger and the possibilities inherent in the new situation:

Comrades, under the guise of national revolution, a new Middle Ages
is being prepared for us. We must not preserve the world as it is; we
must transform it, delivering the state from domination by large-scale
capital and doing so in close collaboration with the workers . . . [16]

Today we would recognize the CVIA as a 'social movement' – but
in the 1930s, with the heavily demarcated culture of party lines and
hierarchical discipline, it looked completely new. And it caught on
rapidly. In the single province of Languedoc, forty-seven local
branches of it were formed that spring. The department of Lot et
Garonne registered seventy-four groups, almost always drawing in
activists from the Radical Party and usually led by schoolteachers.

And it was in this milieu, long before the formal agreement between
the parties, that community activists fashioned the most effective
tools to defeat fascism: a network of grassroots committees; a cross-
party electoral pact; a limited programme for government and a mass
anti-fascist culture.

By 1935, the fascist *Croix de Feu* and its front organizations could
claim 228,000 members. It was, like the Nazis during their initial
surge, recruiting mainly among conservative middle-class voters. Its
principal activities were uniformed parades, car convoys, large-scale,
militarized squad mobilizations and soup kitchens for the poor. Its
strategy was the end of the parliamentary republic by means of a coup,
which its leaders labelled 'H-Hour' and spread constant rumours that
it was imminent.[17]

In response, activists in the CVIA called a mass anti-fascist demonstration in Paris for 14 July 1935, Bastille Day. Since the communists
had spent the past decade denouncing the tricolour and refusing to
sing the 'Marseillaise', the symbolism was immense. Under pressure
from their members the Radicals joined the organizing committee,
which by the time of the demo included forty-eight separate parties,
unions and cultural organizations.

Between a quarter and half a million people marched on that day.
At a huge rally, the crowd took a collective oath to 'disarm and dissolve' the fascist militias and to defend democracy. Crucially, the
staging of the event was designed to reclaim the cultural symbols of

French nationalism, which – just as today – the right believed were their sole property: Joan of Arc, the tricolour, the national anthem and support for the armed forces. Even the communists could now sign up to this because, in response to Hitler's rearmament programme, Stalin had publicly endorsed France's right to self-defence.

The rally's organizing committee evolved into a permanent cross-party leadership body. Just as important was the network of grassroots committees which sprang up beneath it at local and district level: the CVIA groups, cultural centres, writers' associations, film clubs and local formations of the Popular Front. The official party leaderships had scant control over their activities.

Now the CVIA and the trade unions set about writing a new political programme, around which the Radicals, socialists and communists could form an electoral pact. The concrete demands were obvious: an end to wage cuts and public spending cuts, state control of the wheat market to boost farmers' prices, a shorter working week and a programme of state-led investment. How to pay for them was less obvious.

Though other major countries had abandoned the Gold Standard, France still rigidly pegged its currency to gold, limiting the government's ability to borrow and spend. The result was deflation. In theory, once wages and prices fell to a certain level, workers would be rehired, and farmers would find a market for their unsold wheat. Though the British liberal economist John Maynard Keynes had debunked this idea, it was deeply rooted in the Radical Party's ideology.

But as they saw the non-Gold countries recover, key Radical politicians were converted to a state-led solution: borrowing millions of francs from the central bank and quitting the Gold Standard. In January 1936 the Radical Party signed up to the programme of the Popular Front. Both the socialist and communist parties had effectively shelved their most radical demands. In return they created an electoral alliance with limited aims, but which could defend democracy and suppress fascism. But their working-class supporters had more ambitious ideas.

For, in addition to its committee and its programme, the Popular Front had become a mass cultural movement. Its attraction to artists and intellectuals was obvious. For Goebbels had promised to wipe the year 1789 from history: the rationalist, liberal principles of the Enlightenment, along with freedom of scientific exploration and artistic expression, were all under threat.[18] Jazz, modernist painting and experimental theatre were by now banned in Nazi Germany.

As in our time, few mainstream intellectuals relished fighting a culture war. But once it was under way, many allied themselves openly with the Popular Front, and began to produce work inspired by it. One of the most significant examples was Jean Renoir's film *Life Belongs to Us* (1936), commissioned and funded by the communists. Made by a collective of directors and technicians, mostly working for free, the film is a mixture of documentary and drama, showing real footage of the fascist riot on 6 February 1934, and of the 1935 Bastille Day parade. A speech by Hitler is overdubbed with a barking dog, and *Croix de Feu* parades are intercut with footage of SS soldiers marching. But in the middle of it all there is gritty social drama, in the style that would make Renoir's name as a mature director: a working-class family in crisis, bullying in the workplace, the misery of unemployment.

For all its jump cuts and technical crudeness, *Life Belongs to Us* is a highly accurate account of the road French popular consciousness travelled between 1934 and 1936 – from fear and despair to joy, relaxation and confidence. The film's protagonist is not one individual but the whole French people. For those who saw it (it was denied a commercial release), it was like taking a collective look in the mirror and seeing someone more cheerful than you expected.

The Italian historian Enzo Traverso writes that, under the threat of fascism, the anti-fascist movements of the mid-1930s created 'a European public space defined by cultural, ethical and political frontiers'. Networks of émigrés and refugees carried the experience of the Popular Front across borders, and the Comintern's adoption of the strategy globally in 1935 did the rest: 'Against the fascist political religion of force,' writes Traverso, 'antifascism championed the civil religion of humanity, democracy and socialism.'[19]

Everything in French life was now defined by your attitude to fascism: for or against. Even the tiniest street-corner bar would contain signifiers: the playbills and nightclub flyers posted on the walls, the

lyrics of the songs being sung, the newspapers and illustrated magazines people chose to read, and the political buzzwords being exchanged
across the tables. And just as in today's networked social movements,
people made connections: the faces you recognized on the demonstrations became faces in the bar, the cinema club, the local committee, the
self-defence group. The historian Julian Jackson describes the effect:

> Gradually there was a transition from demonstration as protest to
> demonstration as celebration. Demonstrations became family outings:
> the number of women and children participants increased. The work-
> ing class inhabited the street as it was to inhabit the factories – as much
> to assert a presence as to make specific demands. Politics became a
> pageant.[20]

In January 1936, events began that would put the Popular Front into
power, both in France and Spain. In Paris, the Radicals pulled their
support for the pro-austerity government of the right and took interim
control themselves, scheduling an election for April of that year. In
Madrid, with elections set for February, a Popular Front was established along French lines, including communists, socialists, liberal
republicans, nationalists from both Galicia and Catalonia, and an
anarchist trade union federation.

In each country both the liberals and the left understood they were
at the turning point of the decade. Either they would form an electoral alliance, despite their differences, and take power; or an alliance
of conservatism, monarchism and the far right would take power and
finish off democracy.

On 16 February 1936, in an election marred by violence and voter
suppression on both sides, the Spanish Popular Front defeated the
fascist-aligned CEDA. The country had split in half: the Popular
Front squeaked into power with a majority of less than 100,000 out
of 9.5 million votes. The new government banned the main fascist
organization, the Falange, and began a purge of fascist officers from
the army. A wave of political murders, beatings and arson attacks by
both sides plunged Spain into chaos, with both sides warning of a
civil war.

Less than three months later, on 3 May 1936, the Popular Front won a decisive victory in the French general election, gaining 57 per cent of the vote, with the communists making the biggest gains. Leon Blum – the Jewish leader of the SFIO – became prime minister; the communists refused to take up ministerial posts and so Blum handed the most important ministries to the Radicals. But here too the situation spiralled beyond the control of politicians.

In the month between the election and the new government taking office, workers in the metal industry occupied their factories, demanding union recognition, wage rises and the forty-hour week. Soon the strikes spread to department stores, automobile plants and newspapers. By the time Blum took power on 5 June half a million workers were on strike. By 7 June there were 2 million. The owners of the major industries, who had been planning to resist the legislative programme of the Popular Front, capitulated. Overnight they were forced to sign a written national agreement for the forty-hour week, an unprecedented two weeks' paid holiday, wage rises between 7 and 15 per cent, and union recognition. The strikes were ended only when the communists ordered people back to work – and even then with difficulty.

In this month of strikes and factory occupations, the cultural force built up over the previous two years burst out across French society. More than 600,000 people marched across Paris on 14 July 1936 to celebrate not just the election victory, but the real and tangible reforms that were cascading out of the French parliament. The *Croix de Feu*, together with all other uniformed far-right leagues, was banned and dissolved. To mark the first paid holidays in French history, the government issued cheap railway tickets and organized special trains to the seaside for working-class families.

In a novel depicting that ecstatic summer, the communist writer Ilya Ehrenburg describes the moment when reality hit. A young Parisian couple arrives in a Breton fishing village, their heads still full of the chants and slogans of the occupation movement. The ocean calms them down; they barely bother to read the papers. Then, on the radio, in the fourth item after the results of a bicycle race, the announcer reads:

In Barcelona the hotel Columbus was bombarded with cannon-fire. In Madrid troops loyal to the government, together with the workers, have driven the rebels from the La Montaña barracks ... At Burgos, mass executions have begun ... [21]

On 17 July the Spanish Army, led by General Franco, had launched an uprising against the Popular Front government. The Spanish Civil War had begun.

It is fashionable on the modern left to condemn the Popular Front strategy as a failure. On almost every left website you can find articles claiming the Popular Front was 'a bad idea' or 'didn't work' or 'betrayed the masses'. In almost every case the authors are obliged to ignore the obvious truth: without a Popular Front there would have been no left government in either France or Spain in 1936.

In Spain, the Popular Front's victory provoked a civil war which the liberals were unprepared to fight, and in some places a social revolution – which the communists soon showed they were prepared to suppress. To keep the liberals happy, and to avoid upsetting Britain and France, Stalin ordered the Spanish communists to resist the demands of anarchist and far-left workers and peasants for radical social change, enforcing the decision through brutal purges carried out by his own secret police.

In France, after its initial flurry of legislation, Blum's government announced a 'pause' in February 1937, and a partial reversal of its radical measures. It had delivered rights for the workers but was struggling to deliver jobs and growth without a comprehensive economic plan. By June the tensions between the Radicals' desire for moderation and the workers' desire for change was too great. Blum resigned, handing power to the Radicals, and by January 1938 all remaining socialist ministers were sacked.

Despite their ultimate failure, the Popular Fronts are the only historical example of democracies effectively defending themselves against a significant fascist threat. Only through civil war, military intervention and invasion did fascism eventually conquer Spain and France. So even in our own vastly different circumstances we can learn important lessons from the Popular Front.

The first lesson is: *anti-fascist self-defence is not enough*. In February 1934 the French Communist Party, with a membership of 30,000, could probably have kept the fascist squads out of places like St Denis. But once fascism achieves an electoral breakthrough among farmers and the urban middle class, no amount of men with knuckle-dusters can stand in its way. It needs a mass political alliance, and – despite the machine politics of their leaders – the French workers created one from below.

The second lesson is: *parties have to make formal agreements.* From the mass demonstrations to the formation of a government, party activists forced their leaders to sit down in a room with their rivals, negotiate and sign pieces of paper. They understood that, faced with a real and serious fascist threat, the petty rivalries and tribalism that are normal in a stable democracy should go out of the window.

Third, and crucially: *any formal alliance will involve trade-offs.* The left postpones some of its more radical anti-capitalist policies and stops targeting liberals as Enemy Number One. The liberals have to give the labour and social movements a space to operate within, and to actually defend democracy rather than allowing a drift to authoritarian rule. As the French workers found out, it is easier to occupy a factory and force the boss to grant a forty-hour week if that demand is also in the government's manifesto.

But compromise is painful. Both in France and Spain, the communists became utterly determined to prevent either the strikes (in France) or the war (in Spain) from spilling over into a social revolution which had been their stated aim for decades. It was the French communist leader, Thorez, who brought an end to the occupation movement of June 1936. And as the price of unity, the PCF did more than sing the 'Marseillaise', they abandoned their long-standing support for colonial independence movements. In Spain, the communists resisted peasant land seizures and imposed military discipline on the far left, torturing and murdering their anarchist and Trotskyist rivals.

For these reasons, says the orthodox left account of the Popular Front, the strategy of self-limitation led to defeat. But that is only true if you believe a full-blown workers' revolution was on the cards. In Spain it was a possibility during the first eleven months of the civil war; in France – with every party of the new government determined to stop one – it was highly unlikely. Today, if you can name me a country where workers' revolution is imminent, or where there is a socialist party strong enough to defeat fascism on its own, I will gladly sideline the idea of a Popular Front to defeat fascism in that country. Until then, the Popular Front remains highly relevant in the places where fascism is a threat, where the left is weak, and where liberalism is wavering.

Because the fourth lesson is: *Popular Fronts have to be created from below*. In the expanded political space created through grassroots mobilization, the French working class seized what it wanted most, namely control: of the factories, of public space and of culture. Though the formal party agreements were important, the real breakthrough came via the informal merger of 'high' and mass culture, and the coming together of intellectuals, middle-class people and workers on the streets. Networks of popular committees, beyond the control of parties, activating people in pursuit of their own freedoms, are indispensable if the Popular Front tactic is to work.

Finally, the Popular Front *found successful ways of fighting the culture war*. They understood that, once fascism appears in a working-class community, the outcome is going to depend on a battle of ideas, not appeals to shared economic misery. Since that battle would be played out in movies, novels, illustrated magazines, radio stations and tabloid newspapers, they poured their energies into controlling and, where possible, creating these media.

The most important achievement of the Popular Front is obvious: the mass mobilization of people across rigid class boundaries to take control of their own destiny, and design a different future.

The German Jewish leftist Walter Benjamin, caught up in the events in Paris, wrote that while fascism, with its parades and mysticism, had made politics aesthetic, 'communism responds by politicising art'.[22] But the working class, in fact, did something more. They too injected drama and symbolism into their political practice, and demanded the struggle against fascism be fought on the terrain of popular culture, transforming it in the process.

The ultimate precondition for success was a change in the left's strategy, not gradually but by 180 degrees, and sharply. For half a decade the left's main enemy had been liberalism and austerity, its goal socialism or nothing. Now it recognized a more dangerous enemy – fascism. It adjusted its strategy to the defence of democracy, and its rhetoric to 'popular' rather than class politics. It reclaimed the national flag and the narrative of historical greatness from the right. It allowed the working class to achieve in practice what Gramsci, in his prison cell, could only theorize: moral, intellectual and cultural leadership of the nation.

Today the fascist threat does not appear, as the *Croix de Feu* did, in ordered ranks led by an ex-army colonel. It appears in Proud Boy rallies and militia actions in US cities; it infiltrates the anti-lockdown demos staged by conspiracy theorists; it forms cells in the military and the police; it paints swastikas on Jewish graves; and then it surges to the ballot box to vote for people who promise to 'make the country great again', who victimize people of colour and stigmatize social liberalism as an alien ideology.

The only way to defeat it is both politically and culturally, through a political alliance of the centre and the left, combined with a grassroots movement and an effort to weave anti-fascism into all aspects of popular culture.

The lessons of the Popular Front were learned the hard way in the 1930s. But before we ourselves can apply them today, we need to explore the dramatically different class dynamics of the present.

CULTURE WARS, GENDER WARS

Fascism in the twenty-first century is essentially a gesture of refusal. A great human advance towards social, climate and economic justice is so obviously needed, and the means to achieve it so close at hand, that it has triggered the same response that Reich observed in the 1930s: *the fear of freedom driven by a glimpse of freedom.*

But we cannot simply transplant the tactics of the 1930s. Class identities have become fragmented; gender relationships have been transformed; and the ethnic monocultures of the mid-twentieth century are gone. Climate change has placed a ticking clock into the anti-fascist scenario, while the formal hierarchy of parties and unions has been replaced by shifting networks of activism. A mass popular alliance to defeat fascism is still possible, but it has to be built with different forces and techniques.

The most fundamental question is: who is the agent of change?

The Popular Fronts were born out of an act of compromise and political imagination by working-class parties. The working class was the prime mover. Who will stand in for that role today?

Throughout the twentieth century, the working class of the advanced world became increasingly stratified, with the creation of semi-skilled workers, the entry of women into the workforce in larger numbers, the expansion of white-collar work, and through waves of post-war immigration.

After 1945 sociologists began to map these more complicated class structures with multiple layers: classifying people according to their 'standing in society' or their specific mixture of skills and incomes.[23] Even so, the left could still argue that a single 'proletariat' existed, despite being stratified by skills and incomes.

Today, however, there is a growing divergence *within* the life experience of working people. It is based on multiple inequalities: between those with degrees and those without; between those who live in multi-ethnic cities and those who live in 'forgotten' towns; and between those with a secure job and those in precarious work. In every country where right-wing populism has advanced, it has fed on the cultural divisions between those whose identities focus inwards, to their community, and those focused outwards to the world.

On the left, some analysts now speak of two separate versions of the working class: the 'traditional' and the 'new'. Many among the so-called 'new working class', writes Claire Ainsley, an adviser to the Labour leader, Keir Starmer, 'will not define themselves primarily through their work at all. The new working class is more disparate, more atomised, and occupies multiple social identities, which makes collective identity less possible.'[24]

If our aim is to construct a broad social alliance to stop fascism, we need a theory of class that explains why these divisions over cultural values have opened up, and how they might be resolved.

Classic Marxism defines the working class as everybody who lives off their wages and doesn't own assets that generate substantial incomes. Capitalists are people who live off profits and interest, while the middle class consists of people who live off both their work and investments, for example shop owners or farmers, or people whose high professional salaries allow them to enjoy a comfortably consumerist lifestyle. For

Marxists, class is not a 'structure' but a relationship. What made the workers of Paris in 1936 'working class' was not the cloth caps they wore, or the roll-up cigarettes they smoked, but their relationship to capital: their reliance on wages and their need to work to survive.

As late as the 1980s, this definition broadly described reality. There was, in most industrialized countries, a single working-class culture, consisting of language, dress codes, modes of behaviour, implied ethical rules and gender stereotypes. The cultures of the middle class and the elite were equally distinct. Each class had a 'consciousness' of its interests, reflected in political party loyalties. And – though there was mobility between classes – these relationships reproduced themselves and were played out daily, in the workplace.

In the neoliberal era that changed fundamentally. For the first time in the history of industrial capitalism, the focus of exploitation has shifted substantially away from the workplace. To understand how, consider the way my parents lived. They took their wages in cash and spent those wages on consumer goods. They paid off their mortgage in three years (because homes in the 1960s were affordable) and almost never used credit to buy high value goods. They saved money in the bank, and the bank lent it to businesses. The common interests of working people were easily defined because work was the main method of exploitation. If they were poorly paid, or badly treated, it was clear who was to blame.

Consider, by contrast, an average life today. You are paid and spend electronic money; it barely crosses your mind that part of the money is borrowed. As a result, a significant chunk of your salary goes not just on buying stuff, but on paying interest: on your mortgage, your car, your credit card or student loan.[25] Even where you're not servicing debts directly, many of your regular payments – rent, smartphone contract, insurance – are 'securitized': turned into a financial asset generating interest for someone you've never met.

Everything is, in short, *financialized*. The stream of profits generated from the activities of working-class people no longer flows only, or even primarily, through work for wages. It flows, in addition, through:

- direct financial extraction – interest payments, rents, gambling profits, etc.;

- the systematic overpricing of goods and services provided by monopolies;
- data extraction, where tech companies like Facebook collect information about our behaviour and sell that information to advertisers;
- the privatization and commercialization of everything that was once free and publicly owned (or owned by nobody);
- and even through the tax system, where taxes no longer simply pay for state-owned utilities and welfare systems – the so-called social wage – but provide a guaranteed profit stream for large corporations who run public services: a 'social wage' for their shareholders and managers.

Each of these exploitation methods is based on naked power asymmetries. But, unlike in the classic relationship between managers and workers, the terms of exploitation are much harder to negotiate, or to struggle over collectively. You can go on strike against a factory owner; try going on strike against Facebook, your landlord or your bank. The lower skilled and less qualified you are, the easier you are to exploit in these new ways. From payday loans to the quarterly energy bill or insurance premium, those with the least social power generate the biggest rate of return.

From the dawn of capitalism to the mid-1980s, workers' lives were dominated by a single economic relationship – that with their boss. Today there are multiple relationships of exploitation which overlap and collide. As a result, it has become much harder to identify who is exploiting us. The top 0.1 per cent in every country are part of a globalized, super-rich stratum whose wealth is based primarily on rent-seeking and finance – and most of our lives do not bring us into any form of contact with them.

Instead it has become easier to identify somebody lower down the ladder as responsible for your own poverty and powerlessness: the buy-to-let landlord, the staff at the benefits office, the call centre worker at your bank; the person in the queue at the doctor's surgery who speaks a foreign language; the security guard at the supermarket telling you to wear a face mask.

The political effects of all this were not evident until neoliberalism broke down in 2008. But they are obvious now. If we are exploited through multiple channels, not just work, then it is easier for people to see the world beyond work as a more promising arena for struggle. And in the world beyond work, *values and identity matter*.

There have always been divisions within the working class. The skilled toolmakers who I worked with in a factory on Merseyside in the early 1980s had their own separate workshop and refused to speak to unskilled youngsters like me. They thought women had no place in a factory except as secretaries, and that if there was a pay rise on offer most of it should go to them. Many of them voted Conservative. But this classic 'labour aristocracy' would still go on strike if called out by their union. At the pub, or on the football terraces, they were just members of the working class, albeit with more money and higher status.

If we map the new divisions inside the working class, they are today more clearly cultural, and much sharper. A new kind of working-class conservatism has emerged, based not on high skills and status, but on the opposite. Thanks to the automation of manufacturing and the deliberate destruction of trade-union power, people without skills or qualifications find themselves on permanently low wages, and in jobs without security.

There are many such people in what Ainsley calls the 'new working class' – the cleaners who polish the floors of investment banks by night, the Uber drivers and the coffee baristas. But if they live in a city, they are surrounded by diverse communities and increased opportunities, and they have been repeatedly drawn into progressive social movements.

If they live in a small, ex-industrial town, where there is no university, no high-wage employer, inadequate public transport and an ageing population, their life experience is totally different. The two-hour train journey from Euston station, in the London Borough of Camden, to Wigan, where I grew up, illustrates the point. Camden is technically poorer than Wigan, but it is the northern town that feels poorer, more abandoned, facing all the problems of the modern world but few of its opportunities.

It is logical for workers in such places to ask whether inward migration is a good idea. It is logical for them to ask who decided to strip their town of investment and leave it to rot. It is logical for them to ask why China has booming, modern industrial factories while they have a plaque commemorating where the industry used to be.

But it is not logical for them to become fascists. The rise of far-right politics in these communities happened because neither liberalism nor social-democracy could provide convincing answers to their questions. And because the left, now firmly rooted in the educated, city-dwelling and multi-ethnic workforce, either avoided the conversation or, in some cases, declared the conversation itself off-limits.

We live with the results. The toolmakers I worked with in the 1980s grumbled about everything but rarely expressed hatred. Today, expressions of hate are everywhere. Over the past ten years, a political culture has emerged in some working-class communities defined by xenophobia, white supremacy, anti-feminism and Islamophobia. It is hostile, above all, to 'wokeness', political correctness, and what the *Sun* newspaper in Britain calls 'luvvies', people who've received an education and can access culture.

As a journalist who, like Lucie Varga, is determined to go out into the world and listen, I have heard this new, reactionary ethos spread through working-class communities across the planet. It is as strong in Lancashire as in Ohio, its cultural symbols are recognizable from small-town Finland to small-town Australia. Working-class socialists, who exist in large numbers and try to hold the line for progressive politics in such communities, describe the experience as 'drowning in a sea of racism'.

So today, instead of a single, self-replicating class consciousness, we have a self-replicating cultural division inside the working class. *This is a big, new problem.*

I have no nostalgia for the hierarchical, sexist world of the post-war boom, which beneath the surface was rife with racism, domestic violence and child abuse. But the class consciousness produced by exploitation at work did reproduce itself, through the daily routine of the factory or the coal mine. Our common experience of work created the basis for a discussion, even between people with strongly held socialist or conservative views.

Today, it is still possible for people to stage struggles across boundaries of place, ethnicity and gender, and to create a shared, progressive consciousness while doing so. But that consciousness does not so easily self-replicate. It has to be nurtured actively and constantly, in the face of pressures that tend to accentuate the cultural divide, and turn all political arguments instantly toxic.

However, if we ditch the old Marxist definition, based on work and wages, and see the working class as 'everybody exploited by capitalism', through data, finance, rent and monopoly pricing as well as work, it becomes clear that large numbers of people have a material interest in defeating the new extreme and populist right – and the power to do so.

A twenty-first-century fascism would massively enhance the dominance of capital over human beings in every sphere – from the Amazon warehouse to the call centre to the gigafactory. For this reason alone, it makes sense for all sections of the working class to resist the far right. The arguments we once had at work, and in a shared working culture, now have to be had more openly and actively, with the whole of society as the factory floor.

But as we do so, we need to recognize that far-right ideologies are no longer reliant only on racism and on nationalism, but are powerfully fuelled by arguments over gender.

Neoliberalism as an economic model is just forty years old. But its rise coincided with a challenge to a system more than 40,000 years old: women's oppression. Since the late 1960s, albeit with wide regional variations, new contraceptive methods have given women in the developed world the ability to control their own fertility. Even in some developing countries, contraceptive use has surged from near zero in the 1970s towards the developed-world average.[26]

With contraception came the demand for reproductive rights. Even though conservatives and religious authorities waged a relentless rearguard battle, women's rights to abortion have advanced in many countries. In some, abortion is now treated as a healthcare issue, not as a crime or an agonizing moral dilemma.

We are a long way from eradicating the oppression of women based on their biological role as childbearers. But mass access to contraception and abortion has unleashed what economists have labelled a 'reproductive technological shock'.[27] In developed countries, women's participation in the workforce – again subject to cultural variation – has surged: in Britain, the proportion of working-age mothers in work rose from 50 per cent in 1975 to 72 per cent by 2015, while the percentage of working-age women with a degree, which was 10 per cent in the 1960s, is now close to 50 per cent.[28]

Today it is the stated aim of the world's governments – as enshrined in a global treaty – to 'achieve gender equality and empower all women and girls'.[29] Meanwhile, numerous states have enacted legal or constitutional guarantees of women's rights at work, in politics and across society.

But these statistics, impressive as they are, barely tell the real story, which is the rise of women's social and cultural power. From sport to politics, journalism, science, medicine and the arts, the status of women has been transformed in the space of a lifetime. Clearly we are nowhere near meaningful equality between men and women, whether it be on pay or freedom from male violence. But to contemporary fascists, the world already looks like a feminist utopia.

The original fascists did not have to deal with a meaningful advance in women's social power. Their project of violent national renewal took male dominance as an unchallengeable assumption, and set out to strengthen it.

The Nazis banned women from the professions, shut down abortion clinics, prosecuted thousands of women for abortions and 'illegal miscarriages', and minted a special medal for women who bore more than five children. Simultaneously, they forcibly sterilized tens of thousands of working-class women and forced 5,000 to have abortions against their will, in order to 'cleanse the race'.[30] Mussolini passed laws to drive women out of the civil service and 'male' industrial jobs,[31] and churned out relentless propaganda against birth control, saying, 'work . . . distracts from conception. It forms an independence and consequent physical and moral habits contrary to child-bearing.'[32]

Fascism, in short, systematically reversed any reproductive and social rights women had gained during the first decades of the twentieth century. But it arose in societies that were totally male-dominated, and where access to non-traditional lifestyles was limited to women from the elite. And the Marxist parties it was fighting were, while committed to women's rights, functionally male-dominated and hierarchical. For Hitler and Mussolini, the return of women to their traditional childbearing role was a secondary objective. In our century, by contrast, hostility to women's liberation has become as central to fascism as the narrative of ethnic supremacy.

The logic of 'neomasculinity' was spelled out by the American 'pickup artist' Roosh Valizadeh in one of his blogs. Much of it repeats the sexist pseudoscience we saw in Chapter 2. In Valizadeh's telling, gender equality has no scientific basis because men and women have different evolutionary traits. The male traits are 'dominance, independence, intelligence, rationale, analytical thinking', while women are naturally submissive, dependent, emotional and cooperative. Equality laws, he says, have distorted women's true nature, making them oppressive and predatory against men; so it is not women who are victims of sexism, but men who are victims of 'misandry'.

This mythology of male victimization has a direct, practical outcome. Valizadeh advocates that men 'game' all sexual relationships, developing the manipulative skills of the pickup artist to restore the balance. He says men should fight to reverse the social, legal and cultural gains women have made, above all by reimposing the nuclear family, with a male breadwinner as the norm.[33] That's his theory, at least. The practice, for many of the men who follow it, is sexual predation, harassment, rape and domestic violence. For others it is 'involuntary celibacy': the subculture of the 'incel' movement – of men who blame their inability to attract girlfriends on feminism – teems simultaneously with hatred for emancipated women, and subservience to the 'Alpha male'.

From its earliest days, this online 'manosphere' was awash with the same source material as the original fascism: Nietzsche's elitism, Social Darwinism and the mythologized past. What merged it with the political far right was the ideological collapse of neoliberalism.

With the rise of the Occupy movements in 2011 in response to the economic crisis, the pejorative term 'social justice warrior' (SJW) entered right-wing culture, often presented alongside memes depicting SJWs as ugly, crazed or diseased women, or men with feminine attributes.[34] Since traits such as empathy and cooperation are defined by right-wing pseudoscience as biologically female, women were categorized in numerous memes as 'carriers' of a disease-like threat to male power. The SJW narrative crossed into popular usage via the Gamergate scandal of 2014, in which prominent women were driven out of public life for critiquing the sexism within gaming culture, by a sustained campaign of harassment, both online and physical.

From this point, violent misogyny online converged with overtly theorized racism. As the writer David Futrelle put it: 'If you can convince yourself that men are the primary victims of sexism, it's not hard to convince yourself that whites are the primary victims of racism.'[35]

And from here it is a short step to the central myth of modern fascism: The Great Replacement Theory, as discussed in Chapter 2.[36] It was only in 2010 that the reactionary French writer Renaud Camus gave it a name, but the logic of the theory was always there: feminism depresses the birthrate, allowing immigrants to 'colonize' and destroy the white 'race'; the collaborators in this occupation are the politicians who defend the rights of women and black people, and the liberal media who support them.

The importance of misogyny as a gateway drug to modern fascism lies in the broadness of the experience it draws on. Few racists have actually had their job taken by a migrant. But every heterosexual man can feel the difference between the ideology of 'manliness' and the reality, where women are increasingly free to define their own norms of beauty and sexual behaviour.

And while only a minority of racists have physically attacked a person of colour, most violent misogynists have physically attacked a woman. Similarly, though all fascisms involve fantasies of ethnic supremacy, the actual ethnicities concerned differ from place to place: whites in North America, Europeans in Europe, Hindus in India, the descendants of European colonists in Brazil or Bolivia. Misogyny, however, is a universal language.

This is a new problem for anti-fascists. We can, if we wish to, define twentieth-century fascism through its central demand for violent national rebirth. Today, in equal measure, it is a demand for the violent rebirth of patriarchy. If we return to the essence of fascism – *a fear of freedom triggered by a glimpse of freedom* – then the significance of misogyny in driving people towards it becomes clear.

The Russian Revolution was an outburst of freedom. So were the Italian peasant land seizures in 1920. But none of these events matches the scale and depth of the change in women's lives since the 1960s.

Fascism is feeding on a fear of a freedom that did not exist in the 1930s. Today's fascists do not need to dread a workers' revolution, but they have every reason to fear that the millenial generation of women, people of colour, LGBTQ+ people and, yes, workers will demand freedoms unheard of in the twentieth century. And that, in turn, broadens the kind of alliance a modern Popular Front might create.

THE LEFT AND LIBERALISM: A TRUCE?

Since 2008, the socialist left and neoliberal globalists have been at war with each other, and for good reason. The left predicted that, without a radical change in economic policy, the 2010s would be a decade of deprivation and misery, driving some despairing people into the arms of racist, authoritarian movements. Then we watched it happen.

As the Eurozone treaties demanded wage cuts across Southern Europe and mass unemployment ensued, we saw the rise of outright fascist parties like Golden Dawn in Greece, and radical right-wing parties like the National Front (now the National Rally) in France, the AfD in Germany and the Austrian Freedom Party. Yet the liberal centre concentrated all its fire on the left.

In the summer of 2015, I was in Greece to document the moment the European Commission and the IMF destroyed the radical left government there in order to impose yet more austerity. By then half of Greek people under twenty-five years old were out of work. In that two-week standoff, when the banks were closed, I saw elderly people shake with fear; tough, adult men burst suddenly into tears; and extreme psychological insecurity ripple through society as people's cash ran out. I recognized these symptoms of trauma because I'd seen them before, in the war zone of Gaza: the Greek crisis was an economic siege. So yes, the bitterness between the left and liberalism runs deep.

But after Greece, Brexit and the election of Trump in 2016, we saw the beginnings of liberal self-criticism. The Eurozone realized it had come close to provoking a revolution. It pulled back from harsh austerity; rescheduled the debt payments of peripheral countries and expanded the money creation programme of the European Central Bank. Faced with the rising tide of populism, liberal political scientists like Yascha Mounk advocated a controlled retreat from neoliberalism, with new housebuilding programmes, a more generous welfare state, a more progressive tax system, and 'meaningful work'; in short, the traditional programme of social democracy that the neoliberals spent two decades attacking.[37]

Though liberalism had for twenty years shown scant interest in these policies as ends in themselves, they were revived in pursuit of the political goal of saving democracy (and their political careers) from populism. Which is good, but not enough.

Because the neoliberal model cannot deliver any of these reforms consistently and at speed. Politics in most countries is dominated by global finance, the privatization consultancies, big tech and the fossil fuel lobby. The reason such interests decided to put Trump into the White House, Boris Johnson into Downing Street and Jair Bolsonaro into the Brazilian presidential palace was to stop redistribution and tighter regulation from happening.

For a modern Popular Front to work, liberalism would have to do what the French Radical Party did in 1935–6, and what Roosevelt did at the start of the New Deal: switch to a new kind of economics that, at least in part, overlaps with the demands of radical social democracy. The left, meanwhile, would have to put about half its programme, and many of its obsessions, into a box marked 'to be continued'. Difficult and painful though these compromises might be, they are essential in a situation where the alliance of right-wing extremists, populists and authoritarians threatens to create a permanent nightmare of racism, vote-rigging and state violence.

But twenty-first-century liberalism is in crisis. Faced with the collapse of the free market model, and the rise of illiberal conservatism, liberalism seems bereft of purpose. Liberals know they need to resist the new far right. But they sense the fragility of the status quo they are trying to defend.

When liberalism faced such a crossroads in the 1930s there was a clear, functional alternative: the Keynesian system of state intervention, protectionism, borrowing and investment-led growth.

Today, too, there is a clear alternative, summarized in the slogan of the 'Green New Deal' and popularized by the draft bill proposed in 2019 by US lawmaker Alexandria Ocasio-Cortez.[38] It means fighting for an urgent decarbonization programme, putting the state in charge of it, creating high-paid jobs, borrowing billions of pounds, dollars and euros to make it happen – and actively re-engineering the economy to move beyond carbon before the mid-century. Done right, it would inevitably boost the share of the economy going into workers' wages and depress the share going to corporate profits.

But liberalism instinctively recoils from this. There are material and economic reasons: the massive borrowing needed, and the level of state ownership implied, look scary to economists of the mainstream. Plus – from Angela Merkel to Joe Biden and Justin Trudeau – there are always compromises to be made with the fossil fuel lobby.

However, the philosophical source of liberal resistance goes deeper. In liberal political philosophy there is always 'progress' – but it is never towards a goal. Just a calm and steady stream of improvements to human life that happen because of technological change and rising educational levels. Today, humanity has been presented with an unavoidable goal. If we do not reduce carbon emissions to net zero by mid-century, we will leave a legacy of chaos to the next generation; and if we do not defeat fascism, democracy as we know it will die.

There are grounds for optimism. The Covid-19 crisis forced major states to do what they had refused to after 2008: incur serious debt simply to save jobs and companies; take control of the medical supply and healthcare industries; bail out entire sectors whose business models were destroyed; and overtly underwrite government borrowing with money newly created by central banks.

As they fought the pandemic, some in the political centre crossed a psychological barrier: they accepted that, if you can do these things for a public health emergency, you could also do them for a climate emergency and to suppress extreme inequality.

That is the logic behind the World Economic Forum's plan for a 'Great Reset', whereby capitalism is reconfigured towards zero-net carbon and meeting the UN's sustainable development goals, utilizing mild state intervention.[39] It lies also behind the IMF's October 2020 call for a 'New Bretton Woods' agreement, whereby the world's major countries create a new digital currency to underpin the money creation they have done to meet the Covid-19 crisis.[40] But the Great Reset and the New Bretton Woods are meaningless without struggle from below, to redistribute wealth and increase social justice.

The outcome of the 2020s depends, then, on whether liberalism can inject urgency and goal-oriented actions into its agenda, and whether a left emerges that – by mobilizing large numbers of people – can force the liberal centre to create the space and opportunity for radical change. For both liberalism and the left, actually fighting, defeating and shattering the convergent forces of right-wing populism and fascism is an unavoidable short-term goal. But history shows this objective has to involve both struggles from below and coercive action by the state.

MILITANT DEMOCRACY REDUX

Both in France and in Spain the Popular Front governments of the 1930s passed laws and took executive action to dissolve fascist 'militia parties'. But numerous mainstream governments had also done so earlier in the decade, with Finland, Czechoslovakia and Switzerland the most successful. Inspired by this, in 1937, the lawyer Karl Loewenstein, a Jewish legal scholar who fled Germany for the USA, published an influential article entitled 'Militant Democracy'. In it, he argued that fascism was beatable through a combination of mass movements and strict legal measures.

Though the Popular Front had won breathing space, said Loewenstein, fascism had become adept at using democratic structures to undermine democracy. So democrats had to fight back using the state's coercive power and the rule of law. 'Democracy,' he said, 'must become militant.'[41]

Loewenstein listed a menu of legal changes that, though unpalatable to liberals both then and now, were needed to prevent fascist movements exploiting the loopholes in democratic constitutions. In addition to the regular laws against insurrection, he advocated banning uniformed groups; banning squads and militias; and banning political parties if they refused to recognize the Constitution or threatened violence. He called for strict control on firearms and changes to parliamentary rules to prevent the disruptive tactics used by some fascist parties (such as repeated resignations to trigger by-elections).

In addition, Loewenstein urged governments to outlaw hate speech and incitement to violence; and to force political parties to publish financial accounts, in order to trace and intercept foreign funding from other fascist regimes. Finally, he recommended the depoliticization of the army and the police force, and the creation of separate constitutional police units to investigate and prevent anti-democratic subversion.[42]

After 1945 Loewenstein returned to Germany to help in the de-Nazification process, and the principles of his argument helped shape West Germany's Basic Law, which still guides the German government's attempts to suppress the extreme right – though, as we saw in Chapter 1, even there the legal restraints on fascism are fraying.

Nonetheless, 2020 saw three milestones in the use of existing anti-fascist legislation. In March, the German intelligence services forced a 7,000-strong extremist faction inside the AfD party, known as *Flugel*, to disband, having identified its Holocaust revisionism and anti-constitutional rhetoric as a threat to the constitution.[43] The AfD's youth wing was forced to amend parts of its political programme to avoid the same treatment.

In September 2020, after a three-year court battle, the Finnish Supreme Court banned the Nordic Resistance Movement, an openly Nazi organization which had staged anti-Semitic events outside synagogues and uniformed, militarist parades across the Nordic countries.

Then, in October 2020, leading members of the Greek neo-Nazi group Golden Dawn were convicted of running a criminal organization and handed long jail sentences, again after a trial lasting several years, over the murder of the anti-fascist musician Pavlos Fyssas.

These legal victories are, of course, pyrrhic. The German *Flugel* faction claimed it had never really existed; the NRM has gone partially underground and started to operate in a more networked way; Golden Dawn has been replaced by a new, more legalist extreme-right-wing party in Greece. But they illustrate the potential power of democratic constitutions if backed by assertive law enforcement, intelligence gathering and judicial action.

The left, traditionally, has resisted using the state to suppress far-right extremism, on the grounds that, if handed extraordinary powers, most liberal states would rather use them against the left than the right. That is the reflex that prompted numerous left-wing groups and campaigns in the USA to deny the seriousness of the Capitol Hill attack, and to object to a coordinated state crackdown on the far right.

In the absence of pressure from the left, law enforcement bodies and public prosecutors are usually content to let far-right politics fester at the fringes, kept under surveillance in the case of the open Nazis, but generally unrepressed. Since the attack on the Capitol, it has emerged that numerous figures in the Proud Boys were actually being used as informants by the FBI – spying both on the far right and, allegedly, their anti-fascist opponents. So the risks of empowering law enforcement are non-neglible.[44]

But given the scale of the crisis that is likely to unfold towards the mid-century, and the vast opportunities this will offer to the violent far right, we need a more comprehensive approach. No democrat can be happy with the restriction of rights to association, but the risks are too great to ignore. Any modern version of the Popular Front would have to agree, as the French did in the 1930s, a minimum programme of legal restrictions on far-right street mobilizations, online harassment and hate speech – and an outright ban on organizations like the Oathkeepers, the Proud Boys and Generation Identity.

Though there is a highly developed methodology for countering Islamist terrorism, which has in the 2010s also been applied to terror plots by the far right, governments need to stop dealing with the far right only through anti-terror legislation, or even through the lens of 'extremism'. Experts on radicalization have developed a 'pyramid model' showing how a mass, largely passive base creates a second layer of people who morally support terrorism, a smaller layer above them who facilitate it, and a small apex of actual terrorists.[45] What we are concerned with here, however, is a much more fluid process.

A twenty-first-century application of Loewenstein's 'militant democracy' principle would have to begin online. The Boogaloo Bois phenomenon, of armed men wearing ironic militarist regalia at far right rallies and protests in 2020, began on the anonymized 4Chan bulletin board, and was spread by Discord channels to both Facebook and Reddit. The left-wing news site Unicorn Riot, which scanned 240,000 private Discord messages exchanged between the Boogaloos, concluded they were written,

> in great part, by angry racist white men who are at plausible risk of being or becoming murderers and/or rapists. The chat server's logs are rife with blatant calls for genocide, sometimes not even wrapped with a veneer of irony.[46]

Despite banning 200 Facebook groups and de-prioritizing the Boogaloo search term on its algorithm, Facebook has struggled to remove content inciting a civil war; it is readily findable at the time of writing.[47]

The most effective way to attack twenty-first-century fascism would be to classify all internet platforms as publishers, making their owners responsible for the content. Platforms such as Facebook and Google, which only loosely demand real identities and vigorously resist being made responsible for their content, would be forced to police their ID systems; Twitter would be forced to eradicate millions of fake and anonymous accounts. And the fully anonymized bulletin boards would either go out of business or be locked out of the mainstream networks.

In the wake of the Capitol Hill attack, when the tech industry took immediate action to de-platform the microblogging site Parler and shut down numerous fascist Telegram channels, initial studies showed that these actions made a difference.[48] They made it hard for anonymous people to create big, influential ecosystems of hate, and impossible for the algorithms of the big tech companies to guide people into those ecosystems.

There are many good reasons for internet users to remain anonymous: freedom fighters in repressive states, gay people in homophobic communities or women suffering from domestic violence, to name only a few. But since civil society has moved online, the effect of systematic untraceability is to create a two-tier *demos*: real people, who can be harassed, threatened and doxxed; and anonymous users who can perpetrate harassment, hate speech and incitement at will, without the victimized group even having the right to argue back.

We rightly vote in secret, but we do not vote anonymously; the vote has to be cast by a real person with a traceable identity. So why should anyone be able to influence someone's vote anonymously? You cannot stage a physical attack without risk of identification, so why should you be able to advocate a physical attack without such risk?

Given the nature of the internet, with its offshore servers and encrypted messaging systems, it is not possible to enforce identification everywhere. But if a traceable ID could be made obligatory on all publicly available social media – as it is on Facebook – and ficticious acounts abolished, that would shut down a significant percentage of online fascism overnight, and force the rest into underground, private channels with a smaller mass effect.

Though this is constitutionally impossible in the USA, designating the platforms as publishers would force them to self-police. There is a right to freedom of expression, but nothing in the US Constitution that says Facebook is obliged to publish incitements to genocide.

In the offline world, modern versions of the laws Loewenstein advocated still operate in Germany, and could be usefully copied elsewhere: banning organizations that advocate violence; obliging police to break up and disperse uniformed fascist parades; and creating clear rules of conduct for political organizations, signalling, as in Germany, where they become eligible for routine surveillance.

The danger, of course, is that you empower an authoritarian state. But here again Loewenstein's argument remains valid. If you want to defend democracy against a pervasive and rising threat you have to do *something*; better to do it openly, legally and constitutionally. The aim of Militant Democracy 2.0 is to push the extremists back towards populism. They will still have the freedom to stand for elections and publish newspapers, just not to combine those activities with compiling death lists of anti-fascists.

Unpalatable though these measures sound, the ultimate argument for them is the scale of the risk. The fascism we need to defeat today is just as genocidal as the one defeated in 1945. But the means for genocide are, as we will see in the next chapter, easier to obtain.

*

The most important element in the success of the original Popular Fronts was the creation, by the masses themselves, of a powerful and rival ethos to that of fascism. It was not, and could never be, a mirror image of the Sorelian myths that the fascist movements thrived on.

The anti-fascist ethos of the 1930s produced new kinds of art, new styles in cinema, and in the Spanish Civil War a new outburst of soldier-poetry; it drew women into the struggle in a way fascism could never have done. Today, as in the 1930s, the impetus for the creation of anti-fascist resistance movements will come from the left, and from the minorities under attack. But that requires a big change of attitude on the left.

Ultimately the Popular Front's longest-lasting effect was to turn anti-fascism from a tactic into an ethos, and by the second half of the 1930s this ethos had become fully embedded in popular culture. Emulating that is, for me, more important than any electoral agreement or any street mobilization. Trump and his allies spent so much energy delegitimizing the word 'antifa' because a pervasive anti-fascist culture is precisely what they fear most. The task of the 2020s is to make it happen.

9

Everybody Comes to Rick's

Anti-fascism as an Ethos

'Try to get a foreign girl for the part,' says a note attached to the first draft of *Casablanca*, adding that if that was impossible, 'an American girl with big tits will do'.[1] In March 1942 German U-boats were destroying American ships at will off the coast of New England, the US Army had just been driven out of the Philippines and Hitler had made a speech promising 'the complete annihilation of the Jews'.[2] But for Philip and Julius Epstein, the problem was how to make an anti-fascist movie funny.

The Epstein twins – Jewish liberals from the Lower East Side and staff writers at Warner Brothers – had been handed the script of a stage play entitled *Everybody Comes to Rick's*. The story revolves around an American playboy living in Morocco, who helps an anti-fascist resistance leader escape the Nazis in order to win a bet. Their job was to turn it into a screenplay. But without wit and romance they feared it would die a death. Four months after the attack on Pearl Harbor few Americans understood what was at stake. Support for the war was thin.

Locked in a plush hotel in Washington DC, the Epsteins inserted as much comic irony as possible, while urging the director to cast someone glamorous to play the female lead – originally scripted as an American 'tramp' who is the resistance leader's wife but, by coincidence, Rick's former lover. After one look at the draft, the studio hired Howard Koch to do a rewrite. The Epsteins were enthusiasts for Franklin Delano Roosevelt and the New Deal. Koch was a communist and one of the most radical writers in Hollywood.

In Koch's draft all the stakes are raised. Rick saves the resistance leader, but no longer for money or for kicks. In the play, he's a louche, expat lawyer; in the film he becomes a hardboiled veteran from the Spanish Civil War. The heroine is transformed from an American good-time girl into the Swedish radical Ilse Lund. In the play, her character sleeps with Rick transactionally, to get the visas she needs to escape Morocco; in the film, she falls back in love with him. In the play's final scene, Rick hands his revolver to a Nazi officer and cynically claims the money he's just won in a bet. In the movie, he shoots the Nazi and joins the French Resistance.

Koch turned *Casablanca* into a story about how you find the will to resist fascism, even if you're disillusioned and your ideals are shattered. Having fought fascism once and lost, Rick is persuaded to fight again. As he makes the choice to resist, every other character – from the woman propping up the bar to the musicians in the band – has their own choice to make. Even the corrupt French police chief ends up on the right side of history.[3]

The moral lesson of *Casablanca* is that, in the face of fascism, nobody can stay neutral. When it really comes down to it, the defeats, rivalries and betrayals of the past don't matter. As such, the movie is a living embodiment of the ideals of the Popular Front.

There are no death camps shown in *Casablanca*. The violence is euphemistic: three people are shot but we never see them bleed. There is no torture, no firing squads and the word 'Jew' is never spoken. But the presence of evil lurks at the edge of every scene. 'A devil has the people by the throat,' says a refugee from Bulgaria, as she pleads for a visa: it is not the Nazis she is running away from but her neighbours.[4]

By placing the action in the borderlands of the Third Reich, in a liminal space where people's lives are cheap, Hollywood took its audience to the precipice of a moral choice. In every scene the implicit question is: what would you do? Today, every one of us is – metaphorically – a customer at Rick's café. Faced with a global far-right threat, there are few places left to hide.

The last day of filming for *Casablanca* was 22 July 1942. On the same day the Nazis began the deportation of Jews from the Warsaw Ghetto.

Operation Reinhard was designed to exterminate the entire Jewish population of occupied southern Poland at three death camps – Treblinka, Sobibor and Belzec – and a concentration camp at Majdanek, on the outskirts of Lublin. By the time *Casablanca* premièred, on 23 January 1943, the Nazis had murdered 1,274,166 people in these four camps alone: gassed, beaten to death, worked to death or shot.[5]

When the Red Army liberated Majdanek in July 1944 they found the first proof that the Nazis were running an industrial-scale killing operation. The Allies had been sceptical about Soviet claims of mass murder but here was the evidence: a vast encampment of pine huts, surrounded by barbed wire, containing meticulously sorted piles of shoes, spectacles, passports, Jewish prayer shawls and – most importantly – survivors.

Russian writer Konstantin Simonov was the first journalist to file a report from the camp. Soviet journalism followed a formula in which all Russians were heroes, all Nazis evil and all facts certain – so his opening words are all the more poignant:

> What I am about to relate is on too huge a scale and too gruesome to be fully taken in ... I myself am at present in possession of only a fraction of the facts: I have spoken to only one-hundredth of the witnesses and have seen maybe only one-tenth of the traces. But a man who has seen what I have seen cannot hold his peace. He cannot wait to speak ... [6]

For all the mistakes he was about to make, Simonov had expressed a fundamental truth: even today, when we confront the facts about the Holocaust, our rational minds struggle to understand what we are dealing with.

Simonov massively overestimated the number killed in the camp. He wrongly claimed that Leon Blum, who had led the French Popular Front, had died there (Blum was in Buchenwald, and would survive). But his biggest error was to describe the camp as a murder machine for POWs and political prisoners, not specifically Jews. He claimed more Poles were killed than Jews; he listed the victims' passports and countries of origin but did not mention their ethnicity. Though he understood that the camp had exterminated some prisoners on arrival, he made no reference to the fact they were Jews.

Simonov's article was shaped by official Soviet ideology, which de-emphasized the anti-Semitic nature of the Nazis' crimes. But on the other side, there was also willing disbelief.

Allied governments cast doubt on the report. A *New York Times* journalist sent to check the facts noted that 'Jews, Poles, Russians and in fact representatives of a total of twenty-two nationalities . . .' had entered the showers on arrival. 'Sometimes,' he wrote, they were put into the gas chamber, while 'other prisoners were kept for long periods.'[7] Like Simonov, the *Times* reporter omitted the most crucial fact: the criterion for who was murdered. When the BBC journalist Alexander Werth filed a more accurate report from Majdanek that same month, the BBC refused to run it. 'They thought it was a Russian propaganda stunt,' Werth later recalled.[8]

Majdanek stands painstakingly preserved: the spectacles, shoes, luggage, huts, ovens and a vast mound of ashes. The walls of one gas chamber are stained blue and green from the chemicals used to asphyxiate the victims. The watchtowers loom over the Polish countryside.

We, today, know a lot more about what happened during Operation Reinhard: how most of the killing was done in the low concrete bunkers of the main death camps, which the Nazis managed to destroy before fleeing. We can read, if we can bear to, the methods of torture individual guards used as they killed people for fun at Majdanek.

But there is still uncertainty as to who ordered what. By late October 1941 the SS had recruited gas specialists like Josef Vallaster from their medical euthanasia programme and begun building the Belzec camp. But detailed accounts show that the regional SS commander, Odilo Globočnik, was ahead of the game.

According to one historian, Globočnik exhibited 'enormous activism' in pursuit of genocidal racism long before Operation Reinhard. His driving obsession was to repopulate southern Poland with Germans and then to 'encircle' the entire Polish population 'gradually throttling them both economically and biologically'.[9] Records show Globočnik sending requests up the chain of command to Hitler, asking to be allowed to 'send the Jews across the river'. One colleague described him as 'fanatically obsessed with the task':

His daredevil character often leads him to overstep the given limits and to forget the boundaries laid down within the [SS] order, although not for reasons of personal ambition but rather due to his obsession with the cause.[10]

This mixture of orders from above and apparent improvisation from below has prompted a sharp debate between historians over 'function' versus 'intention': did Hitler have a preconceived master plan for genocide? Or did it happen because the lower-level Nazi bureaucracy hated Jews and began the genocide on their own initiative? Both positions carry political implications: if you can blame it all on Hitler and his 'intent', you can theorize Nazism as a one-off, caused by a power-crazed individual, not the product of deeper class and psychological forces. But if you move the focus to the lower ranks, say the critics, you end up moving the blame to 'systems' rather than people, and diminishing their crimes.[11]

If our purpose is to use history as a guide to resistance, both interpretations carry their own insight. Hitler outlined the project of invading Russia and annihilating Jews as early as the 1920s. But the Nazi method of governance – which was deliberately chaotic – left the initiative to second-echelon bureaucrats like Globočnik, who improvised while leaving a purposefully vague paper trail, and then took great pains to cover up their crimes.

The Globočnik case reminds us that, as we resist fascism, we are not always dealing with an enemy with a plan. The thought-architecture of fascism provides a template for action, which can vary in given circumstances. It was the failure of anti-fascists to take the ethos and mythology of Nazism seriously which led many in the mid-1930s to underestimate the possibility of genocide.

Loewenstein, in 1937, argued that the legal suppression of fascism would be more effective than a mass, Popular Front-style resistance, because fascism 'is not an ideological movement but only a political technique under ideological pretenses'.[12] Majdanek and the other preserved memorial sites are proof that he was wrong.

Globočnik was both a fanatical Nazi and systematically corrupt. A building engineer, he joined the Austrian Nazi Party in 1922 but seems to have been inactive until the Wall Street Crash triggered a bout of intense activism. He was arrested five times between 1931 and 1935, for bombing Jewish businesses and running an underground Nazi cell.[13]

In power, the Nazis rejected all proposals to systematize their way of governing. Instead they practised 'politics without administration'. They ruled, wrote the late historian Tim Mason, through 'non-policies and evasions', taking sudden, emotion-led decisions and – when this produced chaos – making up new plans.[14] That system of government could exist only because of men like Globočnik, with an outline of the project already in their heads and a willingness to enact mass murder with or without direct orders. It was designed to empower their racial fantasies and cover up their crimes. So what word should we use to describe men like Globočnik?

When trying to understand the role ordinary Germans had played in the Holocaust, post-war philosophers returned to the concept of evil. Arendt, in *The Origins of Totalitarianism*, used the phrase 'radical evil' to categorize the crime, a transgression which could not fit into the framework of ordinary evil. In the Judeo-Christian tradition, she reminds us, evil is seen as human – both in origin and scale. It is the 'absence of good', a form of backsliding towards our animal instincts. Sins – even serious ones such as rape and murder – are the product of human-scale selfishness and desires.

However, Arendt says, the systematic murder and dehumanization of an entire people, whether carried out spontaneously or by obeying orders, just doesn't fit with the idea of human-scale sin. The radical evil of the death camps, she writes, emerged from a system:

> ... in which all men have become equally superfluous. The manipulators of this system believe in their own superfluousness as much as in that of all others, and the totalitarian murderers are all the more dangerous because they do not care if they themselves are alive or dead, if they ever lived or never were born.[15]

That was true of Globočnik. Captured by the British Army in 1945, he slipped a cyanide capsule into his mouth and was dead within two minutes.[16]

Arendt's concept of radical evil is a challenge for historical materialists. There can be no simple sociological explanation for a character like Globočnik. We need to search for the source of his behaviour at a deeper level. We cannot flinch from a moral critique of fascism. But moral philosophy has become quite alien to the modern left, a problem traceable right back to the positions of Marx himself.

Karl Marx explicitly despised moral philosophy. He believed that all moral systems are the reflections of social systems, power hierarchies and forms of exploitation, and that notions of good and evil cannot be absolute. Yet there *is* an implicit moral philosophy in Marx, and a notion of good and evil. *Capital*, his book on political economy, is also a giant ethical tract, whose premise is that exploiting people in a way that kills their ability to live a fully human life is wrong.

Historical materialism is, in this sense, *teleological*: it asserts that the purpose (or in Greek *telos*) of human beings is to set themselves free – both from material necessity and alienation. For Marxists, therefore, 'good' should logically mean everything that helps us free ourselves from mindless work, racial and gender oppression, exploitation and alienation. We have no need to appeal to a deity or any other external arbiter to tell us that these things are good in human terms.

The implicit Marxist concept of 'evil' is equally grounded in this human-centric view of the world. Evil is what alienates us from our human essence: what stifles our imagination; what prevents us controlling the technologies we create; what represses our sexuality; what exploits us; what kills us. As the French philosopher Michel Henry puts it, 'for Marx, the *economic* is first of all evil' (emphasis added).[17]

But what about radical evil? Where is that in Marxist theory? Because Marx's moral philosophy remained implicit, there is no language – indeed almost no debate – about that question on the left, except among iconoclastic writers like Henry.

But the working class, in the nineteenth and early twentieth centuries, did effectively create their own moral philosophy out of Marxism, despite Marx's derision. They called it 'class consciousness'. Drawing on the Judeo-Christian principles of selflessness, humility and struggle for justice in this world, not just salvation in the next, they created an ethic based on the concept of virtue, with implicit 'commandments'. It asked, just as Aristotle had asked: what does a good society look like, and what should a good person do in order to achieve that society and live in it?

But in the 1920s, the self-designed ethical systems of the proletariat collided with something of a different magnitude: the militant anti-humanism of men like Globočnik. In the face of this new adversary, the old proletarian worldview shattered. Just as no Marxist theorist predicted fascism, no working-class community could imagine it before it happened to them.

This is an error our generation of the left has to rectify. Marxism – both as a political doctrine and as a mass movement – failed in the face of fascism because it had no explicit theory of evil, and when confronted with a systemic, militarized, genocidal anti-humanism, it could offer scant explanation.

If Marxism is to be a comprehensive, radical humanism for the twenty-first century, then it, too, must have a fully theorized concept of 'radical evil'. As with Arendt, its starting point has to be the experience of the death camps.

It is impossible to sense from looking at the wire and concrete how completely people were dehumanized in the death camps. Their purpose was not just to kill individuals but, as the philosopher Claudia Card tells us, to inflict 'social death'.[18] When I met the Auschwitz survivor Marian Turski, in Warsaw in 2018, he took great pains in his faltering English to connect the Nuremberg Laws, which excluded Jews from places like parks and swimming pools, with the final outcome:

> You might think it's unpleasant. Okay, you are not allowed to swim here, so what? In Berlin there are hundreds of places to swim. You cannot sit on this bench but there are others where you can sit. This is how both the victims, the perpetrators and the bystanders are getting used to it. And finally [you have] the ghettoes. Then expelling people. Then to the camps, then the extermination camps.

'What was the worst?' he finished. 'Humiliation. That they treated you not even as an animal but as an insect; as a cockroach; a bed-bug. And this is normal for everybody – what do you do with an insect?' He clapped his hands and stamped, as if to crush something beneath his shoe.

What the Nazis tried to create among the executioners in the camps was Ernst Jünger's 'New Man'. While the prisoners were cruelly dehumanized, the people who worked there were taught to see themselves as machines: as non-human humans. They were prepared to inflict pain and say, as Jünger predicted, 'technology is our uniform'.

Jünger believed the emergence of dehumanized and anti-human people in the twentieth century was not a regression towards savagery, but the outcome of technological progress. Our ability to place machines between ourselves and nature as if they were artificial limbs, and camera lenses between our eyes and the outside world, had produced a 'second and colder consciousness', which 'reveals itself in the ever-increasing ability to see oneself as an object'.[19] Though he became critical of, and distant from the Nazis, he was in this sense their most acute prophet.

The naive moral philosophy of the working class, constructed only with reference to ordinary human failings, could not survive contact with systematic and absolute anti-humanism. Their naïve class consciousness was destroyed. Once again we can think of Jan Petersen's words in January 1933, as he stumbled through Berlin: 'I am dazed.'

In its place emerged anti-fascism, which by the time they started shooting *Casablanca* in 1942 was no longer simply a leftist slogan or even a political strategy, but a global moral philosophy.

Of the fourteen credited actors in Casablanca, just four were born in the USA. Of the seventy-five people who appear onscreen, the majority were refugees from Europe. Paul Henreid, who plays the resistance leader Victor Laszlo, was declared an enemy of the Third Reich and had all his assets confiscated. Helmut Dantine, who plays the young Bulgarian man searching for a visa, was the leader of an anti-fascist youth movement in Vienna, who'd led riots and spent time in a concentration camp. Marcel Dalio, who plays the croupier in Rick's casino, had starred in the anti-fascist movies of Jean Renoir. During the occupation of France, the Nazis put Dalio's face on a propaganda poster entitled 'The Jew'. Madeleine Lebeau, Dalio's real-life wife, plays the onscreen barfly Yvonne; they'd escaped together for real, via Lisbon and Mexico on forged visas.[20]

It is the collective contribution of these real-life anti-fascist fighters that gives *Casablanca* its ethos. Some of the film's greatest one-liners are moral statements. When Rick asks Laszlo, 'Don't you sometimes wonder if it's worth all this? What you're fighting for?' Laszlo answers:

> We might as well question why we breathe. If we stop breathing, we'll die. If we stop fighting our enemies, the world will die.[21]

Somebody on that set – maybe Koch, or Henreid or Bogart himself (who was prone to 'popping lines out of a whisky bottle') – had understood the profound nature of the fascist threat and encapsulated it in one sentence.

Fascism is the organized refusal of human life. It is an anti-morality. Its first philosophical tenet, traceable right back to the words of Nietzsche, is that the elite of Supermen are allowed to become:

> ... exultant monsters, who perhaps go away having committed a hideous succession of murder, arson, rape and torture, in a mood of bravado and spiritual equilibrium as though they had simply played a student's prank.[22]

It is impossible to read that without thinking of Globočnik, and thousands like him, who learned this 'mood of bravado' not from reading Nietzsche but in the SA taverns, at Hitler's rallies, and in off-duty moments of fun, today captured in preserved collections of their sickening personal photographs.

No matter how thoroughly we trace the chain of command back to Hitler, fascism was not just a programme for government; it was a collaborative project, which millions of people participated in, to subjugate their fellow humans and deny their own potential to be free. It was, as the black French Marxist Aimé Césaire wrote, 'colonialism done to Europe'.[23]

Fascism, to put it another way, is the organized denial of our human freedom; driven by the conviction that human beings should be simply machine-like objects who can learn indifference to pain, who have no business striving for freedom and who should be exterminated if they are superfluous to the needs of some self-defined elite.

It cannot be defeated by appeals to reason alone, or even by collective struggle alone. It has to be morally defeated, forced into logical disarray, encouraged to retreat to the 'ordinary' prejudices of racism, sexism and nationalism which – though distasteful – can each be reasoned with and contained.

Wherever it propagates the myth of a coming ethnic civil war it must be *forced into silence* – because the continuous recitation of the fantasy is what prepares the perpetrators to follow through with it in reality.

In 1940, Globočnik ordered 'a large number of Jews' to be beaten to death in the marketplace of Tarnow, in southern Poland. The massacre complete, he marched the survivors to a cemetery, where they would be shot for the entertainment of visiting civilian Nazis from Berlin. His driver remembered: 'The visitors had gone pale; two had got sick in the marketplace and were hardly able to walk.'[24] That's what happens when you are not dehumanized enough.

Leah Silverstein, a Jewish woman who arrived in Tarnow after one of Globočnik's massacres, and would survive to join the Polish resistance, described the attitude of his men:

> They were not even hostile towards us. They were indifferent. You know, it was . . . an inhumane situation already existed there. Relations between people were not already normal; were not human relations anymore.[25]

Genocidal thought can be seen all over the internet, once you know where to look. Just as Globočnik frequently used the phrase 'transferring the Jews across the river', today's genocide fantasists use ironic references to discuss their plans. One of these is 'in Minecraft' – referring to the cult 3D computer game. On the bulletin board 8chan (now 8kun) a typical anonymous post reads:

> Do modern Whites have the capacity to wage a war of independence against ZOG [the Zionist Occupied Government]? . . . I'm talking about waging a war for our own interests and expelling all the poison from our society. If or if not we're capable of doing so, why? This is all in Minecraft of course.[26]

Elsewhere the phrase 'banned from Minecraft' is synonymous with being murdered. For example, another anonymous user writes:

What if we ... make a website of people to be banned from minecraft. Just open it up for recommendations and voting. Let the good men do the work ... A public list of minecraft players and their bannable offenses does the trick.[27]

When investigative journalists leaked a massive database of white supremacist Discord chats, the word 'genocide' appeared 15,063 times. It was used most frequently to boost their victim narrative, asserting the myth that immigration leads to 'white genocide'.[28] But there was great interest in all genocides: the German massacre of Hereros in Namibia, the Ukrainian Holodomor, the Armenian, Bosnian and Rwandan genocides, often illustrated with gruesome pictures. In far-right culture, genocide is an obsession. There is an overt desire to experience it, alongside the casual assertion that white people are already its victims.

Unsurprisingly, if we recall Arendt's comment about the 'superfluity' of all human beings, this obsession with mass death often goes hand in hand with talk of suicide. For in addition to the 'red pill', which is supposed to allow white men to realize the true nature of their oppression, there is also the 'black pill', which is internet slang for realizing that the cause of fascism is hopeless, and that you may have to kill yourself.

Though it originated in the incel movement, among men who believe their physical appearance makes it impossible for them to achieve consensual sex, the black pill has become a metaphor for the idea that multiculturalism and feminism are too far advanced, and that the coming cataclysm will not lead to the desired rebirth of white racism, but its defeat.[29]

This online community of white men, dedicating themselves to genocide and self-destruction, is global, and it is growing. Its existence stands in contrast to the cultural world of fascism in the interwar period, when genocide enthusiasts had no real idea whether they could ever make it happen, and no pictures to swap.

If the young men of Storm 33 in Charlottenburg could have joined Reddit or 4chan, there is little doubt that they would have sat around 'shitposting' memes about Hitler and the Jews all day. But they did not have access to such media. More importantly, they had no previous model of fascism to look back to. They had lurid tabloid newspapers, which stigmatized Jews, Bolsheviks and black people in clear words and imagery. But those newspapers rarely said 'let's kill them all', and could not have said 'and here's how it was done last time'.

There can be no naive or accidental Nazis in the twenty-first century. In response there must be no naive anti-fascists. The time for 'maybe they don't mean it', or 'maybe they're just confused young men' is long past. When historians tell us to 'take fascists at their word', we should listen.

When they talk about genocide *they are thinking of committing genocide*. When they talk about enforced monogamy (i.e. sex slavery for women), *they are thinking of enforcing it*. When they talk about the black pill, that doesn't just mean they are depressed; it means they are thinking of shooting a large number of Muslims, gay people, women or leftists, and then themselves.

Set against the events of 1942, the moral world of *Casablanca* looks inadequate. We, today, know what the refugees, migrants, liberals and leftists assembled on that set could not know: that ordinary Nazis were plumbing the depths of depravity so enthusiastically that they were ahead of their commanders. It is logical to assume that we are similarly underestimating the dangers we face.

So what should an anti-fascist ethos mean today? After 1968 it became fashionable for progressive people to 'acknowledge their inner fascist'; to recognize, as Michel Foucault wrote, 'the fascism in us all, in our heads and in our everyday behaviour, the fascism that causes us to love power, to desire the very thing that dominates and exploits us'.[30]

At one level this is only a sophisticated version of what Wilhelm Reich wrote in the 1930s: 'there is not a single individual who does not bear the elements of fascist feeling and thinking in his structure'.[31] But it begs the question: what do we do as, once again, the inner fascist which may exist in all of us becomes an outer fascist in some of us?

In *Clear Bright Future* (2019), I called for people to 'live the anti-fascist life'. It means living militantly for the ideals of democracy, social justice and human liberation. Acting as if progress is real. Refusing to give in. Refusing to accept that because China, Turkey and Russia have adopted algorithmic control and surveillance, it is unstoppable in mature democracies.

I now think I underestimated the threat. Four years of Trump; four years (if he makes it) of Bolsonaro, plus who knows how long for Narendra Modi: these administrations have opened the fascist floodgates. The effects have been cumulative and global.

The thought-architecture of fascism has to be deconstructed. Confronting people with the truth is still a rational opening gambit. Experts in deradicalization say prevention is better than cure; that 'pre-bunking' is more effective than debunking lies that are already embedded. Everybody in public life needs to go out of their way, unbidden and in advance, to say that 'white genocide', QAnon, 'The Storm' and all theories allied to them are bullshit. But once you've tried rationality, you have to be prepared for coercion.

For those who refuse to stop spreading the mythology of fascism and inciting people to violence the answer is to *remove their platforms*. As they reach out over the networks to find each other, we need to make it easier for them to lose each other. Or to find a route to deradicalization. Or jail.

We should flood the public conversations of the democratic world with pre-emptive propaganda against fascism. Don't wait for the latest pseudoscience to fight its way into your academic journal. Root it out of academia. Ridicule the manosphere. Wherever some think-tank groupie references Carl Schmitt, remind them of the conference where their thoughtful hero called for Hitler to expel all Jews from the legal profession. Explain to students who think Nietzsche is cool that – as the late scholar Domenico Losurdo has proved – there is no 'innocent Nietzsche'; by all means study his rambling aphorisms but understand that they contain the first systematic justification of elite violence against the working class.[32]

Get out in front. Do not let the right lead the conversation. In politics, above all, do not assume that electoral support for right-wing populism is just discontented conservatism that can be appeased, its racism and misogyny ignored.

As for the left, it has a choice to make. What the left might do to win power and achieve social transformation is beyond the scope of this book. But the success or failure of the left's anti-fascist strategy over the next decade is the hinge on which history will turn.

The culture war within working-class communities cannot be avoided. In 2020 we heard from Democratic Congress candidates in the USA that 'Black Lives Matter cost us votes'. Today, we hear from Labour politicians in Britain that trashing the statues of slave traders, or opposition to forced deportations, or active resistance to racist policing, might prevent them winning back the ex-industrial areas lost to conservatism during the 2010s.

All that, unfortunately, may be true. The left deploys no mass media, enjoys the backing of no billionaires. We cannot change the conversation from above, only from below. But as we go, face to face, into the communities that have become battlegrounds between fascism, liberalism and the left, we should remember the words of Daniel Guérin, the French anarchist who toured Weimar Germany in its last days of democracy: only a flesh and blood alternative can defeat fascism.

That means both an alternative vision and an alternative practice; it cannot mean a sympathetic 'there, there', designed to soften the anger of racists, misogynists and conspiracy theorists. A 'flesh and blood alternative to fascism' can be offered only by people who reject fascism, not by people who share its mindset.

If the common experience of working-class communities on both sides of the cultural divide is powerlessness, then the common framework around which their struggles can be unified is justice and empowerment.

Despite its liberal associations, social justice has become one of the most instinctively powerful principles around which people can unite across the 'values' divide. Yes, in its formulation by the US philosopher John Rawls, social justice was a form of political bean counting – asking, how do we inflict neoliberalism in the least damaging way? But the concept has deeper roots in Enlightenment philosophy and Catholic social teaching, and is explicitly embodied in the principles of both the UN and the International Labour Organization.

I once watched Glenn Beck, the right-wing populist celebrity, mesmerize a Tea Party meeting in Indiana with a prolonged sermon about the evils of social justice. Social justice, said Beck, is just communism with another name. If your church starts talking about social, ecological or economic justice, he advised the faithful, 'you should run from it'.[33]

It's an admirably clear and logical position for the far right to take: capitalism has reached the point where even to speak of justice is to challenge the entire social setup, where even to speak of environmental sustainability is to call into question the property rights and political power of large corporations.

It explains why *social, economic, climate and racial justice* can be the framework around which the mutually hostile offshoots from the Enlightenment, liberalism and Marxism can at least for now mount a joint defence operation against fascism.

There has been rising hope, during the back half of the 2010s, that liberalism and the left might find common cause around Green New Deal-style programmes. But as we do so, the militant defence of democracy has to have equal status. Because it is through an attack on democracy that the right will attempt to stop the progressive project.

Active anti-fascism cannot be left any longer to the monitoring groups and antifa activists, heroic as many of them are. Either we now create the modern equivalent of the mass, cultural movement that appeared in France between 1934 and 1937, or we can kiss both democracy and the Green New Deal goodbye.

To visit Majdanek you arrive by rail at Lublin station. When I got there in 2018, I found half a yard of anti-Semitic and far-right newspapers on sale at the kiosk on the platform, with the *Warszawska Gazeta* newspaper in prime position. 'History according to the Jews' read its headline; there was a strapline accusing the Polish president of being Israel's mouthpiece. Inside there was a reprint of a Wikipedia page about the Rothschild family, plus a story implying that the Israeli elite might be amassing property empires in Eastern Europe, because of a genetic tendency to abandon their own people. Then there was another feature on the Rothschilds, again lifted mainly from Wikipedia – and so it continued.

In the magazine *Polska Niepodległa*, historians documenting the role of Polish Christians in the so-called 'Jew-hunt' towards the end of the Holocaust were labelled 'fantasists'. The Polish researcher who

helped me, who was Jewish himself, spread the whole disgusting panoply of innuendoes and hook-nose cartoons in front of me on the
table. Under the right-wing populist government of Law and Justice,
anti-Semitic and far-right narratives are blatant, right here in twenty-
first-century Europe.

For my whole life, possibly influenced by the reaction of my mother
to the Belsen TV programme, I'd never bothered visiting a death camp
memorial. I'd covered mass rape and genital mutilation in Kenya. I'd
watched the corpses of civilians stacked up in the morgues of Gaza.
I'd chased fascists through the streets of London and run away from
them in Athens. Subconsciously, maybe I thought: what can I learn
from the inevitably sanitized remains of a camp?

But once through the gate of Majdanek, and through the doors of
the disinfection block, a profound quiet entered my head. One of the
chambers, where they used exhaust fumes to kill people, is about the
size of a large living room; the other, where they used Zyklon B, is as
long as a railway carriage but a bit wider. If everyone stood close – as
they were forced to – you could kill 200 people in fifteen minutes.

In that concrete box died some people who had cared little about
politics; others were Zionist youths who dreamed of Palestine; members of the anti-Zionist Bund who dreamed of a socialist Poland, and
cosmopolitans who dreamed of a united Europe. The gas did not
discriminate.

Peering through the door of the gas chamber, I remembered Vasily
Grossman's words, in his 1944 report from Treblinka. It took only ten
gas chambers to execute Operation Reinhard, he noted. Before that,
not even the craziest racist knew that slaughter on this scale was possible. In a paragraph so chilling that Soviet censors actually deleted it,
Grossman wrote:

> It is possible to demonstrate with nothing more than a pencil that any
> large construction company with experience in the use of reinforced
> concrete can, in the course of six months and with a properly organized
> labour force, construct more than enough chambers to gas the entire
> population of the earth. This must be unflinchingly borne in mind by
> everyone who truly values honour, freedom and the life of all nations,
> the life of humanity.[34]

In the age of algorithmic control, autonomous weapons, biometric security and nerve agents, how much easier would it be to kill the entire population of the earth?

Before I came to Majdanek, I wondered how it would feel, confronting one of these death spaces, fifty years after my mother switched off the TV to stop me seeing one. Now I knew.

I felt anti-fascist.

Notes

1. Loewenstein, Karl, 'Militant Democracy and Fundamental Rights', I, *The American Political Science Review*, Vol. 31, No. 3, June 1937, p. 432

INTRODUCTION

1. http://theintercept.com/2020/06/19/militia-vigilantes-police-brutality-protests/
2. Nolte, Ernst, *Three Faces of Fascism: Action Française, Italian Fascism, National Socialism*, New York, 1966, p. 16
3. Finaldi, Giuseppe, *Mussolini and Italian Fascism*, Abingdon, 1998, p. 4
4. See, for example, Mudde, Cas, *The Far Right Today*, London, Cambridge, 2019, p. 7
5. Freedom House, 'Freedom in the World 2020', Washington, 2020, p. 10
6. Bardèche, Maurice, *Qu'est-ce que le fascisme?*, Paris, 1961, p. 176
7. Arendt, Hannah, *Eassys in Understanding, 1930–1954*, New York, 1994, p. 111
8. Grossman, Vasily, 'The Hell of Treblinka', in Grossman, Vasily, *The Road: Short Fiction and Essays by the Author of Life and Fate*, London, 2010, p. 179
9. https://www.yadvashem.org/holocaust/faqs.html
10. https://www.nationalww2museum.org/students-teachers/student-resources/research-starters/research-starters-worldwide-deaths-world-war
11. https://www.yadvashem.org/odot_pdf/Microsoft%20Word%20-%20 6622.pdf
12. https://www.youtube.com/watch?v=c91z_ghofRQ
13. https://www.hopenothate.org.uk/islamophobia-in-the-conservative-party-a-year-in-review/

14. https://www.criticalpast.com/video/65675037245_Bergen-Belsen-concentration-camp_piles-of-corpses_guards-arrested_open-grave

15. Cull, Nicholas J., '"Great Escapes": Englishness and the Prisoner of War Genre', *Film History*, 2002, p. 287

16. https://www.imdb.com/title/tt0077025/

17. Traverso, Enzo, *Fire and Blood: The European Civil War, 1914–1945*, London, 2016, Loc 457

1. SYMBOLIC VIOLENCE

1. Varga, Lucie, 'In a Vorarlberg Valley: Past and Present', in Varga, Lucie, edited with an introduction by Peter Schöttler, *Les autorités invisibles. Une historienne autrichienne aux Annales dans les années trente*, Paris, 1991, p. 167

2. Huppert, George, 'Review: Les Autorités Invisibles by Lucie Varga and Peter Schöttler', *History and Theory*, Vol. 33, No. 2, May 1994, p. 226

3. Varga, *Autorités*, p. 69

4. https://www.sfgate.com/news/article/Austrian-village-faces-down-its-Nazi-past-3294093.php#photo-2441641

5. https://www.doew.at/cms/download/a184m/en_war_crime_trials.pdf

6. Schaller, Stella and Carius, Alexander, *Convenient Truths: Mapping Climate Agendas of Right-wing Populist Parties in Europe*, Berlin, 2019, p. 8

7. https://time.com/5366462/india-assam-citizenship/

8. https://www.huffingtonpost.in/entry/anti-caa-protests-azadi-slogan-kashmir_in_5e451ac3c5b62b85f82f0ofa?guccounter=1&guce_referrer=aHR0cHM6Ly93d3cuZ29vZ2xlLmNvbS88&guce_referrer_sig=AQAAABA3URrtwCY8JPUu9K5iUOTonXoidzmBkcU_p8NDCAAvWjE40zWOc88sFXPxHmoQIbAhy1gPwUzh20qx9r_jJylOqt6slC5DZuO8lSR8IO-pyQ4kBN7ABBooLVGmmwNEit81p3j3WfRjtovBlTK2fl8Z9c97yxAxnno2qhrT_-cd

9. https://time.com/5883993/india-facebook-hate-speech-bjp/

10. Report of the DMC Fact-finding Committee on North-East Delhi Riots of February 2020, Government of NCT of Delhi, New Delhi, July 2020

11. https://frontline.thehindu.com/cover-story/moonje-amp-mussolini/article6756630.ece

12. https://indianexpress.com/article/cities/delhi/delhi-riot-accused-thought-themselves-saviours-of-community-chargesheet-6705963/

13. https://www.instagram.com/p/B9Cp-G3gBDV/?utm_source=ig_embed

14. https://www.thequint.com/news/india/delhi-riots-rss-vhp-members-accused-murder-rioting-arrested-delhi-police

15. https://www.nytimes.com/2020/02/25/us/politics/trump-modi.html

16. https://edition.cnn.com/2019/11/25/uk/bjp-kashmir-tory-uk-election-ge19-intl-gbr/index.html

17. https://www.aa.com.tr/en/americas/indicators-signal-trump-triumph-among-indian-americans/1998935

18. Report of the DMC Fact-finding Committee, p. 34

19. Ibid., p. 66

20. Siddiqui, Kalim, 'Hindutva, Neoliberalism and the Reinventing of India', *Journal of Economic and Social Thought*, Vol. 4, Issue 2, June 2017, p. 154

21. https://elasyn.com/2020/03/08/ioannis-lagos-tourgreek-turkish-borders/

22. https://www.politico.eu/article/sebastian-kurz-austria-identitarian-movement-christchurch-terror-suspect-gave-money-to-austrian-far-right/

23. http://www.radicalrightanalysis.com/2020/03/16/fighting-the-great-replacement-in-2020-an-identitarian-road-trip-to-greece-and-back/

24. https://www.independent.co.uk/news/world/europe/sweden-full-leaflets-greece-refugees-jimmie-akesson-a9383996.html

25. https://www.avvenire.it/attualita/pagine/cani-doppiette-trattori-e-neonazi-per-dare-la-caccia-ai-migranti-nuovi-scontri-al-confine-tra-grecia-e-turchia

26. https://www.youtube.com/watch?v=YGChu5vxl3o

27. https://foreignpolicy.com/2020/10/29/how-brazil-was-ukrainized/

28. https://apublica.org/2020/05/especialistas-apontam-semelhancas-entre-os-300-de-sara-winter-e-grupos-fascistas-europeus/

29. Barbosa dos Santos, Fabio Luis, *Uma História da Onda Progressista Sul-Americana (1998–2016)*, São Paulo, 2018

30. Fisher, Max and Taub, Amanda, 'How YouTube Radicalized Brazil', *New York Times*, 11 August 2019

31. https://www.insightcrime.org/news/analysis/spate-murders-brazil-shines-spotlight-militia-phenomenon/

32. https://www.globalwitness.org/en/campaigns/environmental-activists/defending-tomorrow/

33. https://www.worldometers.info/coronavirus/country/brazil/

34. https://www.instagram.com/tv/CF9vKoKHAYZ/?utm_source=ig_embed

35. https://www.nytimes.com/2020/07/03/world/europe/germany-military-neo-nazis-ksk.html

36. https://www.reuters.com/article/us-germany-crime-hitler-iDUSKBN2671ZK

37. https://www.tagesspiegel.de/politik/200-leichensaecke-und-aetzkalk-bestellt-rechtsextremes-netzwerk-plante-attentate-auf-politische-gegner/24505056.html

38. https://www.waz-online.de/Nachrichten/Politik/Deutschland-Welt/Mecklenburg-und-die-Eiserne-Reserve

39. https://www.theguardian.com/world/2019/jun/26/far-right-suspect-confesses-to-killing-german-politician-walter-lubcke; https://www.bbc.co.uk/news/world-europe-55395682; https://www.dw.com/en/hanau-shootings-what-we-know-about-the-victims/a-52460950

40. Klikauer, Thomas, 'Germany's AfD – Members, Leaders and Ideologies', *Asian Journal of German and European Studies*, Vol. 4, No. 4, 2019, p.3

41. https://www.brookings.edu/blog/order-from-chaos/2020/02/28/the-thuringia-debacle-resets-the-merkel-succession-and-proves-the-afd-is-a-force-to-be-reckoned-with/

42. Du Bois, W. E. B., *Black Reconstruction in America (The Oxford W. E. B. Du Bois)* (p. 941), Oxford University Press, Kindle Edition

43. https://medium.com/religion-bites/the-souls-of-white-folk-by-w-e-b-du-bois-354f91ca08ef

44. https://www.gov.uk/government/publications/race-disparity-audit

45. https://www.radicalrightanalysis.com/2018/11/30/catalyst-or-catharsis-inside-the-dfla-secret-facebook-groups/

46. https://www.bbc.co.uk/bbcthree/article/e5ee9e0a-18d7-49a4-a3c2-80b6b4222058

47. https://www.npr.org/2017/07/02/535267439/trump-tweets-clip-of-him-bodyslamming-cnn-network-says-do-your-job; https://www.theguardian.com/us-news/2019/aug/05/cesar-sayoc-sentencing-pipe-bombs-targets-trump-critics

48. https://www.theguardian.com/world/2020/oct/14/greece-golden-dawn-neo-nazi-prison-sentences

2.DREAMS OF THE ETHNO-STATE

1. De Benoist, Alain and Champetier, Charles, *Manifesto for a European Renaissance*, London, 2012, p. 11

2. Confino, Alon, *Foundational Pasts: The Holocaust as Historical Understanding*, Cambridge, 2012, p. 6

3. De Benoist and Champetier, *Manifesto*, p. 14

4. Faye, Guillaume, *Why We Fight: Manifesto of the European Resistance*, London, 2011, p. 29

5. Ibid., p. 70

6. Ibid., p. 31

7. Ibid., p. 167

8. Dugin, Alexander, *The Fourth Political Theory*, London, 2012, p. 94

9. https://www.boundary2.org/2019/09/kevin-musgrave-and-jeff-tischauser-radical-traditionalism-metapolitics-and-identitarianism-the-rhetoric-of-richard-spencer/

10. Teitelbaum, Benjamin, *War for Eternity: The Return of Traditionalism and the Rise of the Populist Right*, London, 2020, p. 1

11. https://theconversation.com/the-long-game-of-the-european-new-right-75078

12. Panofsky, Aaron et al., 'How White Nationalists Mobilize Genetics: From Genetic Ancestry and Human Biodiversity to Counterscience and Metapolitics', *American Journal of Physical Anthropology*, 28 September 2020, p. 2

13. https://unesdoc.unesco.org/ark:/48223/pf0000122962

14. Mehler, Barry, 'Foundation for Fascism: The New Eugenics Movement in the United States', *Patterns of Prejudice*, Vol. 23, No. 4, 1989

15. Piffer, Davide and Kirkegaard, Emil O. W., 'The Genetic Correlation between Educational Attainment, Intracranial Volume and IQ is Due to Recent Polygenic Selection on General Cognitive Ability', *Open Behavioral Genetics*, 11 March 2014, p. 8

16. Evans, Gavin, 'The Unwelcome Revival of "Race Science"', *Guardian*, 2 March 2018

17. Rose, Stephen and Rose, Hilary, *Alas Poor Darwin: Arguments Against Evolutionary Psychology*, London, 2001

18. Murray, Charles and Herrnstein, Richard, *The Bell Curve: Intelligence and Class Structure in American Life*, New York, 1994, p. 548

19. Saini, Angela, *Superior: The Return of Race Science*, London, 2019, p. 104

20. https://www.dailymail.co.uk/news/article-7516365/Cambridge-scientist-sacked-publishing-racist-research-reveals-suing-university.html; https://www.varsity.co.uk/news/17727

21. Barash D., quoted in Panofsky, et al., 'How White Nationalists Mobilize Genetics', p. 6

22. Hoppe, Hans-Hermann, *Democracy: The God That Failed*, Abingdon, 2017, p. 148

23. https://www.unqualified-reservations.org/2010/02/from-mises-to-carlyle-my-sick-journey/

24. Ibid.

25. https://www.cato-unbound.org/2009/04/13/peter-thiel/education-libertarian

26. Mehring, Reinhard, 'Carl Schmitt and the Politics of Identity', in Sedgwick, Mark (ed.), *Key Thinkers of the Radical Right: Behind the New Threat to Liberal Democracy*, Oxford, 2019, p. 47

27. Schmitt, Carl, *The Concept of the Political*, Chicago, 1993, p. 27

28. Schmitt, Carl, *The Crisis of Parliamentary Democracy*, Cambridge, 1985, p. 9

29. https://claremontreviewofbooks.com/the-nazi-jurist/

30. https://www.vox.com/world/2017/8/15/16141456/renaud-camus-the-great-replacement-you-will-not-replace-us-charlottesville-white

31. https://www.bbc.co.uk/news/55017002

32. https://www.nytimes.com/2018/11/13/opinion/cultural-marxism-anti-semitism.html

33. https://www.theguardian.com/news/2019/mar/26/tory-mp-criticised-for-using-antisemitic-term-cultural-marxism

34. https://www.thetimes.co.uk/article/tories-fear-infiltration-by-ukip-members-93t03wkf6

35. https://www.supremecourt.gov/DocketPDF/22/22O155/163550/20201211132250339_Texas%20v.%20Pennsylvania%20Amicus%20Brief%20of%20126%20Representatives%20--%20corrected.pdf

36. https://www.rawstory.com/proud-boys-rally/

37. https://www.buzzfeednews.com/article/janelytvynenko/trump-rioters-planned-online

38. Grand Jury Indictment, US District Court for the District of Columbia, USA *vs* Caldwell, Crowl and Watkins, 27 January 2021, p. 12

39. Evans, Richard J., 'Why Trump Isn't a Fascist', *New Statesman*, 13 January 2021

40. https://jacobinmag.com/2021/01/trump-capitol-riot-fascist-coup-attempt

41. https://www.nytimes.com/2020/11/17/us/trump-found-more-than-10-million-new-voters-they-were-not-enough.html

42. Arendt, Hannah, *The Origins of Totalitarianism*, London, 2017, p. 462

43. https://www.mediamatters.org/twitter/fbi-calls-qanon-domestic-terror-threat-trump-has-amplified-qanon-supporters-twitter-more-20

44. https://www.splcenter.org/hatewatch/2020/10/27/what-you-need-know-about-qanon

45. Smith, Melanie, 'Interpreting Social Qs: Implications of the Evolution of QAnon', *Graphika*, August 2020, p. 13

46. https://eu.usatoday.com/story/news/politics/2020/10/22/qanon-poll-finds-half-trump-supporters-believe-baseless-claims/3725567001/

47. Varga, Lucie, 'The Origins of National Socialism: Notes from Social Analysis', in Varga, Lucie, edited with an introduction by Peter Schöttler, *Les autorités invisibles. One histoirienne autrichienne aux Annales dans les années trente*, Paris, 1991, p. 162

48. Mannheim, Karl, *Ideology and Utopia: An Introduction to the Sociology of Knowledge*, London, 1953, p. 36

49. https://www.vox.com/culture/2017/4/28/15434770/red-pill-founded-by-robert-fisher-new-hampshire

50. https://www.independent.co.uk/news/world/europe/sabmyk-network-qanon-conspiracy-theories-b1820639.html

51. Friberg, Daniel, in Andersen, Joakim, *Rising from the Ruins: The Right of the 21st Century*, London, 2018, Loc 37

3. FIVE KINDS OF TROUBLE

1. Rachel, Łukasz and Summers, Lawrence H., 'On Falling Neutral Real Rates, Fiscal Policy, and the Risk of Secular Stagnation', *Brookings Papers on Economic Activity*, Spring 2019

2. https://ourworldindata.org/economic-growth

3. https://ourworldindata.org/trade-and-globalization

4. World Inequality Lab, 'World Inequality Report 2018', English Version, Executive Summary, p. 9; https://wir2018.wid.world/files/download/wir2018-summary-english.pdf

5. https://www.bbc.co.uk/news/world-55793575

6. See Mason, Paul, *Postcapitalism: A Guide to Our Future*, London, 2015

7. https://www.iif.com/Portals/0/Files/content/Research/Global%20Debt%20Monitor_April2020.pdf?

8. *Global Debt Monitor*, 17 February 2021, Institute of International Finance, p. 1; https://seekingalpha.com/article/4396972-2021-all-central-banks-and-liquidity

9. Dobbs, Richard et al., 'Poorer Than Their Parents?', McKinsey Global Institute, July 2016, p. viii

10. Williamson, John, 'The Washington Consensus as Policy Prescription for Development', Institute for International Economics, 13 January 2004; https://www.piie.com/publications/papers/williamson0204.pdf

11. Fukuyama, Francis, 'The End of History', *The National Interest*, No. 16, Summer 1989, pp. 3–18

12. https://www.strike.coop/bullshit-jobs/

13. Dobbs, 'Poorer Than Their Parents?', p. 37

14. https://wccftech.com/apple-a13-iphone-11-transistors-gpu/

15. https://www.wired.com/story/apple-a13-bionic-chip-iphone/

16. https://creativehq.co.nz/wp-content/uploads/2019/12/ExponentialTech-CreativeHQ-1.pdf

17. Tufekci, Zeynep, 'As the Pirates become CEOs: The Closing of the Open Internet', *Daedalus*, Vol. 145, No. 1, Winter 2016

18. Mason, Paul, *Why It's Still Kicking Off Everywhere: The New Global Revolutions*, London, 2013

19. https://www.bbc.co.uk/blogs/newsnight/paulmason/2011/02/twenty_reasons_why_its_kicking.html

20. Kornbluh, Karen and Goodman, Ellen P., 'Safeguarding Digital Democracy: Digital Innovation and Democracy Initiative Roadmap', German Marshall Fund of the USA, March 2020, No. 4, pp. 4–5

21. https://www.gmfus.org/blog/2020/10/12/new-study-digital-new-deal-finds-engagement-deceptive-outlets-higher-facebook-today

22. Loewenstein, Karl, 'Militant Democracy and Fundamental Rights, 1', *The American Political Science Review*, Vol. 31, No. 3, June 1937, pp. 417–32

23. Ginsburg, Tom and Huq, Aziz Z., *How to Save a Constitutional Democracy*, Chicago, 2018, p. 184

24. Schumpeter, Joseph A., *Capitalism, Socialism and Democracy*, London, 1976, p. 269

25. https://conservativehome.blogs.com/centreright/2008/04/making-history.html

26. Daly, Tom Gerald, 'Democratic Decay: Conceptualising an Emerging Research Field', *Hague Journal on the Rule of Law*, Vol. 11, 2019, p. 9

27. Ginsburg and Huq, *How to Save a Constitutional Democracy*

28. Mounk, Yascha, *The People vs Democracy: Why Our Freedom is in Danger and How to Save It*, London, 2018, p. 17

29. https://ourworldindata.org/co2-and-other-greenhouse-gas-emissions

30. 'The Emissions Gap Report 2012: A UNEP Synthesis Report', United Nations Environment Programme (UNEP), Nairobi, 2012, p. 25; https://wedocs.unep.org/bitstream/handle/20.500.11822/8526/-The%20emis-

sions%20gap%20report%202012_%20a%20UNEP%20synthesis
%20reportemissionGapReport2012.pdf?sequence=3&isAllowed=y

31. Christensen, J. and Olhoff, A., 'Lessons from a Decade of Emissions Gap Assessments', United Nations Environment Programme (UNEP), Nairobi, 2019, p. 3

32. https://www.iea.org/reports/world-energy-outlook-2020/achieving-net-zero-emissions-by-2050#abstract

33. https://www.metapoliticabrasil.com/post/sequestrar-e-perverter?fbclid=IwAR2yJ9k5BJzaHGjjYrVwRdTNyX53D HT1Ng6e4MtnV-sA1xvD-MloWv84hMU

34. Dunlap, Riley E. and McCright, Aaron M., 'Challenging Climate Change: The Denial Countermovement', in Dunlap, R. E. and Brulle, R. J. (eds.), *Climate Change and Society: Sociological Perspectives*, New York, 2015, p. 301

35. Hultman, Martin, Björk, Anna and Viinikka, Tamya, 'The Far Right and Climate Change Denial', in Forchtner, Bernhard, *The Far Right and the Environment: Politics, Discourse and Communication*, Abingdon, 2020, Loc 3341

36. https://www.spiegel.de/international/germany/afd-seeks-votes-by-opposing-climate-protection-a-1265494.html

37. Hatakka, Niko and Välimäki, Matti, 'The Allure of Exploding Bats: The Finns Party's Populist Environmental Communication and the Media', in Forchtner, *The Far Right and the Environment*, Loc 3739

38. http://www.penttilinkola.com/pentti_linkola/ecofascism/

39. Neocleous, Mark, *Fascism*, Buckingham, 1977, p. 11

40. 'Fascist Ecology: The "Green Wing" of the Nazi Party and its Historical Antecedents', in Biehl, Janet and Staudenmaier, Peter (eds.), *Ecofascism Revisited: Lessons from the German Experience*, Porsgrunn, 2011, pp. 13–42

41. Fest, Joachim, *Der Untergang: Hitler und das Ende des Dritten Reiches: Eine historische Skizze*, Berlin, 2002, p. 150

42. https://www.imf.org/en/Publications/WEO/Issues/2020/09/30/world-economic-outlook-october-2020

43. https://ipbes.net/news/Media-Release-Global-Assessment

44. Wang, Lin-Fa and Anderson, Danielle E., 'Viruses in Bats and Potential Spillover to Animals and Humans', *Current Opinion in Virology*, Vol. 34, 18 January 2019

45. https://ipbes.net/news/Media-Release-Global-Assessment

46. Hoare, Quintin and Nowell Smith, Geoffrey (eds.), *Selections from the Prison Notebooks of Antonio Gramsci*, London, 1971, p. 404

47. Munich Security Report 2019, *The Great Puzzle: Who Will Pick Up the Pieces?*, p. 16; https://securityconference.org/assets/02_Dokumente/01_Publikationen/MunichSecurityReport2019.pdf
48. https://www.gov.uk/government/speeches/the-privilege-of-public-service-given-as-the-ditchley-annual-lecture
49. Cornford, John, 'Full Moon at Tierz: Before the Storming of Huesca', in Sloan, Pat (ed.), *John Cornford: A Memoir*, London, 1938, p. 244

4. DESTROY EVERYTHING

1. Jünger, Ernst, 'Fire', in Kaes, Anton et al., *The Weimar Republic Sourcebook*, Berkeley, 1984, p. 20
2. Jünger, Ernst, *On Pain*, New York, 2008, p. 32
3. Erh-Soon Tay, Alice, 'The Status of Women in the Soviet Union', *The American Journal of Comparative Law*, Vol. 20, No. 4, Autumn 1972, p. 669
4. Smith, S. A., *Russia in Revolution: An Empire in Crisis, 1890 to 1928*, Oxford, 2018, p. 153
5. Mason, Paul, *Live Working or Die Fighting: How the Working Class Went Global*, London, 2007, Loc 3225
6. Elazar, Dahlia S., *The Making of Fascism: Class, State and Counter Revolution, Italy, 1919–22*, Westport, CT, 2001, p. 53
7. Laqueur, Walter, *Black Hundred: The Rise of the Extreme Right in Russia*, New York, 1993
8. Wróbel, Piotr, 'The Seeds of Violence. The Brutalization of an East European Region, 1917–1921', *Journal of Modern European History*, Vol. 1, No. 1, 2003, *Violence and Society after the First World War*, p. 137
9. Ibid., p. 136
10. Siltala, Juha, 'Dissolution and Reintegration in Finland, 1914–1932: How Did a Disarmed Country Become Absorbed into Brutalization?', *Journal of Baltic Studies*, Vol. 46, No. 1, March 2015, p. 18
11. Bortnevski, Viktor G., 'White Administration and White Terror (The Denikin Period)', *The Russian Review*, Vol. 52, No. 3, July 1993, p. 364
12. Vtorushin, M. I., 'The Phenomenon of Fascism in 20th Century Russia and its Emergence in Siberia during the Civil War Years', *Omsk Scientific Newsletter*, Vol. 5, No. 112, 2012, p. 19
13. Jones, Nigel, *The Birth of the Nazis: How the Freikorps Blazed a Trail for Hitler*, London, 2004, p. 130
14. Ernst von Salomon, quoted in ibid., p. 135

15. Stephan, John J., *The Russian Fascists: Tragedy and Farce in Exile, 1925–1945*, New York, 1978, p. 19
16. https://avalon.law.yale.edu/imt/1708-ps.asp
17. Madden, Paul, 'Some Social Characteristics of Early Nazi Party Members, 1919–1923', *Central European History*, Vol. 15, No. 1, March 1982, p. 38
18. Farrell, Nicholas, *Mussolini: A New Life*, London, 2003, p. 149
19. https://www.societyforasianart.org/sites/default/files/manifesto_futurista.pdf
20. *Il Popolo d'Italia*, 24 March 1919, quoted in Delzell, Charles (ed.), *Mediterranean Fascism, 1919–1945*, New York, 1970, p. 8
21. Farrell, *Mussolini*, p. 111
22. https://www.bellingcat.com/news/rest-of-world/2019/03/15/shitposting-inspirational-terrorism-and-the-christchurch-mosque-massacre/
23. Hughes, H. Stuart, *Consciousness and Society: The Reorientation of European Social Thought, 1890–1930*, Abingdon, 2017, pp. 37–8
24. Nietzsche, Friedrich, *The Will to Power*, New York, 1967, p. 11
25. Nietzsche, Friedrich, trans. Mencken, H. L., *The Anti Christ*, New York, 1918, p. 43
26. Nietzsche, Friedrich, *Thus Spake Zarathustra*, New York, 1917, Loc 1115
27. https://bigthink.com/scotty-hendricks/how-the-nazis-hijacked-nietzsche-and-how-it-can-happen-to-anybody
28. Pareto, Vilfredo, *Trattato di Sociologia Generale*, Turin, 1988, Loc 1588, quoted in Losurdo, Domenico, *Nietzsche, the Aristocratic Rebel – Intellectual Biography and Critical Balance-sheet*, Leiden, 2020, p. 730
29. Mazel, Henri, *Nietzsche et le présent*, L'Ermitage, February 1893, p. 82
30. Mencken, H. L., *The Philosophy of Friedrich Nietzsche*, New York, 1913, p. x
31. Spengler, Oswald, *The Decline of the West*, Vol. 2: *Perspectives of World History*, New York, 1927, p. 506
32. Chamberlain, Houston Stewart, *The Foundations of the Nineteenth Century*, Vol. 1, New York, 1914, quoted in Mendes-Flohr, Paul and Reinharz, Jehuda, *The Jew in the Modern World: A Documentary History*, New York, 1995, p. 358
33. Ibid., p. 359
34. Le Bon, Gustave, *The Crowd: A Study of the Popular Mind*, London, 1896, p. 3
35. Nye, Robert A., 'Two Paths to a Psychology of Social Action: Gustave Le Bon and Georges Sorel', *The Journal of Modern History*, Vol. 45, No. 3, September 1973, p. 430

36. Sorel, Georges, *Reflections on Violence*, Cambridge, 2004, p. 118
37. Ibid., p. 24
38. Quoted in Mesial, James H., 'A Premature Fascist? Sorel and Mussolini', *The Western Political Quarterly*, Vol. 3, No. 1, March 1950, p. 14
39. Quoted in Sternhell, Zeev, et al., 'The Birth of Fascist Ideology', in Laqueur, Walter, *Fascism: A Reader's Guide: Analyses, Interpretations, Bibliography*, Aldershot, 1991, p. 320
40. Ibid., p. 324

5. STOPPING MUSSOLINI

1. Quoted in Alberghi, Pietro, *Il Fascismo in Emilia Romagna: Dalle origini alla marcia su Roma*, Modena, 1989, pp. 224–5
2. *Il Resto del Carlino*, 4 July 1919, quoted in Zanetti, Walter, 'Lotte agrarie nel primo dopoguerra in provincia Forlì', in Editori Riuniti, *Movimento operaio e fascismo nell'Emilia-Romagna, 1919–1923*, Rome, 1973, p. 211
3. http://digilib.netribe.it/prampolinimag/RicercaMAG.jsp?datadal=1/4/1919&dataal=31/10/1922&idMagMetadigit=1&idMagStru=6919
4. Circondario di Forlì, *Il Pensiero Romagnolo*, 1 July 1920, quoted in Zanotti, 'Lotte agrarie', p. 211
5. Fabbri, Luigi, *Preventive Counter-Revolution*, London, 2005, p. 11
6. Wetzel, Tom, 'The Italian Factory Occupations of 1920', workerscontrol.net, 22 December 2015
7. Spriano, Paolo, *The Occupation of the Factories: Italy 1920*, London, 1975, p. 92
8. Snowden, Frank M., *The Fascist Revolution in Tuscany, 1919–1922*, Cambridge, 1989, p. 61
9. Di Figlia, Matteo, 'The Shifting Evocations of *Squadrismo*: Remembering the Massacre of Palazzo d'Accursio in Fascist Bologna', *Journal of Modern Italian Studies*, Vol. 21, No. 4, September 2016
10. Fabbri, *Preventive Counter-Revolution*, p. 12
11. Revelli, Marco, 'Italy', in Mühlberger, Detlef (ed.), *The Social Basis of European Fascist Movements*, Abingdon, 2016, p. 112
12. Paxton, Robert O., *The Anatomy of Fascism*, New York, 2004, p. 61
13. Segre, Claudio G., *Italo Balbo: A Fascist Life*, Berkeley, 1987, Loc 686
14. Suzzi Valli, Roberta, 'The Myth of Squadrismo in the Fascist Regime', *Journal of Contemporary History*, Vol. 35, No. 2, April 2000, p. 136
15. Ricci, G., *Squadrismo forlìvese*, Forlì, 1942, quoted in Zanetti, 'Lotte agrarie', p. 224

16. Carsten, Francis Ludwig, *The Rise of Fascism*, Berkeley, 1967, p. 59
17. Gallo, Max, *Mussolini's Italy: Twenty Years of the Fascist Era*, Oxford, 2018, Loc 2727
18. Valeri, Nino, 'Origini del fascismo, squadrismo e lotta di classe', in *Lezioni sull'antifascismo*, Bari, 1960, p. 8
19. Quoted in Snowden, *Fascist Revolution*
20. Alberghi, *Fascismo in Emilia Romagna*, pp. 285, 304
21. *L'Ordine Nuovo*, 7 June 1921, quoted in ibid., p. 345
22. Alberghi, *Fascismo in Emilia Romagna*, p. 347
23. Francescangeli, Eros, *Arditi del Popolo: Argo Secondari e la prima organizzazione antifascista (1917–1922)*, Rome, 2008, p. 248
24. Gallo, *Mussolini's Italy*, Loc 2867
25. Sonnessa, Antonio, 'Working Class Defence Organization, Anti-fascist Resistance and the Arditi del Popolo in Turin, 1919–22', in *European History Quarterly*, Vol. 33, No. 2, pp. 138–218
26. Francescangeli, *Arditi del Popolo*, p. 245
27. Sonnessa, 'Working Class Defence Organization', p. 194
28. Carosi, Felice, *Bagliori*, Rome, 1935, quoted in Suzzi Valli, 'The Myth of Squadrismo'
29. Segre, *Italo Balbo*, Loc 680
30. Suzzi Valli, 'The Myth of Squadrismo', p. 143
31. Susmel, Eduardo and Susmel, Duilio (eds.), *Opera Omnia di Benito Mussolini*, Florence, 1956, Vol. 18, pp. 66–72 (my translation)
32. Lyttelton, Adrian (ed.), *Liberal and Fascist Italy: 1900–1945*, Oxford, 2002
33. Larcinese, Valentino, 'Enfranchisement and Representation: Italy 1909–1913', London School of Economics, EOPP/2011/32, p. 8
34. https://ebiblio.istat.it/digibib/Elezioni/RAV0143612Statelezgen-polXXVIleg15mag1921.pdf
35. https://overland.org.au/2018/06/a-brief-fascist-history-of-i-dont-care/
36. Gallo, *Mussolini's Italy*, Loc 3070
37. Segre, *Italo Balbo*, Loc 1031
38. Tasca, Angelo, *The Rise of Italian Fascism, 1918–1922*, London, 1938, p. 200
39. Mussolini, Benito, 'Stato, anti-stato e fascismo', in Susmel and Susmel (eds.), *Opera Omnia*, Vol. 18, p. 263
40. Mussolini, Benito, 'L'ultimo discorso dal banco di deputato', in ibid, p. 292
41. Tasca, *Rise of Italian Fascism*, p. 214

42. https://www.marxists.org/history/etol/newspape/isj2/2003/isj2-099/picelli.htm
43. Ibid.
44. Alberghi, *Fascismo in Emilia Romagna*, p. 550
45. Tasca, *Rise of Italian Fascism*, p. 232
46. Ibid., p. 255
47. Hughes-Hallett, Lucy, *The Pike: Gabriele d'Annunzio, Poet, Seducer and Preacher of War*, London, 2017, Loc 11462
48. Gallo, *Mussolini's Italy*, Loc 3360
49. Quoted in ibid., Loc 3507
50. Engle, Chris, 'Verbal Algorithms and the Human Machine', in Curry, John et al. (eds.), *The Matrix Games Handbook: Professional Applications from Education to Analysis and Wargaming*, London, 2018, p. 88
51. Williams, Gwyn A., *Proletarian Order: Antonio Gramsci, Factory Councils and the Origins of Italian Communism, 1911–1921*, London, 1975, p. 267
52. Tasca, *Rise of Italian Fascism*, p. 304
53. http://www.marxists.org/history/etol/newspape/isj2/2003/isj2-099/picelli.htm

6. 'I AM DAZED'

1. Petersen, Jan, *Our Street: A Chronicle Written in the Heart of Fascist Germany*, London, 2012
2. https://www.oxfordreference.com/view/10.1093/acref/9780191843730.001.0001/q-oro-ed5-00004900
3. Zibordi, Giovanni, 'Towards a Definition of Fascism', in Beetham, David (ed.), *Marxists in Face of Fascism: Writings by Marxists on Fascism from the Inter-war Period*, Chicago, 2019, p. 88
4. Gramsci, Antonio, *Selections from Political Writings: 1921–1926*, London, 1978, p. 38
5. https://www.marxists.org/archive/bordiga/works/1922/bordiga02.htm#n5
6. https://www.marxists.org/archive/radek/1922/radek02.htmi
7. https://www.marxists.org/history/international/comintern/4th-congress/italy.htm
8. Pryce, Donald B., 'The Reich Government versus Saxony, 1923: The Decision to Intervene', *Central European History*, Vol. 10, No. 2, June 1977, pp. 112–47

9. Madden, Paul, 'Some Social Characteristics of Early Nazi Party Members, 1919–1923', *Central European History*, Vol. 15, No. 1, March 1982, p. 5

10. Broué, Pierre, *The German Revolution 1917–1923*, Leiden, 2005, p. 803

11. Valtin, Jan, *Out of the Night*, New York, 1941, p. 58

12. Degras, Jane (ed.), *Communist International: Documents, 1919–1943*, Vol. 2, *1923–1928*, London, p. 77

13. Stalin, Josef, 'Concerning the International Situation', *Works*, Vol. 6, January–November 1924, p. 294

14. https://www.commentarymagazine.com/articles/theodore-draper/the-ghost-of-social-fascism/#5

15. Harsch, Donna, *German Social Democracy and the Rise of Nazism*, Chapel Hill and London, 1993, p. 1

16. Fowkes, Ben, *Communism in Germany under the Weimar Republic*, London, 1984, p. 205

17. https://www.babylon-berlin.com/en/about-babylon-berlin/the-story/

18. Ward, James J., '"Smash the Fascists": German Communist Efforts to Counter the Nazis, 1930–31', *Central European History*, Vol. 14, No. 1, March 1981, pp. 30–62

19. Mommsen, Hans, *The Rise and Fall of Weimar Democracy*, Chapel Hill, 1996, Loc 6224

20. Ward, '"Smash the Fascists"', p. 34

21. Mommsen, *Rise and Fall*, Loc 6665

22. Dimsdale, Nicholas H. et al., 'Unemployment in Interwar Germany: An Analysis of the Labor Market, 1927–1936', *The Journal of Economic History*, Vol. 6, No. 3, September 2006, pp. 778–808

23. https://www.wahlen-in-deutschland.de/wrtwschlehol.htm

24. Schnabel, Thomas, 'Wer wählte Hitler?', quoted in Harsch, *German Social Democracy*, p. 105

25. Reichardt, Sven, 'Violence and Community: A Micro-study on Nazi Storm Troopers', *Central European History*, Vol. 46, No. 2, June 2013, p. 264

26. Brown, Jeremy R.S., 'The Berlin NSDAP in the Kampfzeit', *German History*, Vol. 7, No. 2, April 1989, p. 242

27. https://encyclopedia.ushmm.org/content/en/article/adolf-hitler-1930-1933

28. Harsch, *German Social Democracy*, p. 179

29. Rosenhaft, Eve, *Beating the Fascists? The German Communists and Political Violence, 1929–1933*, Cambridge, 1983, p. 64

30. JJVD Gruppe Nordkap Letter to the Central Committee, 19 November 1931, in Rosenhaft, *Beating the Fascists?*, p. 84

31. Rosenhaft, *Beating the Fascists?*, p. 79

32. Bessell, Richard, *Political Violence and the Rise of Nazism. The Storm Troopers in Eastern Germany 1925–1934*, New Haven and London, pp. 76–7

33. Quoted in Rosenhaft, *Beating the Fascists?*, p. 160

34. http://library.fes.de/cgi-bin/arb_mktiff.pl?year=1930&pdfs=637x638x639x640x641x642x643x644x645x646x647x648x649x650x651x652x653x654; Geiger, Theodor, 'Panik im Mittelstand', *Die Arbeit*, Vol. 10, 1930, p. 682

35. Quoted in Harsch, *German Social Democracy*, p. 109

36. Quoted in Childers, Thomas, *The Nazi Voter: The Social Foundations of Fascism in Germany, 1919–1933*, Chapel Hill, 1983, Loc 4222

37. Petzina, Dieter, 'Germany and the Great Depression', *Journal of Contemporary History*, Vol. 4, No. 4, October 1969, p. 60

38. Guérin, Daniel, *The Brown Plague*, Durham, 1994, p. 50

39. Ibid., p. 57

40. Renaud, Terence Ray, 'Restarting Socialism: The New Beginning Group and the Problem of Renewal on the German Left, 1930–1970', PhD Thesis, UC Berkeley, 2015, p. 26

41. Harsch, *German Social Democracy*, p. 194

42. See, for example, Kuczynski, Jürgen, *Klassen und Klassenkämpfe im imperialistischen Deutschland und in der BRD*, Frankfurt-am-Main, 1972; and Gossweiler, Kurt, *Grossbanken, Industriemonopole und Staat*, Berlin, 1971

43. Sohn-Rethel, Alfred, *Economy and Class Structure of German Fascism*, London, 1978, p. 32

44. 'Neue Dokumente zur Geschichte der Reichswehr 1930–1933', *Vierteljahrshefte für Zeitgeschichte*, Vol. 2, Berlin, 1954, p. 427

45. Stachura, Peter D., 'The Nazis, the Bourgeoisie and the Workers during the Kampfzeit', in Stachura, Peter D. (ed.), *The Nazi Machtergreifung*, Abingdon, 2015, p. 20

46. Satyanath, Shanker, Voigtländer, Nico and Voth, Hans-Joachim, 'Bowling for Fascism: Social Capital and the Rise of the Nazi Party', *Journal of Political Economy*, Vol. 125, No. 2, 2017, pp. 478–526

47. Koshar, Rudy, *Social Life, Local Politics, and Nazism: Marburg, 1880–1935*, Chapel Hill and London, 1986, p. 284

48. https://www.marxists.org/archive/cliff/works/1993/trotsky4/06-germany.html#f43

49. Taylor, Frederick Winslow, *The Principles of Scientific Management*, New York, 2010, p. 46

50. Fowkes, *Communism in Germany*, p. 171

51. Guérin, *Brown Plague*, p. 86

52. Resolution of the ECCI Presidium on the Situation in Germany, 1 April 1933, in Degras, *Communist International*, Vol. 3, *1929–1943*, p. 255

7. A THEORY OF FASCISM

1. https://twitter.com/FFRAFAction/status/1264177258035662848

2. For a full account, see Hagtvet, Bernt and Kühnl, Reinhart, 'Contemporary Approaches to Fascism: A Survey of Paradigms', in Larsen, Stein, Hagtvet, Bernt and Myklebust, Jan Petter (eds.), *Who Were the Fascists? Social Roots of European Fascism*, Oslo, 1990, pp. 26–51

3. Griffin, Roger, *Fascism: An Introduction to Comparative Fascist Studies*, Cambridge, 2018, p. 27

4. Gentile, Emilio, 'Fascism in Power: The Totalitarian Experiment', in Lyttelton, Adrian (ed.), *Liberal and Fascist Italy: 1900–1945*, Oxford, 2002, Loc 1788

5. Ibid.

6. Mussolini, Benito, 'La dottrina del fascismo', in Oakeshott, Michael, *The Social and Political Doctrines of Contemporary Europe*, London, 1959, pp. 164–79

7. https://www.marxists.org/archive/laurat/1940/marxism-democracy/cho4.htm

8. Arendt, Hannah, *The Origins of Totalitarianism*, London, 2017, p. 435

9. Ibid., p. 460

10. Ibid., p. 335

11. Ibid., p. 417

12. Ibid., p. 415

13. Gentile, Emilio, 'Le silence de Hannah Arendt: L'interprétation du fascisme dans "Les origines du totalitarisme"', *Revue d'histoire moderne et contemporaine*, T55e, No. 3, July–September 2008, p. 32

14. Friedrich, Carl J. and Brzezinski, Zbigniew K., *Totalitarian Dictatorship and Autocracy*, Cambridge, MA, 1956

15. Nolte, Ernst, *Three Faces of Fascism: Action Française, Italian Fascism, National Socialism*, New York, 1966, p. 23

16. Ibid., pp. 20–21

17. Ibid., p. 421
18. https://www.nytimes.com/2016/08/21/world/europe/ernst-nolte-historian-whose-views-on-hitler-caused-an-uproar-dies-at-93.html
19. Linz, Juan J., 'Notes Toward a Comparative Study of Fascism in Sociological Historical Perspective', in Laqueur, Walter (ed.), *Fascism: A Reader's Guide: Analysis, Interpretation, Bibliography*, Aldershot, 1991, pp. 12–13
20. Payne, Stanley G., 'The Concept of Fascism', in Hagtvet et al., *Who Were the Fascists*, p. 14
21. Gentile, Emilio, 'Fascism, Totalitarianism and Political Religion: Definitions and Critical Reflections on Criticism of an Interpretation', *Totalitarian Movements and Political Religions*, Vol. 5, No. 3, Winter 2004, pp. 342–3
22. Griffin, *Fascism*, p. 34
23. Ibid.
24. Griffin, Roger, *The Nature of Fascism*, Abingdon, 1991, p. 26
25. https://www.marxists.org/archive/trotsky/1940/xx/jewish.htm
26. Dimitrov, Georgi, 'The Fascist Offensive and the Tasks of the Communist International in the Struggle of the Working Class against Fascism', in Dimitrov, Georgi, *Selected Works*, Vol. 2, Sofia, 1972
27. See, for example, Renton, David, *Fascism: History and Theory*, London, 2020
28. https://www.marxists.org/archive/marx/works/1852/18th-brumaire/ch05.htm
29. Engels, Frederick, 'Preface to the Third German Edition of The Eighteenth Brumaire of Louis Bonaparte', in Marx, Karl and Engels, Frederick, *Selected Works*, Moscow, 1968; https://www.marxists.org/archive/marx/works/1885/prefaces/18th-brumaire.htm#n39
30. Gramsci, Antonio, *Selections from Political Writings: 1921–1926*, London, 1978, p. 38
31. Hoare, Quintin and Nowell Smith, Geoffrey (eds.), *Selections from the Prison Notebooks of Antonio Gramsci*, London, 1972, p. 294
32. Ibid., p. 351
33. Reich, Wilhelm, *People in Trouble* (vol. 2 of *The Emotional Plague of Mankind*), Toronto, 1976, p. 142
34. Reich, Wilhelm, *The Mass Psychology of Fascism*, New York, 2013, Loc 587
35. Ibid., Loc 468
36. Ibid., Loc 1296
37. Ibid., Loc 2219

38. Reich, *People in Trouble*, p. 184
39. Ibid., p. 153
40. Ibid., pp. 164–5
41. Bonss, Wolfgang, 'Critical Theory and Empirical Social Research: Some Observations', in Fromm, Erich, *The Working Class in Weimar Germany: A Psychological and Sociological Study*, Leamington Spa, 1984, p. 1
42. Fromm, Erich, *Escape from Freedom*, New York, 2013, p. 228
43. Ibid., p. 43
44. Ibid., p. 208
45. https://www.marxists.org/archive/marx/works/1844/manuscripts/labour.htm
46. Ashcraft, Richard, 'Political Theory and Political Action in Karl Mannheim's Thought: Reflections upon Ideology and Utopia and Its Critics', *Comparative Studies in Society and History*, Vol. 23, No. 1, January 1981, p. 24
47. Paxton, Robert O., 'The Five Stages of Fascism', *The Journal of Modern History*, Vol. 70, No. 1, March 1998
48. Paxton, Robert O., *The Anatomy of Fascism*, New York, 2004, p. 218
49. Paxton, 'The Five Stages of Fascism', p. 24
50. Hitler, Adolf, *Mein Kampf*, Boston, 1999, p. 449

8. MILITANT DEMOCRACY 2.0

1. Jenkins, Brian and Millington, Chris, *France and Fascism: February 1934 and the Dynamics of Political Crisis*, Abingdon, 2015, p. 180
2. Berstein, Serge, *Le 6 Février 1934*, Paris, 1975, p. 168
3. Soucy, Robert, *French Fascism: The Second Wave 1933–1939*, New Haven, 1995, p. 111
4. Jackson, Julian, *The Popular Front in France: Defending Democracy, 1934–38*, New York, 1990, p. 20
5. Doriot, Jacques, *L'Emancipation nationale*, 10 February 1934, quoted in Allardyce, Gilbert, 'The Political Transition of Jacques Doriot', *Journal of Contemporary History*, Vol. 1, No. 1, 1966, p. 61
6. Soucy, *French Fascism*, p. 210
7. Jackson, *Popular Front in France*, p. 5
8. 'Pour l'Unite d'Action! Les Communistes de St Denis et les événements de 6 et 12 Février', Paris, 1934; https://pandor.u-bourgogne.fr/img-viewer/PAPRIKA/000517/000001/001674/viewer.html?ns=0517_0001_1674_0089.jpg

9. Avramova, V., *Georgi Dimitrov: 90th Birth Anniversary*, Prague, 1972, p. 60

10. Haslam, Jonathan, 'The Comintern and the Origins of the Popular Front 1934–1935', *The Historical Journal*, Vol. 22, No. 3, September 1979, p. 680

11. Ibid., p. 689

12. Horn, Gerd-Rainer, *European Socialists Respond to Fascism: Ideology, Activism and Contingency in the 1930s*, Oxford, 1996, Kindle edition

13. Quotes in Horn, Gerd-Rainer, 'Radicalism and Moderation within German Social Democracy in Underground and Exile, 1933–1936', *German History*, Vol. 15, Issue 2, April 1997, p. 211

14. Hilferding, Rudolf, 'Revolutionary Socialism', in Beetham, David (ed.), *Marxists in Face of Fascism: Writings by Marxists on Fascism from the Inter-war Period*, Chicago, 2019, p. 274

15. Howell, Ronald F., 'The Philosopher Alain and French Classical Radicalism', *Western Political Research Quarterly*, Vol. 18, No. 3, September 1965

16. Quoted in Andrew, Dudley and Ungar, Steven, *Popular Front Paris and the Poetics of Culture*, London, 2005, p. 67

17. Soucy, *French Fascism*, p. 112

18. Confino, Alon, *Foundational Pasts: The Holocaust as Historical Understanding*, Cambridge, 2012, p. 6

19. Traverso, Enzo, *Fire and Blood: The European Civil War, 1914–1945*, London, 2016, Loc 5030

20. Jackson, *Popular Front in France*, p. 114

21. Ehrenburg, Ilya, *The Fall of Paris*, London, 1942, p. 95

22. https://www.marxists.org/reference/subject/philosophy/works/ge/benjamin.htm

23. Savage, Mike et al., 'A New Model of Social Class? Findings from the BBC's Great British Class Survey Experiment', *Sociology*, Vol. 47, No. 2, April 2013, p. 221

24. Ainsley, Claire, *The New Working Class: How to Win Hearts, Minds and Votes*, Bristol, 2018

25. https://www.nimblefins.co.uk/average-uk-household-budget#nogo

26. https://www.unfpa.org/sites/default/files/pub-pdf/UNFPA-SDG561562Combined-v4.15.pdf

27. https://www.brookings.edu/articles/new-mothers-not-married-technology-shock-the-demise-of-shotgun-marriage-and-the-increase-in-out-of-wedlock-births/

28. Roantree, Barra and Vira, Kartik, 'The Rise and Rise of Women's Employment in the UK', IFS Briefing Note 234, London, 2018, p. 2

29. https://www.unfpa.org/sites/default/files/pub-pdf/UNFPA-SDG561562Combined-v4.15.pdf

30. Bock, Gisela, 'Racism and Sexism in Nazi Germany: Motherhood, Compulsory Sterilization, and the State', *Signs*, Vol. 8, No. 3, Spring 1983, p. 407

31. De Grand, Alexander, 'Women under Italian Fascism', *The Historical Journal*, Vol. 19, No. 4, December 1976, p. 598

32. Mussolini, Benito, 'Macchine e donna', in Susmel, Eduardo and Susmel, Duilio (eds.), *Opera Omnia*, Florence, 1956, Vol. 16, p. 311

33. https://www.rooshv.com/what-is-neomasculinity

34. Massanari, A. L. and Chess, S., 'Attack of the 50-foot Social Justice Warrior: The Discursive Construction of SJW Memes as the Monstrous Feminine', *Feminist Media Studies*, Vol. 18, Issue 4, 2018, pp. 525–42

35. https://www.thecut.com/2017/08/mens-rights-activism-is-the-gateway-drug-for-the-alt-right.html

36. https://www.newyorker.com/magazine/2017/12/04/the-french-origins-of-you-will-not-replace-us

37. Mounk, Yascha, *The People vs Democracy: Why Our Freedom is in Danger and How to Save It*, London, 2018, p. 222

38. https://www.markey.senate.gov/news/press-releases/senator-markey-and-rep-ocasio-cortez-introduce-green-new-deal-resolution

39. https://intelligence.weforum.org/topics/a1G680000004C93EAE?tab=publications

40. https://www.imf.org/en/News/Articles/2020/10/15/sp101520-a-new-bretton-woods-moment

41. Loewenstein, Karl, 'Militant Democracy and Fundamental Rights, I', *The American Political Science Review*, Vol. 31, No. 3, June 1937, p. 423

42. Loewenstein, Karl, 'Militant Democracy and Fundamental Rights, II', *The American Political Science Review*, Vol. 31, No. 4, August 1937, pp. 638–58

43. https://www.nytimes.com/2020/03/25/world/europe/germany-populist-party.html

44. https://edition.cnn.com/2021/03/30/politics/proud-boys-fbi-contacts/index.html

45. Muro, Diego, 'What Does Radicalisation Look Like? Four Visualisations of Socialisation into Violent Extremism', *Notes Internacionals CIDOB*, No. 163, December 2016, p. 4

46. https://unicornriot.ninja/2020/patriotwaves-boogaloo-engineering-an-aesthetic-of-violence/

47. https://www.facebook.com/wyatt.pipkin/posts/4752658854776071, accessed 29 November 2020, 10.32 GMT

48. https://www.bloomberg.com/news/newsletters/2021-01-21/trump-s-ban-has-already-had-an-impact-on-the-social-media-landscape

9.EVERYBODY COMES TO RICK'S

1. Harmetz, Aljean, *The Making of Casablanca: Bogart, Bergman and World War II*, New York, 1992, p. 48

2. https://www.jewishvirtuallibrary.org/hitler-speech-at-the-berlin-sports-palace-january-30-1941

3. http://vincasa.com/Screenplay-Everybody_Comes_to_Rick%27s.pdf

4. http://www.dailyscript.com/scripts/casablanca.pdf

5. https://www.nationalarchives.gov.uk/education/resources/holocaust/hoefle-telegram/

6. Simonov, Konstantin, *The Death Factory near Lublin*, London, 1944, p. 3

7. Lawrenceby, W. H., 'Nazi Mass Killing Laid Bare in Camp', *New York Times*, 30 August 1944, p. 1; https://www.nytimes.com/1944/08/30/archives/nazi-mass-killing-laid-bare-in-camp-victims-put-at-1500000-in-huge.html

8. Werth, Alexander, *Russia at War, 1941–1945*, New York, 2017, p. 890

9. https://www.yadvashem.org/articles/academic/the-origins-of-operation-reinhard.html

10. Ibid.

11. Mason, Tim, 'Intention and Explanation. A Current Controversy about the Interpretation of National Socialism', in Hirschfeld, Gerhard and Kettenacker, Lothar (eds.), *The 'Führer State': Myth and Reality, Studies on the Structure and Politics of the Third Reich*, Stuttgart, 1981, p. 25

12. Loewenstein, Karl, 'Militant Democracy and Fundamental Rights, 1', *The American Political Science Review*, Vol. 31, No. 3, June 1937, p. 432

13. Ibid., p. 39

14. Mason, 'Intention and Explanation', p. 25

15. Arendt, Hannah, *The Origins of Totalitarianism*, London, 2017, p. 602

16. Williams, Max, *Odilo Globocnik: The Devil's Accomplice*, Stroud, 2020, p. 356

17. Henry, Michel, *Marx: An Introduction*, London, 2019, Loc 623

18. Card, Claudia, *Confronting Evils: Terrorism, Torture, Genocide*, Cambridge, 2010, p. 237

19. Jünger, Ernst, *On Pain*, New York, 2008, Loc 1065

20. Harmetz, *Making of Casablanca*, pp. 208–25

21. Epstein, Julius, Epstein, Philip and Koch, Howard, *Casablanca*, Los Angeles, 1942, p. 107

22. Nietzsche, Friedrich, *On the Genealogy of Morality*, Cambridge, 2006, p. 23

23. Césaire, Aimé, *Discourse on Colonialism*, New York, 1972, p. 36

24. Williams, *Odilo Globočnik*, p. 95

25. United States Holocaust Memorial Museum, Interview with Leah Silverstein, 22 May 1996, p. 52; https://collections.ushmm.org/oh_findingaids/RG-50.030.0363_trs_en.pdf

26. Quoted by anti-fascist activist @gwensnyderPHL; https://twitter.com/gwensnyderPHL/status/1149061076383883265?s=20

27. Ibid.

28. https://discordleaks.unicornriot.ninja/discord/server/34

29. Wimberly, Cory, 'Propaganda and the Nihilism of the Alt-Right', *Radical Philosophy Review* (forthcoming); https://philpapers.org/rec/WIMPAT

30. Foucault, Michel, in Delouse, Gilles and Guttari, Felix, *Anti-Oedipus: Capitalism and Schizophrenica*, Minneapolis, 1983, p. xxi

31. Reich, Wilhelm, *The Mass Psychology of Fascism*, New York, 2013, Loc 122

32. Losurdo, Domenico, *Nietzsche, the Aristocratic Rebel: Intellectual Biography and Critical Balance-Sheet*

33. https://glennbeck.com/content/articles/article/198/38320

34. Grossman, Vasily, 'The Hell of Treblinka', in Grossman, Vasily, *The Road: Short Fiction and Essays by the Author of Life and Fate*, London, 2010, p. 152

Acknowledgements

I completed this book during the Covid-19 lockdown, so the first acknowledgement must go to my wife, Jane Bruton, who had to endure me writing a book from a desk in our home, instead of – as normally – on the road. Claire Launchbury translated the works of Lucie Varga. Alessandra Castellazzi helped me research modern and historic Italian fascism. Filipe Teles and Ricardo Cabral Fernandes did substantial research on Brazilian fascism. The Erich Fromm Foundation encouraged my work with a generous honorarium via the Erich Fromm Prize 2020. Rainer Funk of the Fromm Foundation gave me advice on the development of Freudian Marxism, as did Andrea and Fritz Lackinger. Journalists Siân Norris and Theopi Skarlatos shared their insights on the far right in Eastern Europe, and made comments on the text. Jan Gebert facilitated my trip to Majdanek, as did the museum itself, as part of a visit funded by Das Progressive Zentrum. Distinguished academics in India offered advice but, like others specializing in research into Hindutva, do not want to be named. Imran Ahmed of the Centre for Countering Digital Hate offered guidance on research within the online digital space, as did activists from Hope Not Hate. The work of numerous online anti-fascist activists, journalists and monitoring groups is acknowledged via specific notes, as are the historians in whose debt I so clearly stand. In the same spirit I should acknowledge the input of their predecessors: the dozens of anti-fascist activists, many of them workers, who during the struggles against the NF and BNP from 1976 onwards, taught me the history and theory of fascism, including Gerry Gable, Adrian Swayne, Bridget Thompson, Dave Stocking,

Mark Hoskisson, Matthew Cobb, Keith Hassell and my late friend and comrade Dave Hughes. Finally, this book could not have happened without the dedication and commitment of my agent, Matthew Hamilton, Tom Penn, my editor at Allen Lane, copy-editor Bela Cunha and editorial assistant Eva Hodgkin.

Index